Live With the Universal Faith

Live With the Universal Faith

This book comes from an ancient legacy via Yo San Ni, Grand Master of the Integral Way

Hua-Ching Ni and Mao Shing Ni, Ph. D.

TAO OF WELLNESS
PRESS
Los Angeles

The authors wish to express their gratitude to all students and friends who devoted their time and effort to editing, proofreading, typesetting and supporting the creation of this book.

Publication of this work was made possible by an anonymous donor.

Published by:
Tao of Wellness Press (An imprint of SevenStar Communications)
1412 14th Street
Santa Monica, CA 90404

Calligraphy by Mao Shing Ni, Ph.D.

Library of Congress Cataloging-in-Publication Data

This book is dedicated to all friends of the Universal Integral Way who enthusiastically choose to share the responsibility for human health by living a constructive life:

The four essences to ensure the survival of humanity are:
Sunlight, fresh air, clean water, and a healthy vision for human life
That includes regaining faith in the Sun.

With this simple spiritual principle,
We are able to manage both our own life essence,
And that of the world.

To All Readers:

According to the teaching of the Universal Integral Way, or Heavenly Heart, male and female are equally important in the natural sphere. This fact can be observed and confirmed in the diagram of the *Tai Chi*. Therefore discrimination is not practiced in our tradition. All work is dedicated to both genders of the human race.

Wherever possible, sentence constructions using masculine pronouns to represent both sexes are avoided. Where they do occur, we ask your tolerance and spiritual understanding. We hope that you will take the essence of these teachings and overlook the limitations of a language in which gender discrimination is inherent. Ancient Chinese pronouns do not differentiate gender. We hope that all of you will achieve yourselves well above the level of language and gender. Thank you.

Warning — Disclaimer:

This book is intended to present beneficial information and techniques that have been used throughout Asia for many centuries. This information and any practices that appear in this work utilize a natural system within the body; however, no claims are made regarding their effectiveness. The information offered is according to the authors' best knowledge and experience and is to be used by the reader at his or her own discretion and liability.

People's lives have different conditions and their growth has different stages. Because the development of all people cannot be unified, there is no single practice that can be universally applied to everyone. It must be through the discernment of the reader that practices are selected. The adoption and application of the material offered in this book must, therefore, be the reader's own responsibility.

The authors and publisher of this book are not responsible in any manner for any harm that may occur through following the instructions in this book.

About the Authors

Hua-Ching Ni, author, teacher and healer, addresses the essential nature of human life and works to further the personal growth and spiritual development of this and future generations. He was raised in a family tradition of healing and spirituality that is being continued by his two sons, Drs. Daoshing and Mao Shing Ni, and by his many friends and supporters throughout the world.

Dr. Mao Shing Ni, D.O.M., L.Ac., Ph.D., Dipl. C.H., Dipl. ABAAHP, has lectured and taught workshops throughout the country on such diverse subjects as longevity, preventive medicine, Chinese nutrition, herbal medicine, acupuncture, facial diagnosis, *feng shui,* stress management, *I Ching,* meditation, *tai chi, chi kung* and the history of medicine.

Dr. Mao has also authored many books, audio/video tapes and DVDs. These include: *Chinese Herbology Made Easy, The Tao of Nutrition, The Eight Treasures Energy Enhancement Exercises, Self-Healing Chi Kung, 18 Step Harmony Style Tai Chi, Tai Chi Sword, Meditation for Stress Release, Pain Management, The Yellow Emperor's Classic of Medicine, Secrets of Longevity* and *Secrets of Self-Healing.* He was also an editorial member for the best-selling book, *Alternative Medicine: The Definitive Guide.*

Table of Contents

Introduction | *i*

Part I *Foundation of the Original Universal Faith*

Chapter 1 Early Influences | 6
Chapter 2 Deviation from the Way | 14
Chapter 3 Essence of the New Direction | 23

Part II *The Search for Spiritual Maturity*

Chapter 4 First Steps | 32
Chapter 5 Seeking the Path of Pure Light | 37
Chapter 6 The Sun is the Source of Humanity | 61

Part III *Fulfill the Hope for a New Humanity*

Chapter 7 Establish a Healthy Human Faith | 70
Chapter 8 Attain Spiritual Clarity | 78
Chapter 9 Support a Healthy Social System | 88
Chapter 10 Create a Healthy World | 104

Part IV *Finding Spiritual Maturity*

Chapter 11 Have Faith in the Light of the Sun | 114
Chapter 12 Deeper Reflection | 127

Part V *Assessing the Spiritual Options*

Chapter 13 Reviewing the Options | 136
Chapter 14 Cast No Shadows | 147

PART VI *Choosing an Effective Direction*

Chapter 15 The Deepest Truth in Life | 154
Chapter 16 Revive the Spirit of Humanity | 163
Chapter 17 Respect the Lessons from the Past | 172
Chapter 18 The Spiritual Strength within Change | 184

PART VII *Focus of the Integral Way*

Chapter 19 Personal Transformation | 196
Chapter 20 Saving Humanity | 213

PART VIII *The Ultimate Spiritual Truth*

Chapter 21 Ally Your Spiritual Life with the Great Sages | 226
Chapter 22 Honor Mother Ocean of Eternal Wisdom | 234
Chapter 23 The Correct Spiritual Expression in Life | 240

Epilogue | 250
Index | 257

INTRODUCTION

Cultural changes relate to the challenges of the time,
Although these challenges and the mental response may differ.
Originally there were no circumstantial challenges,
And the growth of the human mind was benign.

The increasing hostility and cruelty grew from competition,
And did not belong to the original nature of human life.
Evil comes from the circumstances of life,
But biased and prejudiced doctrines cannot be made the norm.

Some established cultures contain excessive religious emotion,
And should be cleansed to further the complete health of humanity,
Because the mental patterns associated with those cultures
Could harm the young minds that need to face new situations in life.

The Universal Integral Way has already done enough work explaining the need for the spiritual detoxification of humanity in the series of seven books on the *Path of Constructive Life*[1] for a modern spirituality that encourages all people to attain the Five Healths. But we should all expect to live a balanced life with a sound body, a sound mind, a sound spirit, sound social connections and sound financial support.

Once the mind has been detoxified there is room for the healthy new strength to grow. The realization of universal morality is the only way to contribute to the spiritual life of humanity, and the practical matters in the

---

1 Titles in the Path of Constructive Life series: *The New Universal Morality* helps to guide us towards the truth in life; *The Power of the Feminine* outlines the importance of feminine energy in spiritual development; *The Path of Constructive Life* shows us how to embrace the Heavenly heart; *Love of Mother Universe* serves the openness of the new generation to live in harmony with Mother Nature; *Five Healths for a New Humanity* prepares us to achieve the complete health required to fulfill our personal spiritual duty; *Evolve Heaven on Earth* encourages us to take our faith in the sun towards a new spiritual direction in life; and the *One Spiritual Reality: A Guide to Universal Harmony* highlights universal spiritual development and personal spiritual fortification.

world. In this context, the constructive contribution from the spiritual life of the early people must also be evaluated so that the useful experiences from past generations are not forgotten.

This book puts aside the old cultural conflicts to produce a common spiritual standard to serve the new generations, although there is still a concern on whether they will be able to face the world any better than previous generations. Therefore, this gift of the fundamentals of the Integral Way has been compiled for their future reference. It can also be used to deepen our understanding of the cultural elements in the teaching of the Universal Integral Way, or to further our understanding of the vision of the Way as a force that transcends the heavy influences of the past. Moreover, it can be used as a resource for spiritual discussion groups.

The simple essence in life
Is also the simple essence of the entire Universe.

Look up to the sky, or anywhere else,
But do not miss looking at the self in life.

The sun is the ruler to all life, and all life is part of the ruler.
Hence, the ruler and the ruled share the abundance of the Universe.

The sun in the sky is the true ruler of our life -
Physically, mentally and spiritually.

PART I

Foundation of the Original Universal Faith

The sun is the ruler of my mind;
The sun is the Heavenly Father to my soul.

Grand Master Yo San Ni

Chapter 1

Early Influences

Early People were led by the Sun

Many people have learned to appreciate the spiritual qualities of the sun during the long period humanity has experienced the light from the sky. Originally this appreciation arose from their basic needs on Earth, but later they developed a sense for the deeper needs in life.

The sun displays the spiritual character that helped people to develop their first concepts and images of a God. This included being the source of the moral force in life that upholds the qualities of justice, brightness, openness, straightforwardness, righteousness, frankness, and cordiality. It also includes being powerful, supportive, loving, life-giving, inexhaustible, ever-youthful, and all forgiving, as well as being without duality or duplicity, discrimination or distortion, and so forth.

The early people then took these deep impressions and required the same qualities for themselves, and especially their leaders. That was the basis of their first spiritual pursuit, but no human creation, such as a conceptual faith, can compare to the deepest nature of the sun. Rather, these attempts have created much confusion.

In the deeper relationship between humanity and the sun, however:

The sun is the life-giver,

The sun gives people their soul of life,

The sun provides their conscious force in life,

The sun directly provides people with the reproductive force of Nature,

The sun offers them its healing power,

And can cleanse the sins of their souls and bring them back to life.

Thus, the sun offers them the power for the resurrection of life.

Our whole world is supported by the sun, and this was recognized by the early people, who were aware that the sun is the source of life. Several ancient cultures were based on the direct teaching from the sun, and objective people also took this direct approach to develop the Way, while the more sentimental people developed conceptual religions.

There are many levels in human life, but the three main partners are the physical, mental and spiritual levels where each partner should attain complete health. If the qualities of the sun are pursued, humanity would develop in a healthy manner. Instead, people have made numerous conceptual detours, although the insistence of the Way throughout all time has meant that this teaching continues through the Integral Way.

In human life the solar force directly translates into the male reproductive force that dominates and drives their lives. That force is also indirectly reflected by the moon to provide the female reproductive force with its associated receptive qualities. Moreover, solar energy helps to develop the human intellectual force that is given equally to both males and females.
Hence, solar power is the essence of humanity, and physically the sun is the true ruler of each life on Earth. Spiritually, however, the sun is the internal ruler of all human life, and its higher conscious capability, regardless of gender and social status.

Original Organic Health of Human Spirituality

Around 8000 years ago,
When people developed the ability to use stone tools,
They followed the one reality in their life - the light from Nature.

From their repeated experiences and difficulties,
They produced the concept called the Way
That centered on the sun that guided their life.

The regularity and constancy of the sun
Suggested that each day is great,
And that the sun was the source of their life force.

Thus, people followed the Way
That was the single constant reality in their life,
But they also knew that the Way is shaped by the uniqueness of the sun.

They had directly sensed that their life and livelihood came from the sun,
And the recognition of living with the gifts of Nature
Expressed the growth of their minds.

Yet they may not have known
That the growth of their conscious power
Is also related to the light from the sky.

The capability of human perception then grew
As each brain was stimulated by the different patterns of light.
And the increased proficiency of their physical force and brain power
Soon meant they became well-established among the other animals.

Later, as their appreciation grew, they began to offer the sky food,
And this showed their progression from merely meeting the basic needs in life.
They then developed the sense of public benefit
That produced a different type of social leadership.

And as their power of perception continued to grow
They came to know more about the gifts from the sun.
The sun had given birth to everything that supported their life -
First the sunlight gave them life, and then indirectly fed that life.

After further growth of the human mind,
Some people realized the sun also gave birth to the planets,
Including their home, planet Earth.

Earth has a marvelous position, close to her Father, the Sun,
Where it is never too hot or too cold,
And provides a wonderful place for all the Father's creations.

He created many species, but was still not fully satisfied.
But after much experimentation he finally created humans,
Who were clever enough to take care of their own life on Earth.

The human species then rapidly reproduced.
Some are better, others are worse, but they keep reproducing,
And planet Earth is now full of these highly mobile creatures.

Their Father is happy to see human life developing on Earth.
Yet, they have chosen to die in the trenches,
Even though they would like to live brightly and enjoy the light.

It now seems that Earth is too small for all these creatures,
And some may have to live under the ocean,
Or move away to some other unknown place.

But know that not all of the stars were created by the Father.
So, consider whether the children of the sun can now move
To a place where they become greater than their Father?

Some people have the power of vision,
And have developed their lives to attain the truth.
Happiness in life comes from embracing the simple essence of life.

The simple essence is:
–原始樸道,
[原樸之道]
Return to the origin before all existence,
And discover how Nature develops herself.
[The early people perceived this as following the Way.]

Nature is the Source of Human Health

The Integral Way is for people who love the depth of Nature, and the teaching service of the Universal Integral Way is dedicated to those who choose to live a constructive life with an enthusiasm similar to the light of the sun. These people also possess the willingness to share the responsibility for achieving and maintaining a healthy humanity. They do this by taking the simplicity displayed by the sun as their spiritual principle as they seek to manage the essence of both their own life and the world.

All cultural inventions arise from the life challenges of the time, and the response from the mind is also conditioned by those challenges. But now we would now like to review the original benign growth of the mind away from such circumstantial challenges. This means going back to the beginning of human culture before the increase in hostility and cruelty that grew from negative competition.

Originally all human nature was benign, and any evil came from various conditions in life. Hence, teachings or doctrines that contain bias and prejudice do not support the normalcy of humanity, which means we must cleanse much of the emotion from the established religions and cultures to restore the health of humanity. Another problem is that some of the mental training in the old cultures can victimize or harm the minds of the young, who must now face many new life situations that require new solutions.

We have already worked on the spiritual detoxification of humanity in the book series on the Path for a Constructive Life, and once the mind has been detoxified, there will be room for the new healthy strength to grow. However, we now wish to review the contribution of the early people, correct or otherwise, so that any new spiritual life can assess whether or not to invent a better approach. We all know that the realization of universal morality is the only way to make a contribution to the spiritual life of humanity, although there is still a concern that the maturity attained from past generations may be forgotten as each new generation deals with the practical matters in their world.

We also know the useful experiences from past human development cannot cover all the needs for the growth of a new humanity, but hope that this review can reduce the time and effort in relearning the old lessons so that future generations can do better than us. In this spirit we now offer our gift on the fundamentals of the Integral Way:

There is the sun in the sky, and there is the sun in all life that is the very soul of life.

The Integral Way Stands Firm

The Integral Way stands for the spiritual effort of humanity that constantly moves upward, and embraces its faith in the hidden potency of the vitality of the cosmos, which gives birth to all form. This cosmic vitality contains its own law which expresses the orderliness of Nature. Without it, the Universe would be a barren chaos.

Struggle among human societies can be seen as one stage of seeking growth, and even though humanity has not achieved maturity this should be our spiritual goal. We all have the duty to seek our own growth, but only the highest level of growth is able to benefit all people. Such growth is limited by our education, life experience, and other circumstances, yet our personal development can go beyond these limitations. Meanwhile, the partial development of human life creates imbalances that then manifest as new problems in the world. In contrast, the Integral Way looks for balance through the complete development of life.

If this balance and unity cannot be found, it is difficult to achieve personal health, success, happiness, and the enjoyment of a long life. Therefore, the highest principle in life is its integrity, and this is what the Integral Way stands for. This includes a strong faith in the health of humanity that is able to respond to the needs of the world, and take people away from their self-created troubles. Hence, we believe the deep predicaments in the modern world need a new and healthy faith to progress the complete health of all people, and that the Integral Way can offer a reliable direction for this new faith.

The most serious mistake made by past societies has been in forming beliefs based on the misunderstanding that our spiritual power is external. Universal vitality gives us life, but our spiritual force grows from the inside out, and is usually covered by thoughts and emotions. Cultivating this hidden life force requires a different effort, whereby each life must attain the mental clarity and healthy emotions to produce a healthy spirit that values the strength of self-reliance, rather than relying on external emotional or conceptual beliefs. If there is no direction, or self-knowledge, there is no more to say on the matter.

This means our emotional and conscious domains must attain enlightenment throughout all our life experiences, combined with the good understanding that can assist mental maturity. Spiritual health comes from the enlightenment of the mind, and not from setting up some statue or name for emotional or conceptual support. Having made the above clear, the Integral Way can offer help as a spiritual friend. And our main goal as a spiritual service is to assist the healthy spiritual partners in your life.

The Integral Way transcends cultural power,
To produce its own clear vision.
At the center is the health of humanity.
Thus, it has evaluated all cultural elements to produce
The teaching of the Way to achieve the integral health of humanity.

After viewing the common conflicts in human life,
And the new sources of social tension and contention,
The Integral Way wants to provide a new direction for humanity
To correct the shortcoming of modern cultures.

The basis of our teaching comes from
The big ocean formed by the small flows of many cultures,
And the legacy from the values within all humanistic efforts.
We also admit that light can sometimes create darkness,
And too many shadows have been created to confuse the new life.

Should we be concerned for the cultural health of the world?
What is the spiritual value of purity and unity?

Why should the health of young life have a solid foundation?
And how should they be prepared to live for a healthier future?
Is the value of a peaceful mind more blessed than ruling the world?
What is our real spiritual support from Nature?
How can we find the deepest unity within human spirituality?
Do we need to form a new spiritual alliance with the early spiritual leaders?
Have the old religions now served their original purpose?
And what is our overall purpose in wishing to serve the new humanity?

The Integral Way wishes to help people understand
How the world became culturally messy,
And why to have faith in Nature,
Rather than hold on to a conscious confusion.
The fundamentals of the Integral Way offer real support
By taking people away from such confusion,
And towards a renewed faith in Mother Nature.
Our many practices can also be used to seek spiritual maturity,
Although such maturity is already shown by following the Way.

The Integral Way helps people to rediscover that their life is
Supported by the simple essence, which comes from the Earth
That also produces the spiritual stability in life.
This would enable all people to embrace
The simple essence of the entire Universe.

Look up to the sky, or anywhere else,
But do not miss looking at the self in life.
The sun is the ruler to all life, and all life is part of the ruler.
Thus, the ruler and the ruled share the abundance of the Universe.

The sun is the ultimate source of the human spirit in life;
The sun is also the symbol of the healthy spirit of humanity.

Chapter 2

Deviation from the Way

People have complicated their means of living and way of life.
The regular, normal Way cannot help them to get what they want,
And the new trends benefit the cunning mind.
This is how the world has become culturally messy.

Common Conflicts

Many conflicts in modern life are an expression of mental confusion. Our life spirit is hidden inside our physical brain and mind, and while our body tends to move downwards, our spiritual potential wishes to keep moving upwards. But most people neglect their spiritual side, and are unable to detect the difference between the physical and spiritual spheres as it seems that everything comes from the mind.

Hence, people tend to live on the surface of life, where there are all kinds of difficulties and challenges, and frequently struggle with the conflicts that arise from their different interests. In this situation they focus on the tangible benefits, and ignore the slim light within the part of the mind we call the lord of life. Yet, the substance of life is simple, and at the end of the physical life, when the body and mind separate from the spiritual self, the conscious light of life suddenly knows that another lifetime has been wasted.

There is a spiritual depth in all human life, although most people mistakenly believe that the expressible side of the conscious is their life, and never know that the spiritual substance of life is inexpressible. Thus, what can be expressed is limited to the life experiences on the outer layer of that subtle substance. Modern psychology is now at the threshold of this subtle reality, but the conventional religions remain far away. Moreover, both of these systems are now established as social services that ask for recompense, although the spiritual truth on the reality of life only 'exists' in the subtle sphere.

Nature has given all people life, but the rest is up to the conscious self that is witnessed by the deep but unmarked book of the soul. The simple picture is that each life must face disintegration when the soul departs from its many outer layers, and at that moment we will know the truth of our precious life. So, do not wait until the last moments of disintegration, but decide not to create trouble for your life, or the lives of others. Rather, use that moment to look at the important balance between fulfilling your internal harmony, and the happiness gained from living a worthwhile life.

The spiritual truth is simple - with harmony, balance, poise and constructiveness, we are already a God in our own lives. But the growth of human maturity is slow, and never comes for some people, while many thousands of years have not been enough for the societies that keep returning to a barbaric darkness. The truth for both individuals and societies is that when one side overly expands a disaster is created. The principle of Wu Wei is to respect and move towards the natural balance of life. Wherever the root of life finds balance through poise, internal harmony, and unity, there is safety in the world.

Nevertheless, there is still general confusion about the distinction between the mind and the spirit. To repeat, the mind is the conscious function of life, and the life spirit is the non-active substance of the soul. But in the broadest sense, the mind includes both conscious activities and the non-active soul. This means that when the mind is confused, the soul may be disturbed, although the mind can also be confused through contact with other people or situations. Generally, the life spirit gives orders to the body through the conscious self that has at least three levels - sensory, reactive, and the deep subconscious. The reactive self includes feelings and emotions, while the subconscious gathers unseen information to report important situations to the brain/mind in the form of dreams.

The three basic motivations in human life are seeking recognition, support, or profit; seeking respect from our peers or society for our cultural and creative activities, including the development of conceptual teachings, such as a religion; and seeking engagement in the moral behavior that extends the humanistic heart. All these motivations can be fulfilled benignly, but when overly extended the first can cause aggression or arrogance, the second may produce self-centeredness or racism, and the third may result in the loss of humanistic balance though zealousness. Trouble comes when people do not know the self and the importance of moderation, which is the key factor in all human relationships.

Humanity supposedly began when two people – a male and a female - appeared on Earth. The female represented *yin*, or feminine nature, and the male represented *yang*, or masculine nature, but each had the same invisible partner, which is the life spirit they called God. Outwardly this God was Nature, and they recognized the sun as the God that had produced all life on earth.

So began the three-way partnership between *yin* and *yang* and their combined life spirit, which immediately started to seek survival. At the beginning, the provisions for life were easily found, but the situation rapidly changed when the couple over extended their reproductive force. The resultant population increase brought about new needs that were later met through struggling with others, including close relatives. First the contention was between individuals, but then people found they needed to cooperate to survive and formed family clans. Later these clans extended beyond the family as they grouped to become the tribes and races which began the struggles that continue to this day.

The first religious faiths were created to assist the internal cooperation within the groups with close blood connections. They then found that religiously organized groups had more force and won more battles, and eventually several of these groups came together to form a nation. This new initiative was then imitated by others to enhance their success in tribal competitions, but their leaders did not see that racial pride based on faith can also sow the seeds of hatred. After many generations, however, it can be seen that the groups who built the strongest conquering force, based on their emotional faith, also paid a high price for their experiences, as the bitter hostilities in the world have never ceased.

The Integral Way promotes humanistic love without bias, and asks no one to give up their ethnic background and conventional faith. Rather, we suggest the removal of any bias that hinders universal harmony and humanistic love as the way to prepare for greater cooperation among future societies. Worldly tension only leads to destruction, and people aware of the deep nature of life should consider how to prevent further contention. So, let us return to the humanistic love without bias where a common conscience could agree on a simple formula to avoid more difficulties in the world.

All worldly tension relates to the three main difficulties found during the struggle for survival - racism, religious prejudice, and a narrow view of nationalism, which are really only one problem with three forms of expression. Much of the basis for the endless rivalry comes from the contentious tendency of the male mentality. Yet realistically, humankind must learn how to cooperate as no group can survive alone. The early people saw the need for cooperation when facing survival in new situations, but at the same time set up religious faiths for competitive purposes. This inherent conflict has proven to be destructive, and should be replaced by embracing harmony and humanistic love.

The Integral Way did not arise from emotional tension, but from the spiritual depth at different stages of human growth. Hence, the Integral Way also accepts the early belief in God. God is a human creation that stands for the belief in everlasting survival. God is complete, and the deepest sense of God is that all people can come together to survive, except for those who have chosen to destroy life.

This is an important message for all those who choose the duty of creating a prosperous and harmonious world with reasonable social management by its leaders:

All humans are the children of the one source that is Mother Nature, and the only truth - yesterday, today, and tomorrow.

Respect those who live a constructive life, even in troubled times.

Grand Master Yo San, Ni [1879-1968 CE]

Social Tension and Contention

Sincerity and trustworthiness are the qualities that hold the key to avoiding further tension and contention, but few people today are able to reduce the tensions of modern life, or the social burdens in their society. What the world requires is the healthy social leadership that would reduce intellectual competition, and increase the sense of humanistic discipline behind the tensions. Such leadership depends on the conscious progress of humanity, while most people are more involved in getting a better deal in life.

Originally people were in a better physical condition than today, because this was part of their survival. But later the patterns of social rivalry changed when the intellectual and physical forces within the male tendency of competition and expansion combined to establish special privileges, where the weak were made to support the strong. This pattern then became the basis of the early governments and religions that eventually became the norm. However, a couple of centuries ago, this unhealthy and often malicious social competition increased and became more related to the desire for expansion than survival.

The creation of many new kingdoms, states, religions, and political parties throughout history, combined with their support schemes, also led to the social practice of being a parasite in life. And it now seems that no one feels shame when some people live on political privileges or favors, or religious support, or the social welfare system created by politicians, while others live off human relationships related to various political and social activities.

Some of these situations are acceptable, such as living off the family when very young or very old. However, other people live off a socialist society where the social burden usually disadvantages the more creative and responsible people. There are some unlucky people that need help in life, although there are more people who have developed social reliance, while much of the intellectual force in modern societies is used to create and sell the social systems that burden their society.

If the moral sense of humanity does not develop with the growth of the human intellect, the modern world may be in trouble. A healthy intellectual force and a constructive life spirit are capable of solving all the troubles in the world, and this is where the teaching of the Integral Way wants to offer help, but we must also fix the health of world leadership.

The picture of the world should be clearer now. Correctly applying our physical force can bring good fortune, while misapplying our physical force only invites trouble:

Your life is equipped with a physical force and an intellectual force where any improvement depends on you.

Make sure your life serves a constructive purpose.

Grand Master Yo San, Ni

Concern for Cultural Health

Conceptual confusion about human spirituality and associated cultures has become an obstruction to improving international cooperation. The Integral Way seeks better spiritual understanding to improve the cooperation among the old spiritual cultures. There is no reason to discontinue our cultural differences, but there is a need for a new standard for spirituality that is above such differences.

All people should expect to live a balanced life with the Five Healths – physical, mental, spiritual, social and financial. Nobody can deny the importance of these five factors in life where an imbalance in one aspect can affect the soundness of other aspects. They form a common ground for humanity, no matter the society, cultural background, psychological situation, or any other circumstance.

Once achieving the Five Healths is our goal in life, the only difference is in choosing whether to live constructively, or destructively, which also means keeping away from worldly confusion. People who live with a constructive attitude are creative and always make both ends meet. That should be one of the standards for healthy spirituality, but first we need to obtain the spiritual clarity that enables our life to exist above any cultural confusion or social fashions.

Today, worldly pressures and demands leave little time to reflect, and most people are unaware or confused about the correct direction for life. The fact that this problem has existed for a very long time shows that the human race has not matured enough to efficiently manage their lives. These matters do affect our health, but the Integral Way chooses to believe that Universal Nature is constructive, and that the evolution process continues to take the world forward and upward, because the Way is both horizontal and vertical, as explored in the vision known as the *I Ching*, or *Book of Changes*.

A partial vision may encourage people to surrender to a life of suffering from physical ailments, an unclear mind, spiritual immaturity, social toxicity, and poverty, as the many social religions and governments continue to shape society towards a problematic destiny. Religious followers may find a false escape in the hope for another world beyond life, but this approach lacks spiritual depth, and meanwhile the political and social struggles deepen.

The Integral Way wants people to live with a clearer vision so they are better equipped to manage life. Generally, the mind masters the body, but this creates danger when the mind does not grow from the experiences in life. This means we must first master the mind to understand the deeper reality of life, including gaining more knowledge and a greater appreciation of the inner partners that work within our consciousness.

In a general sense this deep conscious group forms the non-verbal spiritual life force. It is not as apparent as the physical brain or mind, but still manages that mind, whether or not the life has developed, or remains unachieved. Our personal happiness or pain relates to the condition of this group, which includes representatives from up to seven generations of the blood line. The truth is that life never learns or develops enough, but the will of life continues to strive, and God represents the greater flow of the life spirit in all people.

At the current stage of human development the physical mind largely ignores its partnership with the spiritual mind, and often remains at the animal level. Everyone has a group of internal spirits who participate in the management of the health of their mind. Unhealthy minds can be messy, and a confused mind can ruin a life, while an unachieved mind can only function partially, which is a common condition in the modern world.

There is no physical trace of the group of life spirits that act as a backseat driver in the mind, but these can be traced spiritually. Conventionally, spiritual phenomena are personified as existent but separate beings, and the unified spiritual functions and activities of the mind are often viewed as angels or devils. If these images are personified in a spiritual vision, they come from our own internal group of spirits, although our minds may believe they are external. Rather, these phenomena are produced by our spiritual function that accepts a conscious suggestion to our deeper conscious group to appear as a separate being. This means our life has not yet achieved spiritual unification.

Conventional faiths offer their believers external deities that are really just tools for personal support, or gathering a social force. The clarity attained from overcoming any confusion is the true spiritual power. And as the spiritual strength grows the increased clarity of the spiritual group improves the mind, which in turn improves the bodily life. Hence, spiritual attainment is a matter of developing the personal spiritual function in life, but when the mind has little or no internal help, this function remains at a low level.

True spirituality means approaching life as a source of inspiration, and an opportunity to serve. Thus, true spiritual growth is the result of real life experience, and trying to escape life blocks our internal growth. Buddhism complains about the emptiness of life, although devaluing our life experience also denies our spiritual function as self-awareness is the substance of our spirituality. Moreover, once life is denied, the spiritual function is limited to our basic instincts. Some social religions with external beliefs have good disciplines that may reflect the subtle substance hidden in the mind, but they are still unable to distinguish that being and non-being operate at different levels in life.

There is also the choice of becoming a truthful being in the Universe by fully attaining the Five Healths in life. A level of proficiency in the first three - physical health, mental health and spiritual health - is inescapable, whether or not you choose to retreat from your worldly duties. The other two - social health and financial health - can be expanded or reduced, depending on your personal growth and circumstances.

The Universe is constructive, but if any one of the Five Healths is lacking that life cannot be constructive. The Integral Way supports all people who have attained the Five Healths, whatever their contribution. In the integral truth there is no difference between those who achieve much, and those who achieve little in society. What is important is the value of the well-being achieved from completing all five aspects of a healthy life. Furthermore, any social leader who does not fulfill these five basic requirements in life is disqualified from serving the health of the world.

Some religions have devalued secular life while promoting a Heaven that leads to spiritual failure for many of their believers. Spiritual failure means having the spiritual weakness of not being able to function in a secular life with all its pressures, which eventually leads to spiritual awakening. Other religions have encouraged racial struggle, or suggested living off the life force of others. Both approaches rely on an empty pretext to establish religious practices that lack the truthful foundation that a good life is the basis of a healthy humanity.

The sun is the ruler of my mind; the sun is the Heavenly Father to my soul.

Those who live a constructive life are able to face any challenges in life.

Grand Master Yo San, Ni

Chapter 3

Essence of the New Direction

Becoming part of the new approach to the original Universal Faith in the light of the sun means living up to the standard of the sun spirit, where the word 'spirit' could be used to directly refer to the essence of the sun. In our life the sun within is represented by our healthy spirit of life where there is no self-confusion, and the heart expresses candor.

So far, this spirit has been denied by the physical scientists, who do not see that their interest in research and other factual matters is a spiritual expression of their own lives. But they can correctly deny any reliance on an imaginary faith to support human life because that practice does not uplift our life to the stage where it could reach the subtlety or spiritual refinement that is above the coarse level of the physical life force. However, the latter could be a research subject for an interested mind.

My family research shows that everything has its own spiritual expression, and if only one type of expression is insisted upon this gives other people a general impression of the nature of the spirits in that circumstance. The truth is that being rich is one type of spiritual devotion, being distinguished is another form of spiritual devotion, and even the culture of Las Vegas can be seen as a spiritual expression of life, as can the faith insisted upon by various religionists. Likewise, the fundamental problems of humanity at any time, no matter the culture or beliefs, are all expressions of the different spirits involved.

Hence, each of the many expressions in life is backed by a different spirit. So, what is important in the pursuit for the spiritual health of humanity is whether or not each of these spirits is healthy. I will now offer some simple examples: being diligent in life is a spiritual sign of health, while being lazy is a spiritual sign of weakness. With this understanding we can know that a healthy life is a spiritual choice, and being spirited means being deep, although this differs from the level of expressing various ideas, concepts, beliefs, philosophies, ideologies, or other 'isms'.

Now let us go the depth of life through the work done by my family over many generations. In our new expression of the faith of the Integral Way, the sun is the symbol that represents the complete health or well-being of human life. Yet, there is the reality of a different sun within all life, and seeking this inner sun is our spiritual choice.

The New Expression of the Original Universal Faith

The sun is our model for a healthy, self-reliant life. People who need a ruler at various stages in life can view the sun as the king who supports them without taking anything away. But, because the sun rules by demonstrating healthy moral leadership, it is hoped that all people with power over others will follow this model. The sun is also a model of hope to encourage people on the path of living with the Five Healths as it illustrates a life which owes nothing to anyone, and truly achieves the independence of one of the heavenly light bodies. This accomplishment has no need for social recognition.

The world needs such healthy leadership for all human societies, whether large or small. Thus, our faith is that all universal morality and constructive accomplishments follow the moral leadership of the sun. Following our Heavenly Ruler means we avoid destructive habits, and never express hatred, or have evil thoughts, towards others. Similarly, all constructive human behavior comes from the Heavenly Father-King, while any destructive behavior or evildoing represents the downfall of part of humanity. True humanistic love must come from the Father-King, but tolerance for the differences in life is the most practical way for us to keep the world moving in a constructive direction.

The New Path

The sun is the only spiritual leader to the highest life of humanity. At the same time the sun is the spiritual King of his own Heavenly Kingdom. As his followers we do our best to follow the spiritual qualities of the Father-King, and these constructive qualities that ensure the security of eternal spiritual life, can also bring success in worldly life. Hence, we serve only the one King within the deepest life force, and our assigned duty in life is to comply with the universal subtle law. Loyalty to the King is illustrated by our actions, and the accomplishment of one person equates to the accomplishment of all people.

Following the Father-King in daily life is very simple. In the new approach we express our devotion to attaining the fullest health and most effective life through following the daily, seasonal and annual cycles. We go to bed at the right time and get up early. In between, we do our best to support ourselves and take care of others by always respecting our own and all other lives, whether or not they are directly related.

Towards a New Life

A new life means a constructive life that pursues the Five Healths as outlined in the series of seven titles on the Path of Constructive Life.

The Universal Integral Way has only one important public celebration each year - the Chinese New Year Spiritual Renewal Ceremony. This commemoration spans countless generations, and the custom to make the first three days of the New Year special began during the Xia Dynasty [2207-1766 BCE]. The first day was chosen as the birth of the Sky, the second day as the birth of the Earth, and the third day as the birth of Humanity. At this special time people say Happy New Year to each other when they meet on the road, or elsewhere, regardless of enmity, so this can be called the Universal Day. However, we are also open to new customs as we should all share the joy of life in this world.

In the new expression of the one Universal Faith in the sun and life, and the new path of the Integral Way, we follow the original faith of the early people with the biggest heart of all – the heart of humanity. It is hoped that our new direction will be the real strength that realizes the dreams and visions of these early people, and of all the other sincere people throughout time who have carried the message of the humanistic heart from the light of the sun.

Five Universal Disciplines

The following five precepts, based on Jainism and Buddhism, have been integrated with other basic universal disciplines to form a common social code for treating each other in the world in the hope that we can maintain the inherent decency of humanity:

We do not engage in violent behavior. Motzi believed in no aggression towards others, including aggression by the State. In the Integral Way it is very important that those who engage in serious spiritual improvement work on any violence in their deeper thoughts and emotions, as these are the source of much deviant behavior.

We take nothing from others, whether by force, or negligence, or telling lies.

We respect our own health and the health of our partners by never engaging in improper sexual behavior.

We tell no lies. Lies, whether large or small, have no place in the serious situations of life. This especially applies to matters that could be seen as creating social or political fraud, or establishing a spiritual teaching that could deeply hurt the world.

We do not take any strong stimulants that could turn the world into a graveyard.

Eight Further Disciplines for Moving Along the New Path

The Universal Integral Way is centered on the spiritual growth of life. Thus, keeping up our spiritual study and practices is the main direction in life.

A healthy lifestyle is our best investment.

Conducting each day with a calm mind has greater value than engaging in religious fervor.

Bodily movements that balance the mind and body help to calm an overly active mind, and regular spiritual practices help to maintain a healthy confidence throughout life.

Try to keep away from too many social activities.

Find the time to be alone and undisturbed to benefit from the reflection on life that furthers spiritual growth.

The *Tao Te Ching*, the *Book of Changes and Unchanging Truth*, and other self-selected spiritual books should be used for important life counsel[2].

The spiritual development that comes from helping others can be found through being a mentor or spiritual coach of the Integral Way, but religious fervor is not promoted.

Additional Suggestions for People in Christian Societies

Your spiritual life belongs to the Heavenly Kingdom on Earth, where we all live.

Have the faith that your King is the Heavenly Father, the sun, who demands loyalty and devotion to the health of life.

Like father, like son - you can attain moral power and support from the Father-King, and still recognize Jesus as the head of your church.

In this new approach to the Universal Faith in the sun, Nature, and humanity, 'Mother and Son' would represent the relationship between Mother Universe and the sun, and 'Father and Son' would represent the relationship between the sun and the teaching of Jesus. This means that the sun relates to the deeper Universe like a son relates to his mother, while Mother Universe holds the trust of all human life. Similarly, the life of humanity is like a child to its direct source of support, the sun,

2 Specific resources to support the one Universal Faith in the sun and humanity: All titles in the Path of Constructive Life series [see below]; The Tao Te Ching for public support in the new world; The Way, the Light and the Truth for universal spiritual correspondence; The Esoteric Tao Te Ching, Quest of Soul and some invocations in the Workbook for Spiritual Development to offer further guidance on spiritual fortification.

while Jesus' devoted faith to the Heavenly Father led him to embody the spirit of his Father, the sun.

The Way to Universal Integral Health

The Integral Way is a spiritual path centered on personal spiritual improvement, and its social service forms part of the fulfillment of the universal morality needed to improve the health of humanity. This path is based on the practice of moral duty to others, and living a balanced life. Everyone is welcome to participate in this new path to improve the world, and there are spiritual study groups in various places which support their members as they build and nurture a healthy personality and an effective life.

In the late 1990s, after many decades of reviewing the old traditions, I was internally inspired to teach the Integral Way through the Path of Constructive Life as a new faith to guide humanity away from the continual suffering and confusion people have experienced for over two thousand years. There are seven titles in my series of books on the Path of Constructive Life that establish the foundation for this New Faith:

The New Universal Morality was produced to support the spiritual unity of the world and guide us towards the truth of life. This work explores the concept of God, and the human morality that goes beyond the various racial and religious divisions.

The Power of the Feminine offers support for the gentle feminine principle that is highly respected for resolving human conflict, and for supporting the masculine principle throughout the many challenges we are given in life.

The Path of Constructive Life was written to help people develop a constructive psychology to reduce the conventional religious and social control. This would enable them to embrace the Heavenly Heart and further the spiritual development of humanity.

Love of Universal Mother offers support for the full cooperation between males and females as our society moves away from patriarchal domination.

We also hope that this work will take people back to the wholeness of living in harmony with Mother Nature.

The Five Healths for a New Humanity is intended to support our personal spiritual duty to attain all of the Five Healths that relate to the five forces of Nature – water for balanced development, wood for healthy growth, fire for personal light and warmth, earth for tolerance and balance, and metal for self-affirmation.

Evolve Heaven on Earth is to prepare us to have faith in the Sun God for our new direction. A life centered on harmony, cooperation and balance develops the wisdom, kindness, courage and universal love to allow peace in the world. In this respect all teachings with a good heart are equal in the work to ensure the survival of humanity.

One Spiritual Reality: A Guide to Universal Harmony was written to support universal spiritual development, and our personal spiritual fortification. This book also contains several spiritual practices from the Ni family heritage teachings, which are centered on our faith in the sun, and our connection with the Lady of Wisdom.

The Way was also appreciated by Jesus through the power of universal spiritual correspondence. He helped the West to learn moral love, and his social ethics still form the foundation of most Western cultures. This is similar to the position of Confucius in Chinese culture. But since the time of Jesus some Western cultures have chosen corruption, although the general trend is to lead the world towards globalization.

This contribution is not ideal, however, and has produced many global problems, such as the over industrialization that damages the organic condition of life. Meanwhile, many of the earlier but smaller troubles remain, and any credit for the healthy and prosperous side of Western culture should be given to the many excellent individuals who kept moving forward, rather than to any specific culture or religion. That is, there is a clear distinction between social and religious teachings, and the individual response to life.

The true teaching of Jesus differs from most churches. He wanted to enlighten all people who were attached to a cultural faith, and his life illustrates the maxim that human justice is displayed by the non-discriminating light from the sun. He also publicly transmitted the truth that the relationship between earthlings and the sun mirrors the relationship between a son and his father, while his use of the pronoun 'I' designated all humankind.

All people ought to have faith in the sun, the Heavenly Father, and the new social leaders in the West should lead the movement to create the Kingdom of Heaven in all societies on Earth. My work, *The Way, the Light and the Truth*, may offer them some inspiration. However, the *Tao Te Ching* from Lao Tzu still offers good support to the modern world.

Social change is usually driven by a few individuals, and the health of those individuals predetermines the direction taken, and whether this direction is positive or negative. Positive contributions offer the real salvation to humanity, and these people are the true saviors of their time, although they are not addressed as such. Their strength does not come from the prevailing beliefs, but from the universal heart of life that corresponds to the beneficence of the light of the sun.

The Universal Integral Way supports the clarity of our deep conscious self that is the spiritual soul in life, and whose main source is the sunlight. Let us follow the heart endowed by the sun, and follow the justice of the sun as our permanent Heavenly Father. We now stand at the turning point for humanity, where we look to the sun, the light, the conscience, and the health of humanity. The rest is our own choice:

Follow all our forerunners who followed the sun
With a universal heart, and the strong conscience of life.
We will now exercise our endowed might and latent potential
To do whatever is right for our own life, and for human society.

PART II

The Search for Spiritual Maturity

The ultimate destination of our search for spirituality is spiritual maturity.

Chapter 4

First Steps

Before we reach spiritual maturity we are like a blind person riding a blind horse towards a deep waterway in the middle of the night as they travel through an area where there is no prospect of help. Hence, finding spiritual maturity should be our main concern in life.

First, we should eliminate any religious insistence or prejudice. The Heavenly Father of Jesus, the sun, is the source of life for all humanity, no matter our personal belief. All people receive their life from Earth, and Earth and all life on Earth is part of the solar system. The sun is the source of all planets in our solar system, but human life was conceived, born and developed from the barren Earth that had to work with all available support - internal and external - to develop both itself and humanity. The earliest people intuitively knew that their Heavenly Father was the sun as the males experienced an erection every time the sun began its daily cycle, and the females were aware that their eggs were nurtured by the moon that reflected the energy of their Heavenly Father.

The Heavenly Father possesses three types of potency - physical, mental and spiritual. His physical potency is known by all earthlings, while his mental potency determines the growth of the human mind as the brain is constantly stimulated by the light of the sun and other heavenly bodies. Human civilization is also a product of this stimulation, although the level of civilization differs due to various internal and external influences from human life. At the spiritual level people receive their small soul, the main part of their life, from the large soul of their Heavenly Father. Some people are able to return to their Father, but many lose their soul on the journey of worldly life.

Also be aware that although the light of the sun can form life, different effects are produced when the light beams intersect with other forces in the local environment. Early human life was able to communicate directly with the forces of Nature, but later the growth of their conscious force and conceptual capability enabled them to establish their own world and create their own life faith. In spite of this the Heavenly Father still lives within each human life as their soul and conscience.

The human soul and conscience represents the light of the Heavenly Father through a life which is upright, straightforward, righteous, just, fair, and considerate. When the soul and conscience is strong, the behavior of that life parallels the Heavenly Father, but when the soul is weak the life is usurped by the mind. However, the mind only works for the small self that lacks the all-encompassing approach of our Father in Heaven, so a developed intellect with little conscience can create much trouble for wider humanity.

A growing arrogance that denies the grace of the source of life has made people ungrateful as they develop their own conceptual beliefs that only bring small benefit to a few, but lack the broad, all-embracing nature of Heaven. Many people today also seek to be different from the life they were given by the Heavenly Father, and choose to go against the harmony of Nature. Yet people with a strong conscience should maintain their faith, and live with the openness of the Heavenly Father, in spite of any social pressures and difficulties. We must remember where the soul of life should return, and find more balance between nurturing our natural health and the pressures of worldly life.

At a time when most people were ungrateful to the Heavenly Father, Jesus of Nazareth was grateful and honest and told people: 'I come from my father. The love of my father is great, so I am able to reach you all'. He left us these words with the hope that everyone would love each other because the Heavenly Father loves us all. Ask yourself if you could separate your life from the Heavenly Father and live alone. The answer is clear, so be like Jesus who said: 'I come from my Father, and my Father is in me'.

Some people seek the Heavenly Father elsewhere, but can they go beyond the sky? The early people wondered which one of the heavenly bodies of light in the sky was their Heavenly Father. There are many, but the only one which is the Heavenly Father to the planets and their satellites in our solar system is the sun. Similarly, humans are the only life with the potency from all three spheres of our Heavenly Father, the sun, and no other heavenly body has the strength, or is close enough, to support the human life force. Jesus knew this important reality at a time when other people in his society fervently practiced a hypocritical cultural belief to highlight their difference from other tribes.

When people are open they would admit that creating small faiths is part of the process of attaining growth. But they should also consider whether human life could develop and survive on Earth for so long without the support of their Heavenly Father, the sun. Yet, most religions and other forms of worship neglect the true source of life. No other life on Earth is as ungrateful as the people who do not recognize that the sun is the Heavenly Father to all existence in the solar system. Instead, they prefer the fictitious stories established to dominate or manipulate other people, and neglect the heavenly qualities of straightforwardness, uprightness, righteousness, justice, and fairness.

We all know that Earth could not survive without the sun, so there ought to be tremendous gratitude towards the Heavenly Father we sometimes call God, who supports us all. But people continue to create small conceptual beliefs to support their arrogance and debase others. Arrogance is an emotional poison to wider humanity - when people insist from their pride, whether physical or conceptual, they can become arrogant and belittle others, and this is how the process of spiritual growth has often invited further trouble in the world.

All people on Earth are members of the big family we call humanity, but their only common source is their Heavenly Father, the sun. When the bright sun centers the world it will become a paradise, where all people live together harmoniously, and allow each other an equal opportunity in life. However, people should also be aware that the main source of worldly trouble comes from being overly self-centered when relating to others. When they abandon the openness of their Heavenly Father, they should remember that both their life force and that of all other life comes from the sun.

Some artificial faiths use metaphors or images from the vastness of Nature to help support the small lives of their believers. Most of these metaphors and images represent the sun, but some beliefs adopt other powerful natural images, such as stars, or planets, or thunder. There is no problem with using earthly images like mountains and the ocean to stimulate our creativity, but it is very wrong to insist on a metaphor to support the superiority of some society while ignoring the reality that Nature that is open to all life.

Recognizing the truth that the source of all life is the sun requires spiritual growth, although this should be one of the guiding spiritual principles in life. We also need to recognize that attaining mental maturity, and the spiritual growth gained from real life experiences, provides the true fruit to achieve a healthy humanity.

Realization through Reviving the Universal Faith in Humanity

Do not expect any salvation outside humanity. We have given a clear direction for our new path, but know that most people's lives are commanded by their emotional force. This means that any emotional traps from our established spiritual habits should be reviewed or removed to offer a better support in life. Our hope is that reviving the early Universal Faith in the sun and human life would give all people with a humanistic heart the strength to realize the spiritual vision and dreams from the biggest hearts of all spiritual and cultural heritages:

> The dream of the **Yellow Emperor** was for a Kingdom of Plenty and Beauty [華胥國];
>
> The dream of **Lao Tzu** was for the realization of Universal Morality and Virtue, and a self-sufficient and self-protected Kingdom with undisturbed borders [道德世界];
>
> The dream of **Confucius** was for a world of Great Unity and Harmony [大同世界];
>
> The dream of **Jesus** was to achieve the Heavenly Kingdom on Earth;

The dream of the laughing **Buddha** was to enter the Pure Land [人間淨土];

The vision of the **Messenger** is to achieve a spiritual paradise on Earth;

The dream of **Karl Marx** was for a world that practiced communism without harming others, or the health of society;

The dream of **Dr. Sun Yat-Sen** was to accomplish a world of great harmony.

But also be aware that social accomplishment can cause pain, and that the dreams in sleep come from the life spirits of the heart as a wake-up call from the internal system. The above dreams or visions are different, and associated with personal conscientious concern and the celestial light from sources such as the sun, the moon, and the stars.

The Integral Way now hopes to provide another such vision for modern humanity, and our dream offers the safer choice of a Universal Faith based on personal spiritual fulfillment. No one is able to guarantee being born again or all the conditions in their present life, but our hope is we can all renew our life by achieving the highest standards in the Five Healths, because those already on the Way are able to spiritually return to the youth of life.

人類和諧是總結

Dispel the spiritual confusion of humanity through the principle of Great Harmony.

Chapter 5

Seeking the Path of Pure Light

The Sun is the God of Universal Harmony,
Disharmony in the world comes from human immaturity.
The true Universal Faith believes in the deep truth of Heavenly Harmony,
And when humanity reaches maturity there will be true harmony.

The Way to personal spiritual fulfillment and universal spiritual health can be found in the following messages based on the *Path for Mastering the Grand Life*, also called the *Path of Pure Light*, from Grandmaster Yo San Ni [1879 – 1968]:

Support the One Universal Faith

Reach for Spiritual Harmony

天和真君

Heavenly harmony is the true source of human goodwill

That is more internal than external.

宗教由来是善心, 以[己]为[他] 恐有误.

[把人类自已心灵的投射, 当作 '并非外在的'上帝]

Goodwill is part of human nature,

But our minds are shaped by life circumstances.

Our heart expresses the non-verbal spirituality of humanity;

Our minds create the misconceptions that form various beliefs.

Hence, any 'God' that escapes the heart is an external creation.

The true God is our internal reality that expresses the healthy nature of life,

While universal goodwill expresses the godly nature of humanity.

To live with God means living with our healthy life nature,
And those who live with God live with the true nature of life.

Being straight in life gladdens God,
But the mental misconceptions that externalize God
Created religions that make people try to please an external God.

Real divinity exists in the hearts of all people,
But their minds have made this internal reality external.
The most truthful faith in human life is in universal goodwill.

The original faith in God was an expression of such goodwill,
But when an old mistake made this internal reality external,
Other people went along with this deviation.

天地机密在人身, 向外陈设在劝人.
各种宗教妄立信, 林林总总各赋名.
We all contain the spiritual secrets of Heaven and Earth.
Although many external teachings have persuaded people
To fight against their own fears and uncertainties in life,
This trend expresses insufficient mental growth.

Each culture has a different name for the God of their external faith,
But this did not make human spirituality any clearer.
Instead, the mental confusion has affected the health of humanity.

While many religious cultures in the world are very colorful,
The numerous forms of emotional worship
Are far from the spiritual reality of a truthful life.

名字太多形非一, 转教世人难见真.
族各创教玩名色, 不知同根自相竞.

Many names and too much formality conceal the simple truth,
So that it becomes shallow or remains in the shadows.
This weakness comes from the social rivalry that ignores
The truth that we all come from Mother Nature.

人类精神起混乱, 先须自明後助人.
精神真理只有一, 不知孰底在自身?

Currently there is great spiritual confusion,
But we must all make our own life clear before helping others.
There is no need to search externally,
The one and only spiritual truth resides deep within each life.

虽云三万六千神, 众神聚集成一身.
苏悉谛经七俱胝, 以数自视还赅人!

Folk Taoists claim 36,000 spiritual entities form our bodily life;
Early Indian teachings suggest seven billion of these spirits.
Yet, the number does not affect the true value of a life
That comes from seeking spiritual unity.

知一修一一是根, 清彻无讹须见源.
老子抱一得久寿, 葛洪守一一皆通.

Know, value, and cultivate this unity, as unity is the root of all.
Seeing this without misunderstanding enables us to see the source:
A newborn baby expresses such unity,
Lao Tzu embraced the unity and achieved a long life,
Ge Hong embraced the oneness of his spirit to connect with all.
The real achievement is to clear all internal and external confusion.

黄庭详说各部神, 但修一部得长生.
仍显支离未归一, 因此特地颂天和.

In the Classic of the Yellow Court,
Different inner entities were carefully given specific functions.
This reflected the spiritual truth of the internal world.

Cultivating any one of these spiritual functions
Enhances the entire spiritual force in life
Because the spiritual truth is that all is one, and one is all.

Similarly, the spiritual truth for humanity is:
Each person represents the spiritual reality of all people.
Hence, all people should seek to exemplify the
Original human spirituality before there was any deviation.

Today, most people still insist on their scattered beliefs
Due to mental blockages from their life circumstances.
Yet the spiritual truth remains the great unity at the depth of Nature.

一身实际无数气, 寧可一心略其多.
如何不忽兆万身, 天和真君敕众一.

Our life possesses numerous beings of chi we call bodily spirits,
But it is always safe to be single-minded
When we are supported by our internal spiritual unity.

This position does not ignore the reality of spiritual multiplicity,
And once you have attained the true spiritual knowledge,
You will become the highest holy being.

天真皇人说三一, 三部丹田各亿千.
慑来还三还归一, 天和真君合众一.
The Yellow Emperor visited the Great One of Heavenly Truth
Where he was given the nature of the trinity within the human body.

Our body contains three immortal fields, or Tan Tien [丹田]:
The upper field holds the physical brain and mind,
The middle field oversees the lungs and heart,
The lower field governs the sexual organs and reproductive force.
Together, they support the unity of life.

Internal refinement means returning to our original wholeness
That expresses the harmony and unity from the universal life force.

但在心中存一念, 天和真君所集聚.
太和天君一宇宙, 天和真君一此身.
Our mind should be constantly aware of its relationship
With our physical body through the subtle law of spiritual unity.
This highest Heavenly Law also unifies the Universal Being,
While the Heavenly Law of Harmony is able to unify our life.

修得天和作何用? 修得天和一身一.
不仅一身兼一类, 不仅人类兼宇宙.
What does it mean to cultivate and achieve Heavenly Harmony?
Achieving such harmony not only unifies humanity,
But also brings the unity of humanity and the Universe.

We should never separate our conscious force from
The universal harmony that enables us to view all people
As one life, and identify with the Universal 'Being'.

天和真君致身健, 天和真君使心清.
天和真君保神爽, 处人和睦财养身.
Deep faith in the Universal Being and subtle Law of Universal Harmony
Helps us to attain a healthy body, a clear mind, and a happy spirit,
While our bodily life provides the strength to be materially self-reliant,
And establish a peaceful connection with all other life,

有此五康齐集身, 天和真君实致之.
不是迷信但致一, 科学修行有所承.
These Five Healths come from the depths of universal harmony,
Not the old superstitions that rely on others to care for our life.

It is precious to know the oneness within universal harmony
That also offers some psychological and scientific support for
The life that embodies the Law of Universal Harmony.
This subtle law is the Way.

人之一身有精神, 精神事实非迷信.
尊一守一与抱一, 谨敕众一为真君.
All people possess a bodily life with spirits
That includes their reproductive force and conscious force.
If we respect and unite these forces to create a true universal being,
We would help to ensure the survival of humanity.

天和真君从何来, 就从老子称作一.
People who want the truth about the ultimate law of life
Can study the depth of Lao Tzu,
Who traced the steps of the Yellow Emperor from the early female
Culture that expressed the Way of the everlasting truth of life.

In the true Universal Faith:
The deepest faith of life is in the subtle law of life
Where there is only one law for all lives,
Regardless of circumstances.
Our Lord of Heavenly Harmony is the Sun

The Universal Being

人生各是集合体, 自然造人不由己.
始聚五行是五气, 後生意识未竟功.
Although each life is a collective being,
Being human is not a personal choice.
The five chi from Nature produce all the physical spheres on Earth,
Behind each expression is the Universal Being, or deepest unity of life.

历世历生渐成长, 不是一跃便成人.
陷在生伦无殊他, 灵性外铄万万年.
Human life evolved over multiple generations,
Each of which had limitations as they sought for progress.
This growth included the slow refinement of their spiritual nature
That goes beyond the concept of a life with form,
Because the formless spiritual nature of humanity is immortal.

蠢蠢之灵人类始, 混混噩噩无数年.
不是天生具灵性, 久由外铄庶生觉.
The formless nature of life, called the spirit,
Is projected from the impulse of Nature, the root of all life.
Most people do not gain the sense of their own life nature,
While others choose to neglect the latent depth of their life.

一点自觉分造化, 半由天来半由人.
得来灵性真不易, 不可猛浪变妖妄.

Some self-awareness takes us beyond the merely physical;
This partly comes from Nature, and partly from self-purification.
Do not mistake the transient for the potential of evolving to a higher life.
True spirituality is above the constant whirlpool of worldly existence.

欲知妖妄是何意? 雅称人王滥杀人.
一点灵性得复失, 再从人类往上修.

Demons are those who abuse or slaughter other people.
They are one step away from permanently leaving the cycle of life,
And once that small portion of spiritual awareness is lost,
Their lives will return to a snail-like stage of evolution.

又非一朝一夕事, 历代历劫炼灵明.
人类可轻等鹅毛, 人命可贵抵鸿钧.

True humanity can be viewed as being as light as a goose feather,
But the preciousness of each life equals that of the Universal Being.
Nevertheless, such refinement takes many lifetimes.

常言人妖有分别, [识域]深浅辨人妖.
未完修成人是妖. 只知自利不利人.

Distinguishing the subtle differences between being human
Or being a demon depends on the scope of our conscious power.
This is not the same as gaining knowledge,
Yet it determines the depth of our spiritual growth.

Spiritually unachieved people can be demon-like,
And only possess self-interest,

While the spiritually achieved have dissolved the self
In order to live with the Universal Being of life.

[识域] 浅时人半兽, [识域] 高广半入仙.
古来仙人多久寿, 已具识域深且广.
When the scope of the consciousness remains shallow,
People might only attain half their humanity.
But the consciousness can grow to carry life to its highest level.
A healthy, happy life is the first sign of becoming like an immortal,
Who are known for the breadth and depth of their consciousness.

历世修来得正果, 真性不失非欲牵,
虽然长生仍是欲, 同天同地志不凡.
Healthy fruit grows from nurturing the tree of life,
And producing healthy spiritual fruit requires a regular life
Where the true nature is not confused by human desire.

Although wanting a long and happy life is still a desire,
This differs from pursuing other worldly desires.
Just know that uniting with Heaven and Earth and living
With our true nature can produce a long and happy life.

在生不与他人竞, 但与自竞求改善,
精益求精善更善, 这种根器万万年.
Each lifetime is precious,
And there is no need to compete with others.
Instead, seek to constantly improve the self as the preparation
For deepening the root of life can last for millions of years.

人生归趋不一样, 一点灵气非寻常.
但知逐物气化物, 灵性不偏路久长.
The destination of each life also differs,
And is determined by the nature of our spiritual essence.
Chasing material matters might transform our material life,
But developing poise can clarify its destination, and lengthen its path.

敢为天地作主宰, 不在人间称雄豪.
人因畜志定归趋, 用心可分人高下.
So, give up all interests to be a hero in the world,
And dare to let the nature of life decide its own destination.
People are shaped by their interests in life,
While their conscious choices distinguish the level reached.

生命区分非仅形, 意识宽狭定其人.
同天同地同日月, 须知此人渐化天.
This is not just a matter of each person's form,
But rather the breadth of their conscious condition in knowing life.
If the conscious self is like the sky, the earth, the sun, and the moon,
Surely that life will gradually become like Heaven.

形迹有化性不迁, 这个机密几人知?
五福得来是附属, 须知人生气所化.
Very few people know their overall life can be transformed
By their spiritual energy, though their spiritual nature is constant.
Thus, any condition in life is an opportunity to transform the self.
But also know that the five blessings are only side products,
And even a blessed life can become an attachment.

生命建设在天和, 但修天和沿长路.
万试千难终不失, 修成正果乐如何?

The shape of each life ultimately resides with the
Heavenly Harmony that directs each life on its long journey.
But whatever the challenges, be insistent about the unity of life
To finally attain the happiness gained from the true spiritual fruit.

人能主宰天地乎? 此心同天与同地,
既有此心比日月, 涵包人类有天心.

Can human life really master the sky and the earth?
A conscious life can achieve equality with both
By attaining a heart that is like the sun and the moon,
And always shines openly on all life.

仙人以何为自修, 精勤但只修天和.
内修[三宝]:精气神, 外修[三官]:心口意.

Internally, the immortals refined the three deep forces in life:
Reproductive power, vital support, and conscious power.
Externally, they disciplined the related organs and senses,
Such as bodily desires, verbal expression, and intent.
This enabled them to unite their personal life with Heavenly life.

人亏众力扶此身, 因致天和得内和.
能享五福非独力, 还赖心眼识明路.

A simple healthy life is the convergence of multiple forces,
Thus enjoyment from the five blessings is not the only support.
The inner peace achieved by being in harmony with the sky
Also relies on the growth of our spiritual vision.

心眼识力同一事, 不是赠与是自得.
历代生命皆学费, 得来一点人不同.
The deepest vision of life is not a gift.
It takes many lifetimes to attain such vision,
And is paid for with the troubles accumulated over that time.
But this gain does make the life very different.

太和天君在何处, 今言宇宙古鸿钧.
鸿钧老祖他是我, 同受淘炼我是他.
Where is the Lord of Great Harmony?
In the Universe the ancient people called the vast balance,
He is but me,
And through spiritual refinement, I can become Him.

天地与人通一性, 人与天地同一性.
人能复合天地性, 将谁唤作你我他?
Universal Nature and humanity share the same life nature,
Although people try to separate themselves and live differently.
This creates many divisions among people, even you and me.
The spiritual route is to remove these divisions
And re-unite with the nature of the Universe.

内已无我外无物, 不与侪类同性命.
这点灵性从何得? 应从牲畜去辨人!
Inwardly there is no more self, and outwardly no more world.
Hence, I am beyond the destination sought by others.
Where did I gain this small piece of spirituality?
Through observing the nature of other animals.

同中有异异中同, 不独饮食与女男.
同中求异有拣择, 异中求同总容物.
The similar show differences; the different exhibit likeness.
And not just in eating, drinking and sexual needs.
Be selective and tolerant about differences among the similar,
And when looking for likeness when there is difference.

同同异异异中同, 不自标榜称仙翁.
有所不为是君子, 不为人欲竞人雄.
There is difference in sameness, and sameness in difference.
However, this is not to distinguish one from the other,
Nor establish any rivalry with anyone over anything.
So far that has not been achieved, even by gentlemen.

纵虽有权如天大, 不妄己意乱整人.
不必人上称作天, 怀抱天心即同天.
You may be socially powerful,
But never persecute others by insisting on your own view.
Being like the sky means having no need to overpower others.
Those who embrace the sky can be as broad as the sky.

玄女早有天同教, 放开人生去学天.
做人不是斗权势, 专讲服务不自居.
Long before written history,
Our female ancestors taught people to be open like the sky.
The value of life is not measured by competing for power,
But by our unselfish service to others.

人类何能以同天? 但抱天心行天德.
若问天德是什么? 天不胁人从己意.
How can humanity be like the sky?
From embracing the heavenly heart and fulfilling heavenly morality.
Then, how do we recognize Heavenly morality?
By not forcing others to go along with us.

助人扶世同一事, 毋固毋必毋自我.
不以己命比人大, 将人比己即同天.
Fulfillment also comes from helping the world,
And not insisting on any particular way or opinion,
But valuing all others as equal to, or higher, than the self.
This is how to realize Heaven in life.

人间和乐第一事, 岂用远程去求仙.
和天和地与人和, 人类不朽命同天.
Of utmost importance is finding happiness with other people.
There is no need for a long journey to seek the spiritual truth,
Just harmonize with Heaven, Earth and all people.
The immortal truth is manifested in life,
And the Lord of Universal Harmony is Mother Universe herself.

Support the New Path

Long Live Heavenly Harmony

天若不和天将变, 地若不和地将倾.
人若不和人间乱, 颠沛流离人自受.
If the sky is not in harmony[3] it is troubled,

---

3 Heavenly Harmony or harmony within Nature means that all life in both the internal and external world is in its correct and natural order.

If the earth is not in harmony it encounters problems.
If humanity is not in harmony people suffer, and there is no escape.

上代传下天和经, 人世经验千万年.
传言後人修天和, 整体利益便是天.
The Classic on Heavenly Harmony from the early people
Has been verified by thousands of years of human experience.
Its message is to value the spiritual harmony in life
As a necessary condition to self-improvement, and living with others.
Heaven is found in the common goodness that benefits all.

欲致天和先空心, 去掉己见和私欲.
个己利益莫当先, 倾刻便达大天和.
A healthy life includes the Heavenly harmony from not being
Opinionated, or prejudiced, or motivated by selfish desire.
The priority is to have no conflict with anyone,
And if there is no selfish interest among the family and society,
Heavenly Harmony already prevails.

心若不空和不至, 人类命运难改变.
变来变去仍乱滩, 乱滩之上堆乱坟.
Prejudiced minds have disturbed the harmony within Nature,
And the world remains a place of chaos and destruction.
This ever changing situation only added more graves and tombs,
While making it difficult to change the human destination.

整体利益非一人, 人人合力达天和.
究竟天和作何义? 人类健康乃久长.
Heavenly harmony can bring everlasting health to humanity,

But know that any benefits should be bestowed to all people.
Social divisions based on class are unhealthy,
As harmony within Nature requires complete cooperation.

天与人和是天然, 人与天和乃自然.
上下相和有必然, 左右相和道方坚.

Heaven embracing people expresses its divine nature.
People embracing Heaven expresses human nature.
Harmony between the above and the below is inevitable;
Agreement between the left and right strengthens this position.

Harmony within Nature embraces humanity,
While humanity lives within the harmony of Nature.
A sensitive and healthy response from the deep humanistic heart
Is to be grateful for life, and maintain universal harmony.

Harmony between our private desires and original nature
Can bring long lasting support from Nature.
Some suffering may come from a bad climatic condition,
But people cause more damage than anything created by Nature.

前後相合奔成功, 内外相合得安健.
在人在家与在国, 一理贯通是天和.

Unity between the internal and external factors in life brings peace,
Cooperation among people, no matter their position, brings success.
Whether it is an individual, a family, or a nation,
One thread connects them all: the Law of Heavenly Harmony.

有人违此天和经, 修行拜神皆无益.
原来天和是天则, 岂问谁人任意违?

Once the harmony of Nature is forsaken,
External worship has no real benefit,
And socialistic ventures and other situations where
Some rise and others fall will only have partial success.
But Heavenly Harmony supports the survival of all life:
No one should go against the beneficence of Heavenly Law.

人若不和是生病, 家若违之将破碎.
公司违之巳到头, 国若违之国生乱.

The truth of human survival is clear:
When people disobey Heavenly Law, sickness comes,
When a family violates Heavenly Law, it disintegrates.
When a company defies Heavenly Law, the internal cooperation is destroyed,
When a nation departs from Heavenly Law, this invites disaster.
This matter concerns all conscientious people with a deep moral sense of life.

奉劝世人去私心, 世道健康乃在人.
不论团体有大小, 终之天和是天心.

Ambitious people are advised to eliminate all selfish interests.
The health of the world relies on us all, no matter our situation,
To come together to strengthen the Heavenly axis[4].
This means applying the law of Heavenly Harmony in all worldly life.

---

4 The Heavenly axis is a term to describe the centripetal spiritual force that centers the world.

人类健康是目的, 还凭修炼空此心.
人生得失原有限, 争争攘攘那安宁!
The main purpose of life is to maintain the health of humanity,
And can be achieved by reducing our wildest interests.
In this context, individual gain and loss is a very small matter,
While rivalry or contention seriously disturbs the peace of humanity.

整体健康须尊奉, 决无扩充一己私.
人若通晓天和经, 方知此人善根深.
The complete health of life should be respected above all,
And selfish desires curtailed.
Those who respect the principle of Heavenly Harmony
Are deeply rooted in the natural health of a peaceful life.

有人畜意伤天和, 从此沉沦无尽期.
若是行为出无知, 再来人间遭离乱.
If someone is overly ambitious and intentionally
Disturbs the Heavenly Harmony of the human world,
Their life will fall into a bottomless pit of darkness.
And even if this behavior came from ignorance,
They would continue to experience turmoil and trouble in the world.

不论修己与安人, 但奉天和作天心.
内外一身履天志, 此人属天无可疑.
Whether improving the self or helping others,
We trust in Heavenly Harmony as our standard.
Those who follow the heavenly will, both internally and externally,
Are able to realize their heavenly heart and moral nature in life
That is undoubtedly shaped by the Heavenly axis.

Support for a New Life

Eulogy to the Lord of Heavenly Harmony

大道是天和, 以此称真君.

The great Way guides people to achieve Heavenly Harmony.

Those who attain Heavenly Harmony realize their Heavenly nature.

天若不和天将崩, 地若不和地将裂.
国若不和国将溃, 身若不和身将病.

When the sky lacks harmony it will collapse,
When the earth lacks harmony it will split,
When nations lack harmony they will be in turmoil,
And when bodily life lacks harmony it becomes sick.

天尊 '天和' 天长生. 地尊 '天和' 地长宁.
国尊 '天和' 国兴旺, 人尊 '天和' 人安康.

The sky continues its long life by respecting harmony,
The earth has long offered stability by respecting harmony,
Nations can become prosperous through respecting harmony,
And people will live in peace when they respect harmony.

每晨择时拜真君, 可以掐指或念珠.
真君与人自相应, 天君不召自来居.

Every morning after rising, connect to the Heavenly Harmony
By chanting, praying or using an invocation.
The universal Heavenly Harmony within will correspond,
So there is no need to call out loudly.

天和真君重自证, 一生不与人计较.
太和天君宇宙主, 宇宙深处最宁静.

The power of Heavenly Harmony witnessed by the self
Grows from a life that never struggles with others.

Great harmony is the reality of the depth of the Universe.
This can be reached by a peaceful life that becomes auspicious,
And manifests great harmony to others.
We can all attain this harmony from verifying the deep truth
That people are able to live with the oneness of the Universe.

天和真君四个字, 简而不繁可度生.
人间意念多耗散, 握得天髓念天和.
'*The Heavenly Harmony within*' is quite simple to chant.
This sincere practice can help to stabilize our whole life,
As too many thoughts will scatter the conscious power.
So, gather yourself, and recite 'the Heavenly Harmony within'.

人能专志持真君, 一身强健不散架.
从始到终养元和, 岂同一般鼓励语.
The practice is more than simple encouragement,
As conscious adoption improves our internal strength and health.
Heavenly Harmony comes from connecting with the power
Of life that stabilizes our internal unity.

天不亏人因心虔, 人不自亏尊天和.
内外一如人尊仰, 一生到老品骨香.
Uplifting our piety towards Nature is spiritually beneficial,
And once the internal and external are unified,
We can reach a senior age without any real problems in life.

致心歸命禮: 天和大天君!

Homage to the Highest Being of Heavenly Harmony

Realize the Five Harmonies in Life

人类尊五和, 无一可以缺.

There are five aspects to developing harmony in life, and none should be missed as each is able to counter-balance and mutually help the others.

首要与身和, 役身勿太过.

The first is the physical harmony from not exhausting the body.

二曰达心和, 心欲不可纵.

The second is the mental harmony from not over extending the desires and emotions.

三曰致内和, 精神无偏颇.

The third is the spiritual harmony from not pursuing numerous side interests.

四属与人和, 人际无缺憾.

The fourth is the social harmony from having no regrets regarding the family or society.

五属与物和, 财源自滋生.

The fifth is achieving material harmony without taking anything that is undeserved, or belongs to others.

致此五和者, 人天所同钦.

Achieving harmony in all five aspects is well respected by both Heaven and humanity.

精神统一, 无冲突; 谓之天和.

Moreover, a life with no conflict has attained the spiritual unity of Heavenly harmony.

心理统一, 无冲突, 谓之元和.

Psychological balance and the integration of all aspects in life bring harmony to the organic life force from Nature.

内脏平和, 无冲突, 谓之太和.

Similarly, eliminating imbalance among the internal organs means the attainment of great physical harmony.

道德健康, 无亏人己, 谓之人和.

Achieving moral health through not harming others, or the self, is to accomplish harmony within the human sphere.

经济健康, 无害人己, 谓之物和.

And having no financial or other material burdens in life is the attainment of material harmony.

此五事, 不能求之於人. 但当求之於己.

These five achievements can only be accomplished by our own efforts to live a good life, where there is no expectation of help from others, or the world.

成就五和人生, 然後,人类之五和社会自然可达.

Everyone should seek to achieve these five harmonies. Harmony among humanity can also be achieved naturally and effortlessly as each person fulfills the duty of life.

无遗世殃, 或遗孽於世, 要後人去收拾.

Create no troubles for the world; leave no problems for other people to fix.

但只佳惠後人, 一代比一代进步, 人间天堂可造, 定矣, 必之.

That is how all life can benefit future generations as each generation progresses their spiritual condition. Thus, Heaven is achieved by complete harmony within humanity.

天下人人盼富贵, 世上家家爱荣华. 人性之常非有疵. 但问手段正当乎?

All nations and most people seek to become prosperous, or distinguished. As long as upright conduct and the correctly handling of affairs are part of the success, all healthy interests in life can be encouraged.

人乐五和天相助, 依道而进乃自然. 人人如此世无扰, 减少灾难近天堂.

People who respect the five harmonies have achieved spiritual health and will be assisted by Heaven. It is natural to follow the Way of universal benefit and attain the complete health of Nature. If all people could live with the Way, and not make trouble for the world, we would be close to living in a Heavenly paradise on Earth, and free from any human disasters.

救世安世还在人, 岂可频造苦与难. 只缘不识真富贵, 岂及五和万世安.

The world can be saved, and societies would be peaceful, but most people will not see the real value of peace in life unless these five harmonies become part of the new direction for all humanity.

人类第一是文化, 柔化兽性依仗之. 若以文化掩兽性, 一旦暴露成大祸.

Many people have been helped by civilization. A healthy culture supports the safety of society, and can improve the nature of humanity. Human nature is already an improvement on animal nature, although the animal nature of humankind still requires some refinement. Unfortunately, some leaders may not respect such a healthy culture, and instead create hypocritical systems that hide the residual animal impulses which are the root of much misery, tragedy, and other human disasters.

人发兽性因受困, 因困变厉在弄权 [or 權]. 穷变凶恶还持理, 不尊道德历变剧.

When people engage in these animal impulses and behavior they become inhumane. This form of self-entrapment can also be triggered by poverty or some other predicament where the morality of life is not respected.

人类许从兽中来, 争权犹如狼争食. 一旦狼衰荣华尽, 悔不当初乐五和.

Social power struggles in human society can be likened to wolves fighting their prey, where the desire to conquer is stronger than their limited desire to eat. That may help people to achieve their desires, but there is no longer any pride in human life.

A healthy cultural leadership would place a high value on spiritual development, and once achieved, people would see the triumph of gaining the ability to be above the pressures of their lowliest nature in life. The attractive colors of vain-glory soon fade, and spiritual victory is for the few who triumph over their low desires. Thus, there should be no need to repent - just begin the endeavor of seeking harmony in all five aspects of life.

富贵荣华须自然, 若非自然莫强求. 举世滔滔求荣发, 如浪如潮发痴狂.

However, worldly people wish to be distinguished, and possess much money or power. And they madly push forward, and keep bouncing about like the tidal waves on a rocky shore.

So, here there is the truth on whether or not to take it or leave it in life: if it is natural and causes no particular struggle, accept the riches and distinction. But if these pursuits and gains are not part of a natural life they are not worth any damage to the precious health of life that is above all other matters in the worldly chase for wealth and fame.

富贵高位岂易得, 浮云聚散会有时. 一切假象过眼烟, 人生最贵乐五和.

The pursuit to become very rich, or possess a high social position with absolute authority, has never been easy. Even when achieved, any gain can be like the clouds in the sky that gather and soon disperse, just like all illusions in life. Living with the five harmonies – a healthy body, mind, life spirit, social connections and financial life – has the most value, as these matters do not have an ephemeral nature. Harmony is the main strength to build a healthy life, and offers the wisest choice for everyone.

Chapter 6

The Sun is the Source of Humanity

In the teaching on the *Path for Mastering the Grand Life* or *Path of Pure Light* from Grand Master Yo San Ni:

The Solar System Shapes Our Seasons, Direction, and Sense of Time

日為宗, 月為輔

The sun is the source of humanity, and supported by the moon and other solar planets.

五氣循環:

The rotation of the five elementary forces in Nature shape the seasons on Earth:

春= 生長之氣, 象 木

Spring manifests the force of growth as symbolized by wood.

夏=壯盛之氣, 象火

Summer manifests the force of strength as symbolized by fire.

長夏=雍滯之气,象土

Prolonged summer manifests the force of stability or stagnancy as symbolized by earth.

秋=收斂, 肅殺之气; 象金

Autumn manifests the sharp-edged or stringent force as symbolized by metal.

冬= 歸藏, 聚集之气;象水

Winter manifests the gathering and storing force as symbolized by water.

始祖以冬為始,

Within this natural cycle the early people made winter the time the seasons on Earth began.

冬孕育→春生長→夏壯盛→秋收聚→冬歸藏→再出發

Winter [water] – conceiving; → spring [wood] – growing; → summer [fire] – strengthening; → prolonged or Indian summer [earth]; → autumn [metal] – condensing; → winter [water] - returning to the root, and preparing for a new beginning.

一年為大循環, 一週為小循環

They then used this larger solar cycle to mark one year of life on Earth, and the seven days of the smaller solar cycle, where the natural creative cycle is reversed, to mark one week. Each day represents the sun, or the moon, or one of the five elementary forces as influenced by the five closest planets to Earth [5]:

日, Sunday [Sun] - →, Monday [Moon] - 火, Tuesday [Mars -fire] - 水, Wednesday [Mercury - water] -木, Thursday [Jupiter - wood] - 金, Friday [Venus - metal] - 土, Saturday [Saturn -earth]- and so on.....

二十八宿 :

At the same time the early Chinese people used the twenty eight constellations in the solar system, which also relate to the 28 days of the lunar cycle, to indicate the directions on Earth, each representing one of the five elementary forces, where earth denotes the center:

斗 牛 女 虛 危 室 壁=北方玄亀

North [water] was marked by the seven constellations that form the shape of the Dark Turtle.

角 亢 氐 房 心 尾 箕=東方青龍

East [wood] was marked by the seven constellations that form the shape of the Green Dragon.

井 鬼 柳 星 張 翼 軫=南方朱雀

---

5 Editor's note: Although much of this discussion is based on the approach of the early Chinese people, many of the early people in other cultures viewed these planets as Gods and named them as such. For example, the English names for the days of the week, above, were derived from the names of the ancient Nordic Gods assigned to those planets.

South [fire] was marked by the seven constellations that form the shape of the Red Bird.

奎 婁 胃 昴 畢 觜 参=西方白虎

West [metal] was marked by the seven constellations that form the shape of the White Tiger.

In each group of the seven constellations that represent one of these four directions, the middle or fourth constellation represents Sunday, and accordingly the fifth constellation represents Monday, followed by Tuesday and Wednesday. Similarly, the days in front of the central constellation representing Sunday are Thursday, Friday and Saturday:

木-金- 土- 日-月- 火- 水 [四-五- 六- 日-一- 二- 三]

Thursday-Friday-Saturday-Sunday-Monday-Tuesday-Wednesday, and so on –

七日宗:

The early Chinese people then took all of these inter-related forces to denote the order of the seven days of the week for cultivating our original human nature:

日曜日: 天和力: Sunday [Sun] for harmonizing our physical life with its spiritual nature.

月曜日: 冷靜力: Monday [Moon] for quietening down the self.

火曜日: 親和力: Tuesday [Mars – fire] for brightening the self by seeking the wisdom of life.

水曜日: 均衡力; Wednesday [Mercury - water] for balancing and leveling out the self.

木曜日: 生成力: Thursday [Jupiter -wood] for growing the life force.

金曜日: 凝聚力: Friday [Venus – metal] for gathering the life force.

土曜日: 安定力: Saturday [Saturn – earth] for stabilizing the self.

This means there are seven days in a week where the sun offers us the gift of its brightness and warmth. Hence, everyone should give their brightness and warmth to the people they live with, regardless of the relationship.

Daytime is for working in the light, and as the seasonal changes in the sunlight also shape the length of the night that is the time to nurture the inner light that supports our internal organs. Likewise, on days when the light from the sun cannot be seen, we can nurture the inner light through the three *Tan Tien*. Later, as the internal organs start to glow, this will help our health and lengthen our life.

Some great examples of people who followed the *Path of Pure Light* lived to be around 120 years. These people sometimes sat up all night to await the arrival of the light. So, cultivate the everlasting light within, and understand that whether the light is seen inside or outside, no one should miss any of the great days they are gifted during their lifetime.

生生不息, 源源不斷,
堅守靜土 (学掃地),
脚踏实地 (勿懸脚, 交膝勿徧,勿過久).
日常之正常平安生活即是福.
福從日生, 禍因心暗.

A normal, peaceful day is a blessing.
The source of these blessings comes from the sun,
While disaster comes when the light is missing.
Each day that belongs to Nature and my life
Offers the greatest gift given to me by Mother Nature.
Therefore, I must make the most out of each day
By cultivating and living with the best spirit possible.

The Teaching of the Path of Pure Light

The principles from the *Path of Pure Light*, called the *Path for Mastering a Grand Life* by my father, can guide us to complete health, which means attaining harmony in all five aspects of life: physical health; mental health, including our emotional and conscious health; spiritual health including the growth of a clean and clear spiritual awareness that does not rely on verbal narration when conducting our life; healthy social connections; and the financial health that is preferably accompanied by an interest to assist the weak and needy.

My parents followed this path, and I now outline my own interpretation of this simple spiritual faith in life whereby the foundation is to insist on the fulfillment of these five basic aspects of humanistic health:

大德必得其名,

To live with untiring moral fulfillment is preparation towards receiving a naturally deserved good name. If fame comes from fighting, this disrespect for the moral self can create the first disaster in life.

大德必得其祿,

To live with inexhaustible moral fulfillment is preparation for receiving a naturally deserved material provision in life. If the strong material provision comes from fighting and rivalry, this disrespect for the moral self may bring disaster and affect the health.

大德必得其位,

To live with unfailing moral fulfillment is preparation for receiving a naturally deserved high position. If the high position comes from fighting in a war, this disrespect for the moral self can damage the health.

大德必得其寿,

To live with unyielding moral fulfillment is preparation for receiving a naturally deserved long life. When living long, but still making others suffer, or damaging their health, this disrespect for the moral self can create a long life of suffering.

大德必得其樂.

To live with consistent moral fulfillment is preparation for receiving a naturally deserved happiness. When the happiness is gained from the suffering of others, this disrespect for the moral self creates a poison that takes away any lasting happiness in life.

The world is small, and sometimes insignificant, and human life is even smaller. A thoughtful evaluation suggests choosing a healthy lifestyle, while an unhealthy choice means sipping the poisons in life while eating its unhealthy fruit. But the above path, together with the following five harmonies, provide the definition of an education for a great life as exemplified by several early leaders, such as the Yellow Emperor and the Great Yu:

> How we live now prepares us for the next stage of life. If the preparation is healthy there will be healthy fruit; if the preparation is unhealthy, the harvest will yield unhealthy fruit. Therefore, everyone should correctly prepare for, and live a healthy life.
>
> No one needs to dwell on how to find the rewards in life because these come during the preparation process. We should accept that approach as our new faith in life.
>
> Great fulfillment also requires good opportunities, although even a small life can become accomplished through a healthy life that accumulates numerous small merits.
>
> A life that follows the integral truth would also value the holistic nature of life. In normal circumstances, we should all enjoy the wholeness from being totally healthy and holding no higher interest than this. Any partial interest or pursuit damages the wholeness of our life, while an incomplete life cannot be totally healthy.

> Although each life has five aspects related to our physical being, mental being, spiritual being, social being and financial being, the health of life cannot be separated into five portions because the value of each life relates to its wholeness.

Thus, both the goal and the achievement are to master our own life to attain complete health. In practical terms there should be no conceptual contamination from religious or political desire, as an ordinary life offers the greatest opportunity to achieve spiritual health. Most religions do sell a measure of emotional support, but it is also possible to find this support through having a broad appreciation of life.

For many generations the Chinese people enjoyed the normality of good health without being noticed. These people were the true sages, and some even exuviated at the end of their life, but only a few of their leaders are known. In whatever walk of life, however, whether it is spiritual teaching, healing, political service, or anything else, being healthy is the greatest fulfillment for both an individual, and the health of humanity.

Here ends the book on the teaching of the* Path of Pure Ligh*t called the* Path for Mastering a Grand Life *by Grand Master Yo San Ni. This teaching has been fulfilled and followed by the Ni family throughout many generations and stages of humanity.

Part III

Fulfill the Hope for a New Humanity

The only truthful spiritual attitude
is to worship Mother Nature.

Chapter 7

Establish a Healthy Human Faith

Our hope for a new humanity lies in more people seeking to complete the Five Healths in life, which includes living with a healthy human faith as the first step on the way to attaining spiritual maturity. Healthy people know how to live with the essence of life, and do not unconsciously create trouble in the world through their own negligence. The wisdom of life comes from nurturing the power of discernment, rather than being ruled by the cultural confusion in the world. We should all nurture and express the healthy force of life because there is no other choice when the goal is to achieve a better world.

This is an achievable goal when more people nurture the five healthy forces in life - their physical health, mental health, spiritual health, healthy relationships with others, and the financial health needed to support their life. With this foundation we could expect the social and political health of humanity and the world to grow.

However, we also need to search for more fundamental solutions to improve the health of the world. Personal happiness is linked to the health of society, and rubbing the skin to stop the pain does not solve problems that go much deeper. Most physical health problems are curable, but if these problems relate to an unhealthy belief or a false concept the answer lies in the conscious health of humanity. Hence, this is the focus of our voluntary work.

Attaining a Healthy Faith

One of the differences between humans and other animals is their ability to develop and express a spiritual faith. This may be a personal choice based on a mental attitude, or an inherited belief. Yet, these faiths do not necessarily represent people's deeper attitudes, or provide a fair response to everyone in their society. In contrast, other animals are only able to fight for their direct survival.

Whether or not this ability to develop and believe in a spiritual faith is a helpful quality in our lives depends on the nature of both the religion and our personal choice. Were those matters decided emotionally or rationally? Generally, rationality is a higher force, while religions are often based on a strong emotional attitude towards life.

Most people's rationality is not as strong as their emotions, and educated people usually base their decisions on their accumulated knowledge, which may differ from the uncolored rationality found in a natural life that exists in places far from the acquired knowledge of modern education. We do admit the rational force of intellectuals can be stronger than that of the general population. However, highly developed people, who have achieved wisdom through spiritual independence and freedom, place the rationality of intellectual knowledge at a lower level than the purity of our natural rationality.

But because no other animal is able to challenge our beliefs many people have developed an attitude whereby they accept specific species, or people, or cultures and societies, and reject all the others. Do they have a balanced mind in this situation? Do they treat their own lives and that of others fairly? Are they as truthful and helpful as they believe? Can they advance humanity if they still rely on force to overcome each other? And have they considered there may be other more superior species of life elsewhere?

The Integral Way has pursued the spiritual advancement of human life by applying our innate rationality to the essence of our various religions and customs. Such rationality is also a fundamental principle of spiritual humanism, and can be nurtured by a healthy way of life. Having a good spiritual faith is helpful, but if that faith becomes a fixed mental attitude it can affect the health of our mind. To avoid this problem, the Integral Way takes a different approach to our quest for a spiritual connection in life, and its relationship to our overall well-being and the way we extend ourselves to others.

Of course the hidden spiritual partner of life can still influence our minds, and this factor led to the common practice of believing in a conceptual

God. Some faiths and religions were also created from the social needs of a specific group, such as supporting or protecting their communities. Yet the people who inherited these beliefs may not examine the basis of their cultural heritage, and the perceived religious differences among the many cultures continue to cause confusion, or competition, or even hostility in the world.

Thus, there are two senses to the meaning of faith – an inherited, formalized faith in a conceptual belief, and a broad and open humanistic faith developed from exploring the world. The first meaning is exemplified by the numerous religious cultures in the world, and the second approach can also become a culture as seen in traditional Chinese societies. The latter approach has also influenced the Integral Way to provide a cultural service that continues to grow as we constantly apply humanistic rationality to all our choices.

Humanity has long been divided by various faiths, although the real differences originated in the minds of those who developed the different terminologies, venues, and styles of worship to form a range of ideologies to serve the many human emotions. Yet all teachings based on emotional projections lack the most truthful spiritual knowledge because ultimately our emotions cannot drive the spirituality of life.

This ignorance was also the basis of the boldness in those who described the nature of life before they clearly knew the nature of their own life, and who then established a life faith based on their incomplete knowledge. The creators of these many spiritual faiths would have had some serious dreams, or experiences, and might even have seen spiritual phenomena. But is this enough to create a spiritual faith for others? Was there an objective view on whether these teachings were healthy or unhealthy to the life of an individual, or their society? Can we really expect the growth of a healthy humanity from such incomplete knowledge? What is known is that for the 2000 to 3000 years since most of these teaching were established the world has constantly faced many troubles.

This is why we believe that none of the conventional religions can save the world. Today, the most important spiritual quest would be to improve the health of humanity. Meanwhile, the world acts like a drunken man who zigzags ahead, although he does not where to go, or even if it is safe to proceed. There are some new approaches that boast about their advancement, but they all stay in the small realm of competition, and none offer the safe leadership required to progress society in the modern world.

Some of you may now think I am against having a spiritual faith - that is not my intention. It has long been proven that having a spiritual faith to guide the moral and social condition in life is better than not having one, both individually, and for society. We should all have a spiritual faith, but it must be a healthy one that is helpful to the growth of humanity, rather than establishing further competition. Moreover, a narrow conceptual faith may cause emotional and behavioral difficulties, as well as personal and social trouble, or even conflict, if it is erroneously interpreted by its leaders or believers.

Hence, benefiting the growth of humanity is not a matter of having or not having a spiritual faith. Rather, it is a matter of choosing a broad and healthy faith instead of following one that is narrow, or unhealthy. This was the purpose of my presentation of the humanistic faith of the Universal Integral Way to the public in the middle of last century, as in this faith the highest morality extends beyond any ethnic or social group.

In truth, most people believe their faith is a good faith, although it may not support the health of humanity. But when individuals with a low, or little, or no sense of morality are supported by an established faith as they terrorize the believers of another group in society, and the perpetrators of these events are then respected as heroes, this wrong cannot be corrected. Unfortunately, that example only illustrates the downfall of the spiritual nature of humanity.

Religious injustices may also arise from the social competition between groups or cultures who share the same faith, but where each side supports wrongful behavior. When this spiritual problem occurs, it cannot be corrected by people with a different faith or ethnicity, which is why there is continual struggle among these groups in the world.

Lessons from the Past

The turmoil of the twentieth century had people doubting the value of finding help from religious beliefs, as both sides in the numerous conflicts used similar psychological support for their position. I too felt disappointed by the helplessness of spiritual teachings in this situation, and looked for answers in all the religious classics during the 1930s and 1940s, but none of these approaches seemed able to stop the human conflict, including the aggression amongst the believers of those religions.

I then carefully examined the weaknesses of all the spiritual teachings in the world, and continued this direction of research throughout the Japanese invasion of China, and during her long period of internal political rivalry. My discovery was simple – all popular spiritual teachings are expressed in a manner that can be used to support both sides, that is, both the invader and the defender.

Long before, during the Warring Period in China [403-221 BCE] Motzi stated that all aggression is against the will of Heaven or Nature. He then concluded there should be no invasions, only the necessary defense against an invasion. His vision was that survival comes from the mutual love and care of humanity that is beyond any blood connection. He was respected during his lifetime, although his influence waned as the young impulsive males in his society began to compete for the leadership of a larger, unified country.

After the decline of the Zhou Dynasty [1122-249 BCE] in China, the warring among the many smaller states resulted in fourteen years of absolute authority under the first Emperor of Chin. Historians usually credit him for the unification of China, rather than his tyrannical behavior, although it was the latter that showed the failure of the early humanistic principle that had previously guided Chinese society, and been generally accepted by the public.

It is similar in the West where religions support both the offence and defense in a conflict. This means that cultural strength is weaker than people's impulses, which then drives their behavior at the expense of human rationality. Moreover, the initial approach of an aggressive or offensive force commonly includes destroying the conventional faith or moral beliefs of the defensive society. Once the aggressor becomes the ruling force, however, they quickly see the need to restore the cultural conventions of the defeated population.

People who have suffered from such craziness in the world would sigh deeply at this, and I have to agree that the intelligence of the human race is still at the stage of a rebellious and mischievous teenager. I am now an outdated minority, age-wise, but the health and sanity of humanity remains my prime concern, which means I continue to work on improving the health of people's spiritual faith. This is not just for my amusement, or to fill my life, but for the safety of the new generations in the world.

Clearly people's spiritual faith and conceptual beliefs and opinions deeply affect their lives, and are almost as strong an influence as their genetic and cultural destiny in determining the future direction of both an individual, and their society. Hence, a healthy faith or belief, and how it is projected, is very important to each person and all those affected by them. Although I still respect our spiritual ancestors. I will later describe some of the conventional mistakes that have been made in the past.

Confucius once said: 'people can be guided to do what should be done, and there is no need to give the reasons why'. In this case, he wished to restore the social rites of the early Zhou Dynasty. However, most of the early spiritual teachers, who also told people what to do, did not explain why their edicts should be obeyed. Those people often sacrificed the rational view, and their own spiritual attainment, to serve the public need by updating the social order and ethics in their societies. We can credit them for their service to humanity, but we should not continue in the same manner because most of the functions of earlier religious law have now been replaced by modern social legislation.

Updating the Health of Humanity

After the world wars of the twentieth century many people lost confidence in the religious beliefs that had sustained their strong faith for a better world. Some societies then became open to new teachings in their quest for the spiritual truth. Consequently, many people in the United States and other parts of the Western world experienced decades of confusion from the approach known as the New Age teachings.

I came to the United States during the 1970s, and offered a teaching service at the side of my Traditional Chinese Medicine [TCM] practice. My teaching, usually known as the Way, has a very direct approach to re-uniting people with Heaven, or God, and later became formalized as the Union of Tao and Man [Humanity], or the Healthy Way of Humanity.

This teaching differs from several of the previous cultural approaches in China. I do not represent the Confucianism that concentrates on ethics through practicing various rituals. I do not represent the Taoism that tends to continue some of the practices from early Shamanism, nor do I represent popular Chinese Buddhism or the practice of Zhan [Zen] Buddhism that seeks to return people to their original nature through external worship. I just ask people to directly unite their own human nature with Heavenly Nature.

I call this teaching the Universal Integral Way to include aspects of the other cultures I have explored for many years, as no single teaching is able to help all of humanity due to its incompleteness, or spiritual inadequacy. Although my goal is spiritual integration, I have only selected and revised the spiritual teachings that offer permanent value to humanity. This means I have broadened my cultural perspective in order to correctly deliver the integral truth of human spirituality.

Yet, some of my students are still unable to see that this new position comes from my disappointment in the conventional teachings that have only extended the cultural conflicts in the world. My teaching of the Universal Integral Way is the path to achieving the health of humanity, and my recent books have focused on updating the conventional teachings with the knowledge I have gained from my own training and life experiences. I continue to use the ageless Chinese classics, but my new approach to spiritual teaching should be not be confused with conventional Taoism, Buddhism, and Confucianism.

I arrived at this position after decades of updating the Chinese classics before my internal spiritual strength saw the need to teach the value of a spiritually constructive life to prepare both the current and future generations. They have no need to repeat the suffering from the old problems, some of which have lasted for over two thousand years. I then redirected my work towards the Path of Constructive Life in the hope that a new public spirit would save humanity from continuing the spiritual confusion from the old world.

In contrast, the conventional religions have hidden the human psychological problem of dividing the self, as most beliefs in a conceptual God are based on literary presentations of the emotions that arise from mental confusion, or a misunderstanding that sees the self as a separate reality to God, or any other deity, or group of spirits. Although many of these beliefs were developed to provide emotional support and unity to their society, the reality is that they have sown the seeds of human disharmony. This is because they contain the unhealthy suggestion of a divided self, which is spiritually untruthful.

The worship of Mother Nature is the only truthful spiritual attitude of humanity, since all spiritual phenomena are produced by the human life that was born from Nature.

Chapter 8

Attain Spiritual Clarity

Have a Clear Vision of the Spirits of Life

Attaining a clear spiritual vision in life is another important step on the way to achieving spiritual maturity. For example, all cultures pass through the stage of Shamanism where people believe that external spirits exist outside the self. External spiritual phenomena are actually generated by our own body, while our internal bodily spirits come from the reproductive force within all human nature. However, our brain does not fully understand the nature of these phenomena, and their spiritual reactions and responses, even though they are part of a healthy life and help to shape the spiritual qualities of our personality.

Our brain carries our main conscious power, and our body carries the sense of life with its tiny spiritual entities. Although there is internal communication, the brain generally mistakes the body as its only reality in life while ignoring the associated spiritual phenomena. That wrongful spiritual knowledge about the nature of the human brain and bodily self is the common foundation of all external religions.

Furthermore, most people are commanded by their own thoughts and beliefs, which usually lack a truthful foundation. The result is that wider humanity tends to muddle along without having a clear or serious direction. Yet the truth of life is found within the self, not externally, and believing in an external spiritual 'reality' distances most people from their true spirituality in life.

Believers of an external faith often do things that go against the true rationality of humanity, although this true rationality represents the subtle light of life. Instead, they accept a different authority of life, such as God or Buddha. Yet the light of life, which is part of life, and also grows from each life, should be the only rationality to drive our life. Viewed from this perspective, most conventional teachings illustrate the human tendency of splitting their nature. This division is then reflected in the cultures that further encourage the emotional pattern of splitting the original spiritual unity of humanity, and is the basis of much of the psychological confusion and conflict in the world.

Spiritual health means keeping away from this self-splitting tendency, while having faith in Mother Universe helps to regain the inherent spiritual unity in our life. Mother Nature has always been the only source of life, although each person contains myriad tiny spiritual entities that can affect their vision. Nevertheless, we can still express some useful religious concepts in terms that would help us to regain our original spiritual unity. Thus, God represents our rationality in life, Satan represents our animal impulses in life, and the Devil represents the incorrect use of our faith in life.

Spiritual ignorance regarding the self is not a sin, although it is a weakness in professional life. But when believing in a strong emotional faith is added to this weakness, and used to fuel the ignorance in society, it can be the source of much trouble in the world. In this case, the rising impulses in life may cover the spiritual light from the sun with darkness. At other times, one form of darkness is replaced by another, as found when one religion or ideology replaces another during the process of colonization. Sadly, both instances can cover people's spiritual light, and history tells us that in these situations the health of the human spirit may take several decades or even a couple of centuries to recover.

Know What Being Healthy Means

If we become very rich, complete health should be part of our wealth; if we become socially powerful, complete health should be part of our power; if we become very popular, this should include healthy relationships, particularly with the opposite sex.

Very few people achieve all of the above attributes even though these are common desires, especially among men. But do wealth, social power and popularity alone help our personal health, or the quality of society? That is questionable, which means these attributes are not valuable if they also harm our personal health, or the health of society.

But no matter who we are we ought to have a healthy faith in life, and the spiritual health of humanity is still the most genuine faith available. There should also be universal education, based on healthy spiritual knowledge, to support this faith in order to avoid any further damage to the health of humanity. The faith and teaching of the Path of Constructive Life through the Five Healths focuses on the health of humanity, and offers such spiritual education.

The beginning of the new millennium was chosen to introduce this new faith to the world with the hope of leading people away from the conceptual conflicts of the past. Some of the older spiritual beliefs to help people have also had negative side effects, but the Path of Constructive Life within the Integral Way remains open to all people, including those who wish to maintain their existing faith and practices while adopting the wider principle of yielding to anything that is against the health of humanity.

The Renaissance of the 15th century CE heralded the movement away from the darkness of Roman Catholicism. More recently, the communist movement from Marx and Engels was a reaction to the unjust social practices in Europe during the 18th century. Neither of these solutions has achieved the religious dream of worldly salvation, but the Path of Constructive Life offers a spiritual solution that avoids any negative competition by emphasizing the humanistic cooperation that would bring real improvement to the world.

In the West a few wise leaders have been able to effect some social improvements that applied both traditional and more recent ideas to resolving conflicts without starting a cultural revolution. Even so, a truly spiritual solution ought to benefit the entirety of humanity. All social and religious initiatives originally had the intention of saving the world, but these ambitions have usually become faded dreams. Moreover, some of the newer social campaigns, designed to overcome the inertia in society by attracting the wider public, still adopt the old religious style of propaganda to present an extreme position. This only illustrates that little real progress has been made to the overall growth of humanity.

Much social work touches the surface of humanity, but real spiritual work goes much deeper. Our suggestion is to find time every day to feed our souls with something that benefits our life, as spiritual achievement should be a human duty that is valued by all people. Although we all live in the confused world, this should not condition the destiny of our lives. Fostering the soul with the five faiths of a constructive life is one way to condition our life for health, rather than sickness. So, privately say the following lines to nurture your soul:

> *I have faith in my physical health.* This faith gives me the strength to fulfill the first moral duty in all human life, and not burden others with my health. If I fall short in this direction, I will make it the first priority in my spiritual improvement.
>
> *I have faith in my mental health.* This faith gives me the clarity of mind to conduct my life in a clear and clean manner, and create no confusion or trouble for either my own life, or the lives of others. My healthy mind should fulfill this moral duty, but if I fall short in this direction I will make it a priority in my spiritual development.
>
> *I have faith in the healthy condition of my soul or psyche [soul-mind]*, which invigorates my life spirit and enables me to face the world alone in an upright manner, and fear and doubt nothing. Hence, I am able to fulfill a totally moral life in any position within society.

The health of my body, mind and soul form the solid foundation of my being, and maintaining them is a moral duty in an independent life. Therefore:

> *I also have faith in my healthy connections and relationships* with all other people, whom I love out of my moral sense of life. This means I hold no hatred or hostility towards anyone as I fulfill my share of achieving the total health of humanity.
>
> *In addition, I have faith in my healthy and self-reliant financial life,* and no matter how difficult, I am able to support my own life and the lives of my

family. I am also willing to help others reach success once I am equipped to do so.

I promise to treat each of these faiths fairly because all preparation for our internal health helps to extend our external health. Everyone face difficulties and challenges, and should understand that overcoming these crises is a normal part of life:

If we feel physically low or demoralized from an external condition that causes us to lose interest in people and being creative, this shows we devalue the world and may even dismay others in our surroundings. At those times we should ensure our physical health, or at least continue to practice some constructive movements and exercises.

If our mind is disturbed or annoyed we may become less effective in life, so we then need to adjust our mind before we fall. This means we need to cleanse our mind regularly with the correct spiritual practices to ensure our mental fitness in the world.

If we lack a healthy spiritual motivation in life and wish to withdraw, rather than share the duty of serving the world, we should engage in the spiritual cultivation that provides the strength to tackle our troubles and regain our happiness in life.

If we lack sympathy for those who suffer the darkness created by a cruel leadership in the world, we should not support that dark force in any way. This situation could also be caused by having no clear understanding of the direction ruling the lives of others. At these times we need to dedicate our lives to improving the spiritual direction of the world. There is no need to lead a war - just help people to attain peace, and never lose interest in becoming a constructive model of life. Ultimately, no one can escape such fulfillment.

If we continually stretch our financial margins in life we may also need to strengthen our self-discipline to ensure more effective spending. And when we continually have more than enough, we can offer this strength to help others in the world.

Achieve the Five Healths for a Great Life

Although the social service of the Universal Integral Way focuses on achieving a healthy world with healthy social leaders and politics so that everyone is able to enjoy life, our own Heavenly Paradise can be fulfilled by achieving the Five Healths in life:

For physical health we can consult *Mastering Chi*[6] as we practice the various gentle movements that directly improve our health and well-being;

For a healthy mind we can consult *The Foundation of a Happy Life*[7]. If any of the Five Healths is lacking we are usually unhappy, no matter how much the deeper conscious self tries to manage our well-being. At these times we need to work at cleansing and balancing the conscious reality in our life;

For a healthy life spirit we can consult *The Centermost Way*[8];

For healthy human connections we can consult *Stepping Stones for Spiritual Success*[9] to ensure our social success is also a blessing for the world. Also consult *The Majestic Domain of the Universal Heart*[10] to ensure that our life amongst others reflects the most auspicious possibilities for humanity;

For a healthy financial life we could consult *Enrich Your Life with Virtue*[11] so that every dollar we make to support our life and the life of our family honors humanity.

---

6 *Mastering Chi*, Hua-Ching Ni with Dr Daoshing Ni and Dr Mao Shing Ni, 1994

7 *The Foundation of a Happy Life*, Hua-Ching Ni, 1999

8 *The Centermost Way*, Hua-Ching Ni, 2001

9 *Stepping Stones for Spiritual Success*, Hua-Ching Ni, 1990

10 *The Majestic Domain of the Universal Heart*, Hua-Ching Ni, 2002

11 *Enrich Your Life with Virtue*, Hua-Ching Ni, 1999

The Integral Way also wishes to contribute to everyone's emotional health by smoothing our worries, anxieties, mental weaknesses and other emotional concerns as we practice the various bodily movements. The principle is to use these gentle movements to pacify the mind and attune the emotions, and thus enhance all levels of our health. While a healthy body can support a healthy mind, another level of emotion can be supported by joining with others in the daily, seasonal, or yearly spiritual renewal ceremony found in the *Workbook for Spiritual Development*[12]. If this is inconvenient, just read the practice alone to broaden our spiritual perspective, and enhance our sense of being able to unite with the oneness of universal life.

This contribution from the Integral Way comes from the earliest belief that humanity and Heaven form one life. That source is also the basis of the teaching of the Union of Tao as expressed in our Shrine of the Eternal Breath of Tao [or Life]. Our teaching manifests the spiritual unity with Nature, although respecting this unity may take many decades.

However, spiritual separation is still a common practice. This was first illustrated by the early, but direct, worship of idols, and continued by the later worship of conceptual symbols. Both of these practices express spiritual ignorance and, as Jesus pointed out, spiritual culture is often full of hypocrisy. In a truthful world everyone would directly believe in the truth, the light, and the Way because in the highest spirituality there is no separation from Nature. Yet, people continue to separate themselves from the genuine qualities of life when their spiritual practice and respect should be directed towards the spiritual unity of the Way of Nature.

The Shrine of the Eternal Breath of Tao displays some early human images to symbolize the spiritual truth that Heaven contains humans, and humans contain Heaven. People were born from the dark into the light, however, and their development is often obstructed by internal conflicts, some of which are inherited from up to nine generations of ancestral genes. Hence, there may be spiritual elements in our life that are not supportive, or easily harmonized, although the invocations in the *Spiritual Workbook* help us to

---

12 Workbook for Spiritual Development of All People, Hua-Ching Ni, 1983

rise above the murky waters of our deep emotions, and allow us to cleanse the spiritual core of our life.

These invocations assist the benign spiritual functions of life, and there is additional support for our spiritual practice in the *Guide to Universal Spiritual Harmony*, as each of these functions can be seen as a different deity that helps to determine our personal character. But note this is an internal practice, rather than a form of external worship.

Many of the established religious teachings do offer something to help the growth of humanity, but they should not stop making progress because health, like wealth, relies on the principle of accumulation. At depth, the sense of wealth and the sense of health are interactive, and our wealth in life is displayed by the way the Five Healths support our complete being, including our spiritual health and cultural wealth.

Material science tells us which conditions at the shallow level of life produce the results that determine the condition of our material life. Spiritual science goes much deeper, but still expects certain results from particular conditions, and this is how our personality becomes molded towards success or failure. So, raising our level of rationality in life helps our selection making processes. A good public faith can also assist this process, but my hope is that we could all be more selective about the social conditions needed to manage our health, rather than just accepting the many conditions that bring suffering.

We all live with the ever-changing seasons each year, and the different moods affect our lives. For the new humanity who live a constructive life: spring is for hope, summer is for happiness, autumn is for blessings, and winter is for joy. People who choose to live a constructive life may also like to gather the ten bright stars that symbolize the ten auspicious lights of a healthy character that allows the development of a brighter destiny:

A Bright Star for great friendship;

A Bright Star for love;

A Bright Star for financial wealth;

A Bright Star for happiness;

A Bright Star for success;

A Bright Star for being knowledgeable, or contributing to useful knowledge;

A Bright Star for beauty and wisdom;

A Bright Star for the warmth of the family;

A Bright Star for being honest, upright, and reliable;

A Bright Star for a long and healthy life.

These qualities bring satisfaction, and the ten stars also symbolize the moral characteristics that guide the life of any constructive individual. If we aspire to live a constructive life, but are unable to find any of these stars immediately, do not be disappointed. A brighter future comes to all people who improve the deeper conscious self in their life. When each person looks into their heart for the three permanent qualities of truth, goodness and beauty they will soon find that all ten stars will surround their life.

A fully developed human is physically and spiritually complete. Most of our knowledge about physical life has been developed through the physical sciences, which are generally accepted, while the spiritual side of life has largely been developed through the many spiritual faiths. Each faith offers a range of services, and people are required to develop themselves to make the right choice for their own happiness and well-being in life. Physical science has not yet reached its final achievements, but the spiritual sciences and services in any generation have the duty of continuing to seek the complete health of humanity.

Practicing the five faiths for a healthy life can relieve our everyday pressures, and reduce the conflicts from negative competition, although we should also help one another to attain a healthier condition in the world. The conventional congregational approach is one way to assist each other to learn and achieve the Five Healths as we continue to engage in our practical life in society, and eventually this approach would take many people to the Heavenly paradise on Earth sought by many generations.

There are many different versions of the same dream, and all good dreams for humanity can be achieved over time. I now hope that I have now finished the intellectual service on this subject. Other important questions can be answered by participating in the Renewal Ceremony from the *Spiritual Workbook for All People* because the main source of all spiritual inspiration is the direct experience of a sincere heart.

Chapter 9

Support a Healthy Social System

What is a Reliable System?

Another step on the way to achieving spiritual maturity is to recognize the nature of a healthy and internally reliable social system. Many societies are interested in a united justice system, such the International Court of Justice, because they cannot manage their own conflicts and hope that an objective authority would be able to resolve any confusion and deliver absolute justice. This quest dates from the time people began to form communities, although a solution has yet to be found.

Often the lack of justice, particularly between striving countries, or among ethnic groups, has led some people to believe that might is right, and that belief has made the world a dangerous place, and threatened the health of humanity. Other people seek justice from the sky, and although their questions have never been fully answered this position is the basis of various forms of spiritual justice, many of which have an ethnic or racial bias.

At least three of the popular religions have established a spiritual justice system based on their faith in the same God, although each developed a different interpretation. Yet all three behave as if they were a spokesperson for God, even though each expresses some narrowness or bias. Judaism does not fully accept Christianity and Islam, while both Islam and Christianity hold some prejudice towards the other two beliefs. In this situation God has lost any independent judgment towards people, which means there can be no real sense of spiritual justice until those faiths find spiritual unity.

There are also two other types of spiritual beliefs. Buddhism represents the faiths that do not seek spiritual justice, but strive to be above all entanglements by emptying the mind and withdrawing from worldly life. In contrast, the profound Lao Tzu represents the beliefs that recommend letting matters become resolved naturally. This is not the same as the scholarly attitude of waiting for the judgment of history, but comes from having the deepest faith in Mother Nature, which offers a cure to every worldly entanglement.

Whatever the choice, the different approaches show that the world needs spiritual justice. Put simply, it is a matter of right or wrong, and when applied to life, it is a matter of being healthy or unhealthy. Although many people have examined the spiritual justice systems throughout history, none of them have been effective in reducing the numerous conflicts among people. Perhaps the answer is to stop wasting time looking for the best external system, and instead seek an effective and healthy life through attaining all of the Five Healths. Once these are fulfilled, any external spiritual search becomes meaningless.

History clearly shows that the spiritual justice systems that decide who is to be punished and who will be rewarded by living in Heaven have largely been in vain. Earning a peaceful conscience is much more practical because a healthy conscience supports both our personal health, and the health of society. Other societies believe the authorities offer them protection from any evil-doers. We support that thought and hope it is true, although all political and religious systems are managed by people, and people can be corrupted.

The deities from Nature are beyond manipulation, but the religionists who seek offerings or donations on their behalf have opened these images to corruption. This form of religious fraud is found everywhere, and people's faith in a religion is increasingly being used to help various social struggles. That pattern becomes stronger every year, and when there is a conflict the people on both sides imagine that the deities are supporting them.

During the 18th century, some new ideas about social justice, initiated by Marx and Engels, attracted large crowds wishing to test a system that suggested that their unsuccessful life came from others taking all the opportunities for material support. Inhumane means were then used to suppress the people who had more, whether or not this was fair, but by the 1970s the experiment had clearly failed to produce either justice or social health. A healthy society requires harmony among all people, and not just one social class suppressing everyone else.

The earliest people developed within a cooperative system. Similarly, our internal organs and mental and spiritual functions naturally cooperate. Once this fails, life ceases, which also applies to the life of a nation and wider humanity. Social salvation is a Western invention, but the Oriental belief in individual salvation is still applicable in the modern world.

People with a healthy mind do not expect or rely on external support from any religious or social system, although a healthy society supports the needs of all its members. In the traditional societies, people believed that their rewards or punishment in life came from the sky, and being good or bad, and right or wrong, would be judged in the temples. Today, people ask the government for help, but the real health of a society is built by all the healthy people who are able to rely on themselves.

A healthy life force and a good faith in life are mutually supportive, while those who practice religion to salve their conscience as they live in a dubious manner illustrate the negative use of a faith. There is also no happiness from polarizing people through an internal practice. So, the focus of the Integral Way is on achieving complete health, based on the openness and broadness found in the ageless, humanistic teaching of the Way.

Conversely, religions based on what is good and bad, or right and wrong, have reinforced the pattern of an almost irreversible dualism that is the basis of all human conflict. This dualistic approach to life constantly practices an unhealthy form of discrimination, but few people take the time to look inwardly when they experience any spiritual or emotional polarization. That is the source of much human unhappiness, and may even cause a nervous breakdown.

Moreover, people generally separate their desires and emotions from their sense of safety and morality. The intellect can go in either direction, so there is often an inner war on whether or not to live on the side of morality or immorality. This means most people still carry a weak desire for the spiritual light of salvation from God that arises out of their fear of spiritual darkness. That fear is also the reason many people attend church regularly where they are unlikely to find the self-awareness to know they are being socially manipulated, either consciously or unconsciously. Their real duty, however, is to seek the light of life, rather than continue programs that were established well before they were born.

When there is no need to rely on a church it is clear that the material desires associated with the emotional force of life can become the darkness that forms the lower mind, sometimes called hell. On the other hand, the sense of safety associated with the moral sense in life can grow to become the light that forms the higher mind, which some religions call the salvation of God. This polarity actually does occur in the human mind, and while no real God is involved, it can be part of the nature of a specific life.

The ageless Way promotes the reality of a life from Nature that is far away from any conceptual belief, and the definition of a healthy life from the Way of Eternal Truth is to walk along the middle path between extreme holiness and being sinful, while avoiding any serious polarization.

We have now seen that the cultural mistakes from the strong discrimination found in the past have brought more tension, pressure, competition, and external polarization in the world. This also had a serious effect on people's nervous systems, and their overall health and well-being.

But in the old farming societies of China and India, life was basically self-reliant, and the original communal festivals suggested their inherent spirituality rather than offering social competition. These people lived a hard but happy life, and their religions supported their festivities. Societies like this can still be open to social improvement without any need to introduce the radical social concepts that often create new tensions and polarize people.

The sense of good and bad, and the division between the rich and the poor, is much sharper in the social doctrines of the West. This is because their religious documents relate to the constant need for survival and the ensuing tribal struggles. But when these somewhat negative cultural beliefs were introduced to the East they attracted young leaders from the naïve farming societies, who turned those influences into social solutions that eventually created national disasters. Furthermore, the younger West was influenced by the mentality of the spiritual teachings from the Middle East that spread an erroneous vision of religious salvation, which has not really helped the growth of humanity.

In reality, the East and the West are mutually reliant, while the world needs continual cooperation, not more competition. Yet today, our global relationships are still dominated by cultural contradictions, and some racial struggles continue to be fueled by various religious teachings. These forces also contribute to the deterioration in the healthy nature of humanity.

So, how can we expect an improvement in other human relationships? My hope is for the world to review the old humanistic culture from China, and that China would regain her old values of a peaceful society, free from serious discrimination. Such social improvement would not need any involvement by God, but God could take credit for the healthy humanity who made this happen.

The Way of a peaceful, harmonious and humanistic life was not invented by Lao Tzu, although he did illustrate the practice of the Way during his lifetime. However, his profound views on human life are opposite to those generally found today as people continue to practice the polarization that has already damaged the health and happiness of humanity, as well as jeopardizing the survival of the human race.

What then, is a Healthy Culture?

The culture of the Way is unique in that it is concerned with the survival of Nature and all lives, and suggests that each life should be in harmony with both its internal nature and its relationship with all other lives, as well as with greater Nature. Hence, all life is valued, and open to the benefits from the life giving energy of Nature.

This wisdom is also elucidated in the *I Ching* or *Book of Changes*. Culturally, the Way does not exalt the good over the bad, but suggests we never contend with others in our practical life. Objectively, we all share the sense of survival with Mother Nature, and therefore should be at peace with all other life. Subjectively, we all need to fulfill our duty to lead a good life, which includes appreciating all the people in our own life. The Way has always respected having faith in Nature, as the moral nature of Mother Universe is to give birth, and support all lives and all things while asking for nothing back.

This is the Way that should be followed by all people. Harmonizing with others is the only way to live, and cultural polarization, whether internal or external, is the way to endless confrontation and social disharmony. When any strong sense of difference is expressed as black and white, or good and bad, or right and wrong, this sharpens the struggles among humanity, and cunning people can then use that influence to divide society and create trouble. Achieving harmony comes from tolerance, rather than using differences to establish an emotional precipice. Hence, the Way that has long observed human society chooses to respect and teach the value of harmony in all human connections.

Then, how did society lose this natural harmony? When King Jie was dethroned by King Tong, 湯, 3500 years ago, the latter demonized the young emperor. King Jie was actually more interested in his personal life than his public position, and while this was a small problem to society his opponent used that defect to attack and dethrone him. This event harmed social harmony, and later influenced the way King Wu dethroned King Jou, 紂. Now this method has become the stereotype of modern political behavior, whereby politicians attack their opponents at every opportunity. This makes King Tong the pioneer of all politicians who engage in the form of social rivalry commonly called 'dirty politics'!

Records show that since King Tong the Chinese dynasties have changed around every 500 years. Prior to this, there was harmony among the tribal groups and all people respected and enjoyed a peaceful life. That widespread social harmony was interpreted as the Way, and any leadership changes in society occurred naturally. For example, the Xia Dynasty was established after the Great Yu overcame the deluge about 4000 years ago, when he, and later his son and other descendants were gifted with the symbolic leadership.

King Jie had also inherited this symbolic position as the center of harmony from his ancestors, but when he was dethroned by King Tong there was little improvement to general society. Similarly, when King Wu dethroned King Jou, the last emperor of the Shang Dynasty, for his personal corruption and neglecting his social duty, the life of the people showed little improvement, except for the establishment of the social rites.

Most modern democratic societies change their tenure around every three to five years, as agreed by society. Here, I am not saying we should maintain the former styles of leadership, but I do expect real improvements to society instead of the merry-go-round changes in power at great cost to each nation and its people. No dynasty lasts forever, but the changes illustrated above did not uplift the quality of society, nor reduce the contention as exemplified by later events in the Zhou Dynasty. History may cite King Jie and King Jou as typical examples of over-indulgent emperors, similar to King Louis the 14th in France, but are those who gain power or financial strength today any different?

In contrast, Lao Tzu's perspective does offer hope to humanity. He did not admire the initiators of any of the new dynasties who gained power by physical competition and demonizing their opponents. Rather, he saw that the public prefers a peaceful world where people can live happily without going against the nature of their life. He also saw that a healthy society does not express any of the social preferences that divide people. Moreover, Lao Tzu's view mirrors that of the earliest people, who limited any social establishments that unnecessarily interfered with people's lives. These constrictions are unnatural, and therefore cannot serve the health of humanity.

Confucius had a very different view. He had observed that the Chinese nation no longer respected the earlier social rites from Duke Zhou, one of the few real statesmen during the long history of China, and sought to restore this style of management to the now larger society comprising over 500 small kingdoms. Although he failed to achieve this goal, he should still be recognized and respected for his personal courage.

Confucius lived at a time of great social tension, and collected the teachings from his cultural heritage that he believed should be preserved. Although he focused on the constructive side of humanity, and particularly on the humanistic social order, he did not really address the naturalness and organic strength of society. Thus, his audience with Lao Tzu, who respected the natural course of humanity above all, had no apparent effect on his decision to allow an artificial social order to govern the five great relationships.

Strengthening what is already outdated is not helpful, and this point divided the two great sages and their different schools. That separation still stands, although we now know how to use each approach to complement the other. Overly strong governance can harm the organic condition of both society and Nature, so the health of humanity should never be sacrificed for a political ideology. Large families can still share their assets, similar to the early communal tribes, but can Nature share the poverty and suffering of all the starving people in the world?

Confucius also idolized the nature of humanity. In his model people are absolutely loyal to their king, even though the soundness of the ruler is not questioned. They unquestioningly fulfill their filial piety, no matter the moral condition of their parents, while parents always care for their children without considering the suitability and value of such care. Women obey their husbands and do not engage in any other decent interests in life. Likewise, younger brothers listen to and help their elder brother regardless of the latter's moral condition, while friends always assist each other without considering the real interests of both sides.

Hence, Confucius promoted the application of humanistic love, but when his approach started to damage the health and safety of humanity it no longer fulfilled the goal of improving human morality. For this reason he also raised the strong antipathy of the younger generation in China last century, who then rejected him. I hope I have not misrepresented his teachings, and only suggest improvement, like all the other old teachings. Even so, Confucius has enjoyed fame in China over many generations.

A hundred years later, however, Mencius revised Confucius' teachings by proposing that the principles of propriety, suitability and humanistic love should all be applied when managing human affairs. This is still applicable today, although the five great human relationships were originally the work of Emperor Shun, 4000 years ago. At that time the natural healthy practice was: dutiful parents had good healthy children, a loyal king was served by loyal ministers, a supportive husband had a helpful wife, a loving brother had cooperative siblings, and faithful people found faithful friends. When everyone fulfills their moral role in life there is no need to command, or demand.

Thus Lao Tzu's approach was to wonder whether the cultural trends of his time were really better than the natural moral condition among the earliest people. Life produces a sweet taste for all people who love life, and no external social code can increase this. We should also be happy whether we are alone, or in the company of others, although the sweetest taste of all comes in a life that is ready to make sacrifices for others. This does not mean we should live with ungrateful beasts, but those who make a contribution to others without seeking credit experience the best in life, which includes the long lasting appreciation of Lao Tzu.

I appreciate nothing more than the nature of the people who fulfill their life without asking for a moral favor or anything else in return. When human connections remain at the level of a social or business exchange, what is left is merely the obligation to fulfill a contract, or an even worse condition where people refuse or try to escape the terms of a contract. In this respect the Chinese have witnessed a worsening of their humanity for several generations through the influence of several culturally inferior invaders.

Moreover, Confucius' ideas on the moral standards for humanity had already been lost long well before his time as he wondered if humanistic morality had disappeared forever. He has my sympathy in knowing he was helpless regarding the fate of his compatriots, but he kept working to fulfill his moral duty, and his five standards for human relationships remain a useful generalization of a healthy humanity where people with a dutiful heart create a good family, and a peaceful country.

This is a great life practice, but in subnormal situations does anyone have the right to demand or enforce these natural moral fulfillments on others? In a perfect world wise kings attract wise ministers, kind parents nurture dutiful children in a good family, a faithful husband earns the support of his wife in a harmonious team, and loving siblings or friends gain help from each other. That is, when people respond to each other dutifully and responsibly they express the true nature of humanity. But can people with an artificial moral education, taught to only love their party or nation, or always be faithful to their religion, still maintain their original healthy nature, upright personality, and a righteous and independent view of life?

Confucius described his disappointment in the volumes known as Spring and Autumn at a time when kings and ministers did not behave wisely, and fathers and sons did not perform their filial duty. When the decency of humanity is put aside, society merely expresses the physical competitiveness inherent in the male nature. As Lao Tzu once said: 'when society is sick, some people fight for unworthy causes, but the most unworthy position is to be a monarch who does not fulfill their moral duty to the people'.

Today, maybe the worst of all are the people who engage in immoral competition to gain special privileges. So, we now need to address the origin of the false culture of pursuing unworthy causes. This began when gifts, such as land and social privileges, were given to generals, dukes and other officials, who then lived off the efforts from others. Winners of the numerous physical competitions were also rewarded with the opportunity for military service and adventure. Both circumstances robbed the public in order to pay for these favors, which were also generous enough to make people risk death.

This approach is counter to Lao Tzu, who asked people to value the healthy nature of their life that includes the natural health of humanity. It also contradicts Confucius, who asked people to maintain the ethical standards of society. Both men were correct, but neither has ever been fully accepted. Chuang Tzu was another wise man who believed in an organic, natural society because an unnatural establishment is often stressful and may harm the world, but he remained independent from the social problems of his time. Previously, the inner work of the Yellow Emperor had also viewed people as part of Nature, and he fully believed in their ability to fulfill their basic needs in a manner agreeable to others.

Motzi had yet a different point of view and asked his followers to sacrifice personal profit for social righteousness, while the scholars from the School of Public Prosecution theorized that people were born evil and needed to be forced to obey orders. Other cultural standards, often overly high or unreasonable, were also established, such as the religions with saints who lived in the thin air of life. Some of these stories are the basis of much charming literature, as well as widespread social hypocrisy, although the teaching from both Lao Tzu and Jesus does not agree with any of the more extreme approaches.

Take the example of the early Zhou Dynasty when the young and ambitious Duke Zhou created his version of the social rites. These rites were expected to modify the loose sexual behavior of males during the early matriarchal society, but instead this once normal human connection became strained. Mencius then modified this stern discipline when he suggested his approval of male-female contact in certain situations, such as when a man's sister-in-law is drowning he could then rescue her by offering his male hand.

The younger Confucius was enthusiastic about Duke Zhou's initiatives, but these were not favored by Lao Tzu, who maintained his view that each person should fulfill their life correctly and harmoniously, and that the healthy nature of life has a higher value than any social rites. We concur with the highly rational and reasonable views of both Lao Tzu and the inner work of the Yellow Emperor because social troubles cannot be stopped in competitive situations, or when the natural health of society is disrespected.

Helpful teachings can encourage people to regain their natural health, not by adding anything, but by eliminating cultural poisons. This differs from the current political practice of developing new and often expensive programs to fix the mistakes from previous programs. That approach has increasingly burdened the social health system and created an unhealthier society. But Lao Tzu mentioned frugality, meaning effective management of both our own life and our nation, although few people value his view.

Lao Tzu was also the first to recommend the feminine principle for managing highly aggressive males, who are always ready for action. He had a lot of respect for women, compared to Confucius and the other cultural leaders at this time of tumultuous social tension, most of whom were unable to see that much of the trouble came from male aggression. Moreover, Confucius' words can be easily distorted to mean that everyone must conform to the male-centered obedience of the social rites. And this did occur during the Han Dynasty when the Confucian approach was rigidly revised to strengthen the male society as they defended the northern border of their homeland from the aggressive nomads.

Since then, this rigid interpretation has often been applied as an excuse to enable ruthless emperors and overbearing fathers to persecute the benign lives of the young. That approach was suitable for Duke Zhou to discipline males at a time when humanity was moving into a new phase and required some moral guidance, while Confucius wished to emphasize the old rites at a time when the male impulse was, yet again, becoming overly strong. But after Confucius' death the patriarchal societies became very aggressive as the smaller monarchial kingdoms battled against each other until the most brutal of all, the Chin, were victorious.

Over expression of the male impulse in any patriarchal culture rapidly antagonizes other patriarchal cultures, and in the above situation led to almost 300 years of extreme turmoil as the Chin cruelly swallowed all the other small kingdoms. The first Emperor of Chin then gave himself absolute power, and achieved his dream of being the king of all kings. He had wished to be the first of a long lineage, but only ruled for 14 years.

In the natural societies of old China the many small kingdoms had recognized the Way, and all communities, large and small, lived together harmoniously. But as the population grew, so did the competition to expand each society. This may be a natural male tendency, although being overly impulsive damages the light of life and the respect for Nature. Furthermore, males were repeatedly sacrificed to satisfy the desire of their leaders to increase their power by expanding their territory.

Eventually this tendency within males transformed into a form of social respect and admiration, which is also evident in the male-centered religions where God is seen as a male ruler who controls all. A similar tendency is found in politics, especially at times of war, when many people die to satisfy the male emotion of increasing their power by winning a conflict. Yet, Lao Tzu's advice to the male rulers of his time was that fighting and war are not the only way to run the world. Rather, he offered a vision of a world where all the male interests in aggression were softened to benefit the wider population.

A Constructive Approach

When working to improve the world it is safer to keep away from the external competition that supports the male need for self-aggrandizement. If this conquering tendency continues there is not much hope for a better and safer world, and the earth could shrink, or even disappear into a black hole over time. It may not come to this, although the force of Nature is not totally predictable. Nonetheless, people have definitely over estimated themselves regarding the scope of their many religions and other beliefs.

Constructiveness means having faith in the health of Nature, and constructive people seek to improve their internal qualities. External improvement comes from internal improvement and we should all work on this aspect of life. We cannot expect the world to improve immediately, but each person, either alone, or with a group of friends, can find a way to assist the spiritual improvement of humanity. In this context, I now offer my version of the five great healthy human relationships for today's world:

> *If the political situation is healthy* and the leaders conduct their duties in a healthy manner, offer healthy support, but walk away from any form of leadership that does not conduct their duty in a healthy way;
>
> *If your father is not as strong as you expected*, still offer him your dutiful support;
>
> *If your spouse is faithful and dutiful*, offer her or him your faithful support;

> *Siblings with a true heart* will naturally offer each other mutual support;
>
> *True friends will also be faithful*, and naturally offer each other mutual support.

We have now seen that over the past 3000 years human nature has become polarized with conceptual beliefs about good and bad, or right and wrong, and so on. Lenin used this technique to divide the social classes and win the Russian revolution. China then copied the method to start the second Chinese revolution in the 20th century, although both revolutions failed through unhealthy leadership and the loss of natural harmony.

But around 6000 years ago Fu Shi had already seen the need for cooperation between all opposing forces to accomplish a constructive life and healthy relationships. This includes good cooperation between the masculine nature and the feminine nature for effective improvements in the world, as well as the constructive survival of humanity. World harmony and spiritual health are still very far away for most people, although it is possible to fulfill our own internal harmony by uniting our lower mind with our higher mind, and our lower self with our higher self. This is the way to spiritual unity and a complete life, and allows the union with God that then advances the union of Tao and humanity.

It has also been proven that once a person attains complete spiritual health, this activates different spiritual functions, and when those people face difficult life situations their spiritual mind is able to take them away from the trouble. To achieve this we need to nurture our spiritual strength and watch our mentality and emotions, because healthy spirituality requires the unity of both our intelligence and our feelings. That is, complete spiritual health supports the non-verbal spiritual unity that governs all aspects of life.

This approach is very different to that of the conventional religious teachings which use a dualistic approach to illustrate what they believe is the nature of an unhealthy spirituality. Thus, they often personify elements of the human mind and emotions and teach polarizing concepts such as God vs. Satan, or Heaven vs. hell, which then disturb the internal harmony of the body. This is because there are numerous experiences in life that are not easily classified using those expressions. Furthermore, these concepts do not help to restore the natural unity of life, and can even intensify an internal conflict in people who rely on the external belief that God is the savior of their soul. But the worst aspect is that these conflicts can be expressed externally, and lead to a divided society and world.

The Integral Way does not push people towards a higher moral condition through severe disciplines, such as lying on nails, or walking on fire, or wearing heavy chains to wipe away loose thoughts and other 'sins'. Many people who seek such perfection become crazy, but the above practices arise from the male peacock complex that wishes to show a spiritual strength that is merely an emotional force to invite respect from others.

Spiritual health is not for show, and can only be expressed correctly by having complete health, which includes all of the Five Healths, and the associated healthy character and moral behavior in life. Religious people may wear colored robes and high hats, and murmur strange words and sounds, but all that is far from having spiritual health. Moreover, true spiritual health cannot be achieved through any external help that establishes reliance because that is just an emotion from a different level of the life spirit.

Each culture reflects its society, and vice versa, but once a culture merges with a religion the spiritual truth may be obstructed. Religious and social faiths are merely conceptual constructs for the crowds who look for truth in the wrong direction, although the emotions that made them fragile remain at a superficial level. Thus, the society who nailed Jesus to the cross used a similar psychology to the Indian sages who persecute themselves to prove their divinity.

True spiritual health is non-verbal, but offers real spiritual protection to an individual, and to all societies that pursue spiritual health instead of social manipulation and control. Spiritual health also makes life durable. Similarly, the complete spiritual health of humanity would produce the true divinity. However, those who destroy the health of Nature destroy life, and those who destroy the health of society destroy the health of humanity.

This means our true spiritual health is found in life, and life is for living with complete health, although some Buddhist sutras say: 'I do not want to become Buddha until all people become Buddha'. But know there can be a long period of emotional expression on the search to becoming Buddha before the mind becomes mature. Also remember that an integral life is a constructive life that follows the broad direction of never neglecting the universal moral duty of life. Hence, there is no need to surpass the morality of any of the sages, as once all Five Healths are attained we have already reached the highest moral standards of humanity.

All life is born with sufficient spiritual health to achieve this goal, but religious teachings have turned people into beggars who constantly seek help. This has damaged the spiritual dignity of humanity. So, do not seek to climb the peaks of life - worldly or spiritual - because those challenges are for immature minds. Just stay on the broad and healthy path that enjoys the spiritual honesty and sincerity which comes from living the integral truth.

The integral truth does not want to point to any serious mistakes made by an individual, even though worldly cultures and their leadership do affect both the internal and external condition of people's lives, and may even heighten the dualistic condition of humanity. A black and white presentation to an immature crowd has plagued many unworthy lives, but whose life is really unworthy if they raise a God, or a false culture, to determine the precious life of benign people who are not really interested in these religious or social concepts?

An internally reliable system means having no more inner holy wars, as this divides the mind, and one side of life can betray the other. The healthiest way is for both sides to merge towards the inner unity that precedes external unity. The Integral Way hopes all people can achieve that unity, and the freedom from both internal and external wars.

Chapter 10

Create a Healthy World

Conditions for a Healthy World

The following twelve conditions would improve the health of the world:

Improve Human Rationality: This would include respecting our rational strength, and adopting reasonableness as the prime consideration to guide social behavior. Human rationality could also be the common faith to replace the current confusion among the many external beliefs. This also needs approval from our internal partner, although not all life has that power of discernment. But everyone is born with the power of knowing right from wrong before experiencing the cultural confusion that disturbs our vision. So, first we would try to cultivate the health of the public conscience as a higher and more realistic divinity than any religious custom.

Have Faith in Heavenly Justice and Nurturing a Healthy Conscience: This would include knowing that human rationality is the source of the many points of view that cause contention among people, and having faith in the commonality of the sky, which is sometimes called Heavenly Justice. This position is not a form of hero worship, but reflects the highest level of selflessness in a rational human being. Thus, we would all nurture our healthy conscience, while social activists would benefit from examining the health of their own conscience before they supported an external cause.

Offer a Pure Public Service: This means people with a political position in society would offer a pure service rather than looking for material support, as the latter indicates some confusion in their public spirit. Societies which lack the intellectual force to improve their social management could invite expertise from outside, instead of constantly engaging in an internal power struggle.

Separate Politics from Religion, and Social Programs from a Pure Spiritual Offering: In a healthy society national politics and religious services would be totally separate, while religions would be viewed as a range of social programs that do not engage wider society. Social work within a community would also be separate from any pure spiritual offering that wishes to improve the ethical condition of society.

Improve the Political Culture: This means societies with a democratic system would insist on a just level of competition where political rivals would present a range of different views, and then allow the public to make an objective choice. In this system there would be no political manipulation or demonization of any opponents, nor any more of the civil wars that express the lowest nature of humanity. This approach would improve the political culture of the world. Similarly, a great nation would never initiate aggression against another nation, no matter the excuse, though the international society would likely punish those who do.

Improve the Overall Harmony of Humanity: A healthy spiritual faith represents the health of society. Thus, a healthy religion would never support racism, or nationalism, or any other form of social or psychological warfare that could damage the harmony of humanity. Moreover, a true religion would not sell fictitious emotional support because the ultimate purpose of spiritual work is to be self-supporting, and contribute to world peace and harmony. However, social, racial or national pride could still be used to boost people's morale as they work to attain a completely healthy life.

Only Support Healthy Public Funding: This would mean Governments could not use their financial force to develop weapons for social expansion, or needless aggression, but would invest in healthy social ventures, such as funding all public education up to junior college.

Support the Health of Our Environment: This would include not allowing Governments and other interests to destroy the forests and bodies of water to accommodate an industrial project, public or private, as this could directly damage the health of all life.

Respect Healthy Family Values: This means we would continue to respect the values where the duty of the family includes building the healthy character of young life. Parents would also share responsibility for the education their children receive at school, but those who feed their children fattening food as an expression of love, or allow them to play with guns or other dangerous weapons, would be seen as irresponsible.

Value and Strengthen Society: All people would value their homeland and seek to improve it, while each nation would be open to immigrants who could strengthen their society, and help the lives of others. Countries that accept immigrants would attract people through their cultural and moral situation, rather than their social welfare system. Moreover, political parties would not make immigration an election issue as this can poison the health of society.

Value Cultural Health: Museums would continue to be built to display cultural relics and other items with historical or constructive social value. But any negative social influences from movies, television, cartoons and electronic games and so forth, would be regulated by their producers, who would respect and consider the adverse effects on both individuals and the cultural health of society. A healthy society would also send people who destroy public facilities and services, or the nature of their healthy culture, to reform camps, but these places would not be used for people whose only misdemeanor was having a different viewpoint.

Continually Pray for the Health of Humanity: For example, begin all personal spiritual requests with a prayer such as…..

My deepest faith is in the health of humanity,
There is no other salvation when we create our own health problems.
Hence, all people share the duty for establishing a healthy humanity.
To fulfill such duty, I must attain the Five Healths in life,
And will cultivate a sound body, a sound mind, a sound life spirit,
Sound human connections, and a sound financial strength in my everyday life.
With utmost sincerity, I can then live with the health of humanity.

Social Correctness and the Spiritual Truth

Some of the oldest spiritual faiths and social structures promote God as the highest spiritual ruler of humanity. Yet, many religious professionals manipulate the faith of the people they serve by presenting themselves as an agent or go-between for God.

Our new spiritual approach suggests recognizing God as the natural strength or potency of life that comes from the constructive and everlasting power of Nature. And since God represents the potency of Nature, it is beyond our capacity to describe it, and also beyond any human emotion or conceptual differences, such as gender.

Religions can still be seen as an expression of the values in society, but this has very little to do with the deep spiritual truth of Nature. Sometimes a spiritual faith is also associated with the confidence of a specific ethnic or cultural group, and we do recognize that generally these beliefs are a sincere attempt to find the truth. However, be aware that over confidence in a belief can create trouble – personally, nationally, and globally.

Our spiritual faith believes in the healthy nature of life and humanity where:

> *God represents the health and normality of Nature*, and therefore also represents the healthy nature of the Universe;
>
> *The human potential for a completely healthy life also represents God.* Hence, people with all Five Healths - physical, mental, spiritual, social and financial - manifest the health of God;
>
> *God is also the inexpressible healthy power of life*, so we should all express the health of God.

Our spiritual practice has the purpose of uniting with the healthy universal potency of God. At that stage the divine energy will naturally move all bodily functions, such as our mental behavior, spiritual projections, social connections and financial support, in a manner where nothing goes against God, or the healthy nature of the Universe.

So, how do we unite with God? God is our internal unity, as well as the external unity of all human spirituality. This means there is a need to make an effort in both directions, and once these merge there are benefits to both our own life and wider humanity. At the personal level this can be achieved in one lifetime, although unifying human society will take longer. While there have already been many efforts in this direction, we need to be careful, or these attempts could obstruct the achievement of a totally healthy humanity.

At the level of our conscious capability, God is also the totality of the truth, goodness, and beauty of the Universe. Hence, God is found in all people whose healthy lives manifest the goodness and beauty of universal truth. However, the strength of our consciousness is not capable of comprehending the totality of the truth, goodness and beauty that is only found in the depth of Nature, and the wider Universe.

In spite of this limitation, people willing to unite with the truth, goodness and beauty of God can reach the constantly constructive nature of the God that is also the nature of the Universe. There is a destructive force in the world, but this is merely an accident without fault or blame, because the highest quality of God, and everyone who unites with God, is to be self-reliant and ready to help others. Hence, the agent between God and human life can never be a religious or social professional, as this role can only be fulfilled by the refined mind of a totally healthy person able to reach the same wavelength as God.

Happiness and success in life, no matter the personal fortune or nature of society, relies on a sound mind. And while spiritual potency cannot be described, we can describe the qualities of the human mind. A healthy mind is creative, calm, balanced, poised, even-handed, detached, relaxed, and leisurely during a busy life. All those attributes can elicit a response from God, while the prayers that are just desires find little or no response.

God stays with a constructive life, so every time we want to request God's help we need to look at what is missing in our life. But the people who really help God find their own solutions, because God is the potency of life, and life merely expresses our motivations. Thus, God is behind all life that is supported by healthy behavior, healthy thoughts, healthy spiritual projections, harmonious social connections, and healthy finances.

This also means that attaining a healthy and constructive mind is the most worthwhile pursuit to bring happiness, which is merely an expression of the healthy qualities of a sound mind. A strong body is important, but that does not assure happiness as many people who pursue extreme physical strength, and the societies that pursue physical force, can lack self-control, and might even become self-destructive.

Although this approach to having faith in God is simple, nobody can accomplish a constructive life through worship or prayer unless this is combined with the everyday offering of our healthy qualities in life. And when there is direct connection with the source of life we will no longer experience exhaustion. Complete health encompasses all of the spiritual and material aspects of life, but a healthy person knows how to engage in a comfortable range of activities without over burdening the natural order of their healthy life.

The highest rationality in life is the internal messenger from God, and that messenger only rides on a mind that has attained peace, calmness, balance, poise, and creativity. Thus, rationality or reasonableness represents the God in our life. But we should also have the highest respect for the total rationality of humanity, which grows with the development of every healthy life. Producing the rational mind that is closer to God also requires being free from the many pressures and emotions that twist our minds and block us from seeing God, as well as all the other external influences that hinder our clarity and independence, such as being tempted by immediate profit.

A life that is ruled by God via the internal messenger of rationality has reached the highest potential in human life with its divine qualities of self-commandment, calmness and composure, poise, justice, fairness, and a peaceful nature. Hence, the best fruit that can be harvested from life is our rational mind, while the above qualities can be found in the best brains of humanity.

An unprejudiced mind that has achieved all of these qualities and united with God has reached the ultimate state of divinity. My work, *Enrich Your Life with Virtue*, contains 25 constructive spiritual qualities that are worthy of our attention and absorption if we intend to regain these qualities in our own life. But for those who seek real examples of people with the divine qualities of the highest rational mind, consider the following three great sages:

Fu Shi, who lived around 6000 years ago, and discovered the eight trigrams that express the balance within Nature and human life;

Shen Nung, who lived around 5800 years ago, and developed an agricultural system to better support people's lives, as well discovering the value of plants as a source of human nutrition and effective medicine;

The Yellow Emperor, who discovered the use of the compass and the value of practicing humanism in society.

My spiritual background is the Union of Heaven and Man [Humanity], where we trust that the early people and their leaders had no evil intention towards others, because they were born with the complete health from Nature, and did not experience any social or conceptual confusion in life. These people had no need of spiritual cultivation, and were naturally benign and straightforward. They are the genuine models of a healthy humanity.

Later generations engaged in spiritual cultivation because they frequently faced the external influences and unclear social situations that contaminate the mind. During the long history from the original people to the present day, however, the depth of Chinese culture has continued to place utmost value on the Heavenly nature of humanity. Having a Heavenly nature means experiencing no confusion in the world, because all people are born with an innately healthy nature, and a heart free from evil intent.

Most people today have forgotten or lost these innate qualities, so regaining the original nature and healthy qualities of life should be our immediate concern. This is also the source of the meaning and spiritual position of the teaching from the Union of Tao [the Way] and Man [Humanity] in California. We simply unite our life with Heaven. We should also unite with God, instead of with the downfall of the world, to spiritually uplift humanity for humanity has lost its way of updating the natural spirituality in our lives.

The ancient Chinese called God their Heavenly Grandpa, which is sweeter and closer to human life, but the idea of the Heavenly Father is deeply rooted in the minds of many modern people. Therefore, the non-competitive Grandpa has yielded to his son.

PART IV

Finding Spiritual Maturity

The new path for humanity embraces the brightness of the sunlight.

Chapter 11

Have Faith in the Light of the Sun

Most of the public faiths that originated 2000 to 3000 years ago now cast shadows over the spiritual truth of life, and the inherent harmony of humanity. I hope that the following discussion will help to cleanse this confusion, and open the way to a common faith.

A spiritually correct faith improves the health of humanity, while a confused faith can cause more trouble. People have a strong psychic foundation, and the health of their psyche determines whether or not they are happy. Unhappy people may become destructive, either in their own life, or in society, while having a healthy faith helps life. So, the Universal Integral Way has taken up the challenge to renew the healthy faith in humanity, and direct people to the light of the sun.

Conceptually, God is in charge of the world. At a deeper level the sun is the source of the entire solar system that includes all life on Earth. Most religions have created a faith based on that reality, and offer symbols that suggest the sun. Yet, having too many symbols and terminologies has meant these religions often miss their true source, the light of the sun, which enables the brain to create such symbols. The troubles that arise do not come from the imagery, but from using people's faith for social manipulation.

The Integral Way respects these symbolic systems, but not any social manipulation by their religious leaders or believers, or a government, or anyone else. Our approach is to work with all symbolic systems and religions, but our main effort is to help people break through their conceptual barriers to see the permanent reality of the bright sky, and the value of returning to the ancient worship of the sunlight.

In places that only worship one God it is easier - just let the people know there is no conceptual God, only the God that is the sun in the sky, and that all religions are really symbolizing their common faith in the sun. This approach to a universal faith also accommodates most differences among the various local customs.

In the East, some people have become confused by the many different statues and forms of worship. In reality, there is no conceptual conflict, only personal preference, as all statues represent the worship of morality. For example, Buddhism worships peaceful golden statues, while folk Taoism worships some of the heroes from the past, or symbols of imagined deities in the sky.

The richest symbolism is found in Buddhism, although the Integral Way remains open to adopting these symbols and terms while maintaining the important principle that the real spiritual inspiration comes from the light of the sun. But all other natural sources of inspiration, such as the North Star, or other stars, or the planets within the solar system, still symbolize our spirituality, which comes from the light of the sun.

The health of humanity could be saved by recognizing that all spirituality is based on this source, although the personalization of the sun with concepts such as God or Buddha is more easily accepted. While not totally truthful, those symbolic teachings do offer some progress towards a healthy humanity by encouraging the human instinct to be good, and do good deeds, but this suggestion also came from Nature through the light of the sun.

Religionists cannot tell people how to please the sun, but once the sun is personalized it becomes much easier to control their congregation. Some teachings, however, do contain practices with an unhealthy image, or even support human darkness by using concepts such as God or Buddha as a 'business sign' to shield any mismatch with the reality that the nature of the sun in the sky cannot be changed.

A good common faith would help to shape the progress of humanity, and give people the strength to avoid the temptations from adopting confused beliefs, or chasing easy money. Yet, the simplest and most truthful faith is in the sky, which also suggests seeking an upward movement for our spiritual life that is a fundamental element in the depth of human nature.

The new spiritual faith of the Universal Integral Way recognizes the sun as our Heavenly Father, while the spiritual faith of the Heavenly Father is in Mother Universe, also known as Mother Nature. The Messenger for Mother Universe is the Lady of Wisdom, who can take any form or gender to enlighten and inspire all spiritual seekers with a healthy mind and good intentions. All other effective spiritual beings are respected and included in these three names with the hope that this healthy vision can restore the spiritual health of humanity, and relieve much of the conceptual confusion in the world. Hence, we acknowledge that:

> **The Heavenly Father to humanity is the sun;**
>
> **Mother Universe or Mother Nature supports the Heavenly Father;**
>
> **The Lady of Wisdom, or Messenger of Mother Universe, has the power to inspire a healthy human mind, and enable good communication with Nature.**

The Awakening Force

In this new universal faith the concept of Buddha is used to represent the awakening of our healthy being, rather than linking the life giving force of the sun to an image of a fatherly, but austere, God. The sun should be free from any such conceptual manipulation. All life is supported by the sun, and whatever is done to support earthly life has the Heavenly Father's approval, but no one should exploit the Father, or Earth, or kill another life. This means the Integral Way prefers that the life giving force be untouched by the human mind and its perverse activities that illustrate the slow growth of human spirituality.

In the Integral Way the sun is the life giving force, the moon is the reflecting force and Buddha is the name for the awakening force of humanity. First there is life, then the reflective inner light, while Buddha carries the divine nature of a complete and healthy human life that is no longer a refugee trying the escape the world. Thus, renouncing the world, or being totally reliant on physical survival, betrays the health of the spirit of life.

Buddha is also seen as the force for attaining complete health where there are five directions to assist the development of our physical health, mental health, spiritual health, healthy social connections, and healthy financial capability. Nature endows people with the potential to develop all five directions, although any higher achievement relies on the gift of special opportunities. These Five Healths are not totally a gift from Nature, but also require the correct effort. We recommend a fair achievement in all aspects for a balanced life, while insufficient achievement in any area may cause trouble.

The five directions to attain a balanced life can also be enhanced by suggestions to the five spiritual essences symbolized by the Angel of Life, who represents the spiritually awakened. This could be you! But we should all allow our lives to be assisted by the Angel of physical health, the Angel of mental health, the Angel of spiritual health, the Angel of social health, and the Angel of financial health.

Moreover, we should respect all people who have already become spiritually awakened. Yet know that practices which involve the worship of external divinities, or other unrealistic fantasies, can lead to a spiritual loftiness that blocks our personal awakening. Real spiritual awakening is the duty of life, and should never be a challenge. When we worship the five Angels in life they will respond to us, although we may wish to change their title to be Buddha, or use the practice as a form of psychological self-suggestion. Whatever the title or form, as long as the mind is not scattered, we will surely achieve.

Also know that our mental health has three distinct aspects - emotional health, conscious health, and conceptual health. This means there are really eight healths, and a responsible person has the duty to live a healthy life physically, emotionally, consciously, conceptually, and morally - meaning a healthy conscience - as well as spiritually, socially, and financially. These aspects are further enhanced if we seek assistance from the relevant Angel, or other Holy Being, or suitably apply the power of self-suggestion.

By now we should be able to identify the eight aspects of our life that relate to the eight trigrams which symbolize Nature, all of which can be assisted by our Holiest Being:

The Holy Being of our physical or bodily health;
The Holy Being of our emotional health;
The Holy Being of our conscious health, and general thoughts and activities in life;
The Holy Being of our conceptual health, and deeper thoughts and creativity in life;
The Holy Being of our healthy conscience;
The Holy Being of our spiritual health, including the influences from our inherited genes;
The Holy Being of our social health;
The Holy Being of our financial health.

But when we only pray to one of these eight Holy Beings this can bring more tension and block our progress, as it means we want that aspect too much and turn the prayers into an emotional demand. Be relaxed. The eight Holy Beings are really the Holiest Being that is our own precious and pure life force. In Buddhist terms this means our conceptual cleanliness produces the true Buddha, where all Buddha become no Buddha.

To become truly awakened means cleansing ourselves of all weak spots, emotionally or consciously. First, we must return to our original healthy nature, and remain independent from conventional confusion. Further spiritual support then comes from increased self-awareness, and the efforts made, as healthy thoughts automatically benefit other aspects of our life. Do not allow any 'leaks', however, as the unconscious worries or fears in any sphere of life could unintentionally create a personal disaster, or even damage others.

We could also increase our conscious power by learning the way of Jesus, and simply identify with either one or all of the Holy Beings. In the deep spirituality of Nature, one is many, and many are one. This requires deeper understanding, and the application of the spirit of non-attachment to all aspects of our Holy Being, to enjoy what comes to us naturally. That was the true achievement of Buddha. Furthermore, when one is many, and many becomes one, the spiritual conflict between a regular life and an achieved life, and the tension between pantheism and monotheism, will no longer exist.

Real help comes from adopting an integral approach, rather than creating separate deities for different needs, where any spiritual correspondence comes from the life of the worshipper, not the form of worship. But every day we still need to find time to pray to the ten Holy Beings with a clear mind and good concentration. Here is an example:

My life breath produces and respects the ten Holy Beings,
Who represent a spiritually awakened inner life:
The Holy Being of happiness;
The Holy Being of wealth;
The Holy Being of prosperity;
The Holy Being of brightness;
The Holy Being of clarity or no obstacles in life;
The Holy Being of no dark practices;
The Holy Being of health;
The Holy Being of uprightness;
The Holy Being of righteousness;
The Holy Being of self-completion.

Some people may find praying directly to Buddha, or Jesus, is a more effective method to awaken themselves, but those who prefer, or have a conscious obstacle, can use 'Holy Being' to replace Buddha in the following example:
I am a happy Buddha, 快樂佛;
I am a wealthy Buddha, 富足佛;
I am a prosperous Buddha, 發達佛;
I am the Buddha of brightness, 光明佛;
I am the Buddha of no obstacles, 无障佛;
I am the Buddha of never partaking in dark practices, 无暗佛;
I am a healthy Buddha, 健康佛;
I am an upright Buddha, 正直佛;
I am a righteous Buddha, 公義佛;
I am the Buddha of self-completion, 完成佛.

The vehicle at this stage is our conscious intent, as all human societies remain at the level of the conscious mind. Over the past 3000 years, however, much trouble has been caused by the cultural developments that disrespect the true, non-verbal spirituality in our life. These problems arise from an imbalance between the deep soul, that may be half conscious, and the non-verbal life force. Few people have attained sufficient knowledge of their inner life to be aware of the difference between the conscious soul and the spiritual soul. Our conscious soul relates to the living brain, and our spiritual soul relates to the entire life force. The latter also provides the essence to the substance of life, while our expressible conscious soul is a function of our spiritual soul. But the most important fact is that they intersect.

Chen Tuan experimented with his own long life as he lived in solitude on the heights of Hua Mountain, 華山, where he made the important discovery that the total health in life is closely related to the health of the conscious soul. This means we should not fill our minds with the vulgar side of life, or become attached to the troubled, sick, and miserable images shown on the news, or other modern media. Negative images can condition the mind to disrespect its physical life, and may even cause a disease like cancer.

The Integral Way is unable to cleanse all cultures in the world, but we do suggest the practice of safeguarding our own conscious health. If our minds lack self-discipline and suitable protection, how can our body and its organs be healthy? So, we all need to look after our conscious self and attain the confidence to pursue a healthy life. Identifying the conscious self is not enough – the real duty is the management of our conscious contacts.

Moreover, the true self, the spiritual self, can be supported by reversing the above prayers to praise Buddha [or another Holy Being] at certain stages of our development:

Buddha is happy, 佛快樂*;*
Buddha is rich, 佛富足*;*
Buddha is prosperous, 佛發達*;*
Buddha is bright, 佛光明*;*
Buddha is without obstacles, 佛無遮*;*
Buddha is without darkness, 佛無暗*;*
Buddha is healthy, 佛健康*;*

Buddha is upright, 佛正直*;*
Buddha is righteous, 佛公義*;*
Buddha is complete, 佛完成.

Some people may still wonder who Buddha is. According to Hui Neng, the sixth master of Zhan Buddhism, Buddha is our original life nature. Hui Neng was a wood cutter who found the deepest truth in life. Namely, that worshipping names like Buddha is an untruthful pursuit, but it cannot be wrong to achieve spiritual independence through maintaining our original, complete nature while living a decent life. Later, however, he negated this enlightenment by using Buddhist formalities in his own teaching. This may have been his spiritual duty, although it also means he is no longer a complete spiritual model of the teaching from Lao Tzu and Chuang Tzu.

All people could be spiritually healthy and live with their original, complete nature before their worldly experiences contaminated and distorted their lives. Hence, the above spiritual practices and protective disciplines from the East have continuing value in life.

Our Relationship with the Sun

Much of the above relates to Eastern spirituality, which also includes Lao Tzu's concept of the relationship between Mother and Child. At another time and place, Jesus was enlightened by his Heavenly Father, the sun. We will now consider these two spiritual concepts - the relationship between the Mother and Child from Lao Tzu, and the relationship between the Father and Son from Jesus.

Lao Tzu said: 'The world has a beginning that is the Mother of the world. Knowing the Mother it is easy to see her offspring. By knowing the offspring but keeping to the source there will be no exhaustion in life'. The key point is to value life by keeping to the source, or giver of life. Their connection is the Way. This is how Lao Tzu explains the relationship between Nature and human life. But Jesus saw this connection as a father and son relationship, where the conscious self identifies the sun as the life giver, and the son represents each life.

These concepts make the source of life much clearer, although most people do not know that the conscious self is able to usurp the throne from the non-verbal substance of life. This is because the upper conscious only knows itself and its partner, the subconscious that creates dreams. Yet, all three functions - upper conscious, subconscious, and non-verbal substance of life - form our complete life, including the many entities associated with our bodily functions, plus the genes from several past generations.

All this confuses an underdeveloped life, and the conscious self can make a decision to take, forsake, or generally mismanage the precious gift of life. Some religions also misuse the conscious self through meditations that disrespect bodily life because they have not achieved the internal harmony that sees balance as the highest principle in life.

So, how do we know which part of our inner life is our Mother or Father, and which part is the child? That is, which part practices self-discipline, and guards our moral and ethical standards? Any dilemma comes from an overly expanded mind that is too serious about conceptual beliefs. Our minds continually develop, but are never really ready to judge external society, even though its influence, including socially inherited beliefs, remains strong. Hence, personal spiritual development is very important, and the reward is the ability to break away from any dark social conventions. Meanwhile, most people are stuck, or just follow the flow of society, while the general confusion grows.

To fully value life we must first understand the relationship between the internal and the external aspects of life, and then find the truth of both. There should be unity within, and harmony without. All that is attained above the verbal or narrative level of life, and any spiritual achievement should not be shown to others. Also withdraw from disputes and enjoy the resultant peace. Inner peace is an achievement, but inner unity is an even higher attainment. Although verbal teachings in a social setting are the custom in most places, true spiritual progress is made alone. Adopting the right path and healthy concepts in our life, however, can help us to be above any of the darkness in our culture.

The predominant faith in the West is the Way of Jesus. His way of teaching is direct, with no need for middle men. Accept the pure heart of Jesus, but do not claim any special relationship with God, as this suggestion could make an unclean mind crazy. Also accept that his difficult personal practice may not be suitable for most people. But anyone willing to fast in the desert to undertake the test of God, the sun and the Heavenly Father, is qualified to say they are God after triumphing over all the temptations from the devils of hunger, thirst, heat, fear, solitude, sleeplessness, sexual and other desires, and the many strange thoughts of a mind under the baking sun. If they survive all those tests, they can say whatever they like!

The Way of Sakya was more moderate. He sat under the shade of a Bodhi tree in the forest for six years before being enlightened or, more truthfully, defeating his improper desires. Hence, he won the battle in the type of life where there are many crazy pursuits when seeking immortality. His disciple, who stayed with him, also attained a peaceful mind without the disturbance of evil desires. That was their real test, and their real life.

The young Jesus and older Sakyamuni can still be spiritual models for people attached to the ups and downs of life. But the Universal Integral Way has taken all past spiritual experiences to produce a new Way, which is to be just where we are, and find spiritual improvement through constant prayer. This means living a general life, and paying attention to our attainment as we achieve all eight aspects of the Five Healths. Studying the books from the Integral Way can also further our spiritual understanding, but first learn how to use the *Book of Changes and Unchanging Truth* as this pivotal work supports all the other books that help us to make the spiritual adjustments in life. Another useful practice is to keep a diary to check our spiritual growth every three to five years.

Jesus' heroic spiritual challenge took years of preparation to see the results from those 49 days in the desert, while the approach by Sakya was more like a farmer slowly tilling the land of the self. The Integral Way is to recommend the path of natural accomplishment, since there is no need for any especially designed practices to experience life. Most lives are already full of ordeals, and there are plenty of unexpected spiritual encounters.

Anyone who wishes to take on a special spiritual challenge should complete this early in life, although our everyday personal spiritual disciplines should last a lifetime as the purpose of life is to learn. At different stages there will be different lessons to be learned, and numerous matters to overcome, but there are no set tests. We cannot expect our lives to change overnight, and the more spiritual and mature approach is to live humbly and be ready for challenges at any time. The spiritual reward is the health attained from any experience, whether productive, or unproductive.

Spiritual and Psychological Maturity

Psychological maturity takes time and the right amount of life experience. Spiritual maturity is even more difficult and may take longer. Few people today have a clear view of their own life, and what is right and truthful, while most remain at the mental stage of people 2000 years ago. Yet, the spiritual maturity that is the genuine solution to all worldly problems is still possible, and should be the common goal of humanity.

Jesus, Sakya and Hui Neng were relatively young men when they rose in society. Jesus started teaching when around 30 years old. Sakya was 29 years old when he withdrew from worldly life, although it took him another twelve years to prepare himself before he faced the public. The young Hui Neng lived and hunted in the mountains for around 19 years before being popularly recognized. If they had been given another opportunity later in life, when they had matured, it is unlikely that their teaching would be the same.

We can still respect these great spiritual heroes, whose visions represent the stage of mental and spiritual growth during their time. For similar reasons, the Integral Way draws from the experience of all important spiritual teachers throughout history, although we now suggest the following direction to guide modern spiritual life. This approach is suitable for people at any age, and all stages of spiritual growth:

> *Develop spiritual independence*, which means not being reliant on an external teaching. All people were born the same and can find their own way to

achieve spiritually. Although the level of spirituality in each life is unique, everyone can attain some achievement.

Develop the moral courage to live fully, which means uniting our spiritual life and our secular life, and not forsaking the responsibilities on either side. Genuine spiritual accomplishment comes from going through worldly life without being defeated.

Develop the spiritual achievement that comes from the world to help the world, but do not take away the joy from secular life, or allow the pride of spiritual loftiness. The correct path is to give spiritual service by supporting a healthier human culture.

Have the courage to live with the plain truth of life, which means conducting our healthy life force honestly and earnestly, while our ability to make a living strengthens. At the same time, we need to constantly embrace and uplift our spirit.

Maintain the spiritual position of not rejecting conventional customs, nor accepting them as the final truth. This means working on our own spiritual progress, and acknowledging that each spiritual teaching represents a stage of human attainment.

Concentrate on pursuing the Five Healths so that no aspect becomes a burden to our own life, or to our society. Simply live with the well-being from complete physical health, the open and objective mind from good mental health, the spiritual transcendence from rising above all worldly matters, the social health from appropriate social connections, and the good financial health that supports our personal and family life.

Develop and strengthen the psychological support that grows from making spiritual development our main goal in life. There are various levels, so gather and test the practices that are the most effective to support the Five Healths in our own life.

Fortify the spirit by improving the mental and emotional health. There are many practices in the *Workbook for the Spiritual Development of All People* that can help to fortify our spirit, and one of the most effective is the secret prayer:

天官賜福, 地官赦罪, 水官解厄;
吾奉昊天大帝, 隨愿成就!

The Governor of the Sky blesses me,
The Governor of the Earth pardons my negligence,
The Governor of Water unties all my entanglements.
When my life embraces the greatness of the Sun
All good wishes will be granted!

Chapter 12

Deeper Reflection

We should now be clear that the purpose of the Universal Integral Way is to help us to achieve all eight aspects of the Five Healths, which are the basic standard for all human life. Serious students of the eternal life would also keep a written record of their daily self-inspection, and some may choose to make a seasonal or yearly confession to our Heavenly Father using a water body, or a mountain, or a forest as a witness. That is a suitable practice, depending on both our spiritual nature, and our ability to receive direct inspiration from the Messenger we call the Lady of Wisdom.

Deep spiritual faith in the Heavenly Father, Mother Universe and the Lady of Wisdom will help our spiritual health, and we may see improvements in our general life. Personal cultivation includes finding time to be our true self, so it is important to nurture this habit. Effective cultivation also means not being scattered as we quietly mind our life, and after some time we may be able to see a light with our eyes closed. The white light reflects the Lady of Wisdom, the purple light reflects Mother Universe, and the golden light reflects the Heavenly Father. Once proven, there is no need to tell anyone - it is our blessing in life.

Moreover, the Five Healths that form the main goal in life can be used as a standard for measuring their attainment. But also know that complete health has many different levels, and some of these cannot be generally known. This means we should just mind our own health and respect the health of others - there is no need for any comparisons. Originally the word health meant moral, and good morality always yields spiritual improvements in life. Universal moral life is known as the Way, or *Tao*, while personal spiritual benefit is called *Te*, where the ultimate gain, or reward, is complete health.

There is also another secret about the sun and human life. Every generation some wise people may appear in society and accomplish meaningful deeds. These people are the achieved souls who rode on the sunlight to reach

Earth, and when their duty is fulfilled those precious souls will again ride on the sunlight and return to the sun. A clean life with a clean soul is important to make this journey to participate in worldly life.

All people on Earth, however, must first attain the highest condition of conscious health, which is strong, and as clean as the high mountain ponds. This level has already been achieved by various seekers of the highest spirituality, although it is only their conscious attainment, and their total achievement of life is yet to come. The next step is to incorporate good deeds for the undiscerning public, and in time the conscious self automatically transforms to be the divine inner light. But do not use the imagination to seek this inner light as that can cause conflict – it is just a matter of coming to it naturally.

Furthermore, although this light comes from the internal transformation or sublimation of the general condition in life, it cannot be seen in a physical sense. But when it becomes stronger and reaches the same wavelength as the true divinity of the Universe, the two will merge. While fully understanding this requires the real experience from achievement, at that stage, where the life may choose to leave the world and return to the heart of the Universe, the white light meets the light of the moon and the stars, the yellow light meets the light of the sun, and the bluish-purple light meets the light of the Lady of Wisdom, who is our Messenger from Mother Universe.

The sun is in the sky, Mother Universe is infinite space and time, and the Lady of Wisdom is the moon and the reflecting stars, sometimes symbolized as a Goddess with a thousands arms. The source of all light is where our life comes from, and where it should eventually return. The spiritual truth is this much, but it is unseasoned and unflavored compared with the many highly seasoned and flavored cultures in the world. Hence:

The new approach to the *Universal Faith* in all our lives is to have direct faith in the sun, and a healthy confidence in humanity;

The *New Path* is straight, with no deviation from living the truth of Nature, and where the best support is self-support, and the best opportunities are in giving to others;

The *New Life* is unblemished, and comes through the achievement of self-reliance, good health, and practicing moral merit without discrimination or calculation;

***Moral Merit* is the realization of the benignity of original life, where fulfillment comes from viewing all people as one life.**

Moreover, all possibilities to develop the human mind come from this light. Repeated stimulation from the sunlight through the eyes causes the brain to respond to the various wavelengths from that light, and this process was particularly strong before people developed shelter. This also means the mind is very sensitive to changes in the external environment, and can even perceive the large to be minute, and the small to be enormous.

Thus a developed mind could perceive the origin of Mother Universe. The Universe experienced a long period of darkness before producing the bodies of light, and although the sun is not the only body of light, it is the father of all earthly life. Therefore, the greater Universe can be perceived as the mother to her son, whom we call the sun.

We should all be able to use the power of the sunlight to attain a healthy life and a clean brain, but most people have allowed various concepts to distance them from the truth, or even cause them to become sick, or confused. That is, their minds have stolen the part of the life force that seeks health and longevity, and widened their separation from the light, although they are still capable of cleansing this mental confusion and returning to the reality of life.

Yet, whether or not we realize it, our life force comes from Mother Nature, and that life force is the substance of our life. No mental vision or concept can ever change this. So, I now ask all children of the Heavenly Father to return to embracing the sun, the immediate source of our life and intelligence. This renewed relationship will then enable us to receive considerably more benefit than holding on to any artificial belief.

Also be aware that a great life can be found in the mountains where there is good water and fresh air. Artificial faiths arose when and where the land was destroyed to support people's excess desires, but the faiths that have created the worst disasters compete with the real God in the sky and Mother Nature, and have already corrupted many people in the world. We must now have the faith that our path and our life can do better.

The truth about our real God cannot be found in the many thick books written on this subject, although we are able to identify at least three characteristics of this God:

> *God is omnipresent.* There is nothing more omnipresent than the sunlight. God, the sun, is the direct source of the creative force of Nature that is reflected in all life, and hence the indirect source of all human creativity;
>
> *God is omnipotent.* The all-powerful, creative force of Nature, as reflected through the sun, is the source of the reproductive force in all life.
>
> *God is omniscient.* The all-knowing sun follows its own path while keeping each planet on track. It also provides the sensory capability in all life on Earth.

Ancient people admired the fact that that the Sun God is all knowing and all powerful, but this has been misused by the churches, who usurped the power of the sun in Nature, and transferred this natural faith of the people into several beliefs through the powerful image of a personified God. Some churches even maintain a contrary practice that requires their believers to confess their sins to the priests, which then negates the very omniscience of their God, as well as illustrating the general weakness of that religion.

If we still deny the position of the sun in all life, where do we think our own life force came from? We could say the air, or water, or food, or even the check from the Social Security Office that keeps some people from stealing or looting, but would any of these things exist without the sunlight? Do we also truly believe it is possible to find humanistic love from any other source? Many hardened human hearts have been softened and inspired by the light of the sun, our Heavenly Father, when they finally wish to learn how to help others.

Therefore, we should not be confused by the many conceptual beliefs in the world, as we have identified the highest and most positive belief to be that in a universal, impersonal God. Rather, we need to identify the godly qualities in each belief that have been proven to assist the health of humanity, and which would contribute to universal harmony and prevent us from falling further into the darkness, or complete chaos.

Two of these qualities are exalting the public spirit in all people, and providing a healthy image of a spiritual leadership that includes positivity and constructiveness. The sun possesses both of these higher qualities. Yet, all conceptual interpretations of the Sun God have failed, thus far, to provide the world with the spirit of constructiveness. So, perhaps we could learn directly from the sunlight by adopting an updated faith in the Sun God, as the sun remains a God to all people, regardless of any conceptual interpretation.

Originally, people held on to their true faith in Nature, and had no motivation to create a fictitious belief. Later, there was a need to update the ethical condition among people, or coordinate a social force for a specific purpose. Unfortunately, these solutions often involved social manipulation. But there is no conceptual belief higher than our natural faith in the sun to exalt the universal public spirit. Furthermore, the Sun God is no lesser than any of the other moral models conceived throughout human history.

Many of the long lasting and trusted spiritual qualities identified with the sun have come from the general public perception over time. The sun was also the spiritual teacher to several of the most respected Chinese leaders and sages in the past. Yet, people who possess the characteristics of the sun often attract strong hatred, and for that reason our faith in the one universal God in the sky should only mean having faith in the forever impersonal sun.

Some the higher spiritual qualities of the Sun God also form the nature of universal morality, of which the following are more than enough for most people to learn:

Powerfulness, 權勢; majesty, 王範; nobility, 高貴; greatness, 宏偉; wealth, 財富; awesomeness, 威嚴 ; health, 健康; straightforwardness, 坦

率; candidness, 開明; frankness, 坦白; never covering things up 无隱; directness, 直行; uprightness, 正義; righteousness, 公義; just 公正; all-benefiting, 利而不害; unselfish, 無私; non-attachment to triviality, 不支離; non-involvement in tedious details, 不煩瑣; completeness, 完整; fulfillment, 完善; dedication, 奉献; uniqueness, 貞一; no hypocrisy, 無偽; no regrets, 無憾; no puzzlement, 无惑; no enemies 無敵怨; no worries, 无憂; happiness, 快樂; all-accomplishing, 美満; ever present, 無所不達 無所不在, 無所不與, 無所不照, 長寿無極; .... and so forth.

Is there any other choice?

By now we should all know we were born as part of the sun, and that spiritually the sun is our complete life. We already know we were born into a timeframe governed by the sun, which we count in hours, months and years. Moreover, we can all be described by our birth sign within the twelve zodiacal divisions of the year that are also part of the twelve yearly cycle of the sun. In this context, no one is spiritually complete.

Hence, to achieve a complete life and counteract any defects, we should allow the sun to rule our direction in life, and seek any further spiritual support through personal cultivation. Having faith in the sun, and being able to deeply communicate with the sun also chases away depression, but remember that the sun does not grant all wishes – the real gift is the time we are given to achieve the healthy wishes that are right for our life.

Compared to a fictitious God or the numerous deities from various beliefs, the sun lacks promotion as a force to change our personal fortune. But the people who are attached to these conventional beliefs might now like to consider whether their deity is really higher than the sun. Some wishes may be granted from worshipping a fictitious image, although many temples and churches still house groups of mixed spirits from the egos of past worshippers. People with faith in the sun will be protected, while the real help comes from our own attitude, and an understanding of what is correct and most important in life.

There are also the people with a big ego, who wish to be the king of kings. No one is able to change the ambition of another person, but we do need to assess whether or not their leadership comes from the sun by distinguishing the nature of their behavior. For those with good spiritual qualities, offering healthy, upright public leadership at any level offers a great opportunity to serve others, just like the sun. Similarly, any leadership which matches the spiritual qualities of the sun is great leadership, and worthy of respect.

The Heavenly Father of humanity, who is the real king in the world, can be reached by his light. The light of the sun is the true life giver, and all people are expected to be qualified citizens of its Heavenly Kingdom. While it seems that few people clearly know that the duty of life is to realize the Heavenly Kingdom within, those who possess the Five Healths have already realized their personal Heavenly Kingdom, and do not need to go anywhere else to harvest the spiritual rewards of life.

When all that is achieved naturally there is no need for any special spiritual teaching, or organized leadership, and this has already been observed by a few people like Lao Tzu and Chuang Tzu. People who still seek help can find a spiritual self-fortification practice in the *Guide to Universal Spiritual Harmony*. Those looking for further fortification in life can refer to the *Esoteric Tao Te Ching, Quest of Soul,* and *Nurture your Spirits,* while some invocations in the *Workbook for Spiritual Development* also meet this need.

Also be aware that even though our soul comes from the sun it is easily contaminated by the world, either through our life experiences, or the genes we inherited. Hence, there is the need for faith in the sunlight to cleanse the new soul. Yet, many people continue to forsake the moral leadership of the sun, and allow others to seize the throne of heavenly peace and happiness for their own enjoyment and personal power. Consequently, most natural leadership has long been lost, or overtaken by ignorance and arrogance.

Nonetheless, the sun is still the king of all life, and its spiritual qualities form the healthy Way of humanity. No other teaching expresses this in such a straightforward manner as the Integral Way, where the Tao Te Ching provides the main guidance for achieving the Heavenly Kingdom, and Jesus is seen as the son or natural leader of that Kingdom. As Lao Tzu said - 'my words are very easy to understand, so how can people have such difficulty understanding and achieving them in life?'

But also be very clear that my [Om Ni's] words now offer a direction for serving the Way in a worldly spiritual paradise centered on the sun, where all life is able to embrace the light of their father. So, learn to value the sunshine, fresh air and good water on Earth. Modernization has not provided all the answers to people in either the developed or lesser developed world. Social progress does not mean destroying the forest and farms for the factory, while the natural support in life is often lessened by increased industrialization. These trends should now be re-evaluated.

The Heavenly Father has long been the 'cure-all' medicine for rural people, who knew where to find the best herbal and other natural remedies for their illnesses. Now, in spite of many new inventions, this form of help is rarely seen, and has been replaced by expensive pharmaceuticals that rapidly exhaust the wealth of these simple people. They should have no shame about living simply and naturally, while it is one of the great shames of life to chase them into a hitherto unknown direction.

The Universal Integral Way stands at the turning point of human history. We look to the sun, the light, the conscience, and the health of humanity. We also support the clarity of our own deep conscious self or spiritual soul in life, whose main source is the sunlight. But whatever the source, or degree of contamination, we must all worship the sun to cleanse our new soul. The rest of our life remains as our choice!

Let us follow the heart endowed to us by the sun.
Let us follow the justice of the sun as our permanent Heavenly Father.
Follow the sun, follow the light, and follow the conscience.
Follow all those with the heart of the sun, and a strong conscience in life.
Exercise your endowed might and potential,
Do whatever is right for your life,
And whatever is right for humanity.

PART V

Assessing the Spiritual Options

When the original teachings are killed, the essence of the sage's wisdom is lost.

Chapter 13

Reviewing the Options

Human spirituality is very subtle and the modern intellect tends to turn away from addressing the matter. People then have the problem of not knowing the real purpose of their life, for it is clear that the intellect is only a tool to support that life. Moreover, because the material foundation of life is common to all people, many of them prefer to take a materialistic view, and replace the spiritual side of their life with goods and activities that satisfy their emotions. Thus, they miss the whole point of life.

Some people do retain a spiritual interest in life, although they may find the conventional spiritual expressions confusing. I respect these souls, who have not been spoiled by the conventions of a religion, and my lectures and books have the purpose of helping them to overcome their confusion. I also hope they will become good teachers, both for themselves and for other people who experience spiritual difficulties.

Yet, there is only one spiritual reality in human life - the light from the sun and the stars that has helped to develop our minds and our souls. Within this simple reality our mind continually communicates with our soul at the conscious level, or at the level of our deeper consciousness that also includes the ability to communicate with our conscious soul through dreams. At the conscious level, however, the activity of our brain, which produces our thoughts and decisions in life, is always pushing our conscious soul to one side. But when the higher mind is sufficiently rested to allow the conscious soul to function, it is able to send messages, through a dream, to the conscious level of our brain.

The early Wayfarers sought to achieve the dreamless mind, where the good work done by the physical brain leaves nothing behind that needs to be supplemented by its partners in the deeper conscious self. As the internal mental condition is very personal, however, most people are never really clear about which of these partners is active, although some external knowledge can help to improve our internal mental condition. This is where the spiritual teaching from the Universal Integral Way can offer a service.

So, we will now externally examine several spiritual beliefs and cultures. All people live with the same non-verbal spirituality that is the deeper substance of life. The ultimate reality of this life is whether to live or to die, but there are numerous cultural interpretations. Yet, most people do not know how these beliefs have influenced the world for thousands of years, or that having incorrect beliefs is an invisible killer. Our hope is that offering the true spiritual knowledge would help more people to make the correct choices in life.

The following selection of spiritual beliefs and cultures share the deep reality that the sun communicates with all life, even though most people wish to apply their own consciousness to interpret this universal fact. That is, all religious cultures are based on a quality found in the sun. While this illustrates the universal supportiveness of the sun, the various interpretations and supposed spiritual phenomena come from human emotion, rather than reflecting the reality of Nature. Hence, seeking the light can also create darkness.

An unbiased vision of the spiritual confusion in the world over time does have value, but also be aware that our own discernment, combined with a broad and open mind, is now required to objectively view some of the spiritual options currently available.

The Integral Way and Buddhism

Buddhism is well established as a form of worship over much of Asia, and has had a long relationship with Chinese culture. The now predominant Mahayana Buddhism established Buddha as a symbolic authority outside life, although this teaching also has the psychological effect of uplifting people's respect for life. Therefore, it remains an indirect form of teaching the spiritual truth.

Many Buddhist teachings now offer various rituals to serve the wider society, but the Lotus Sutra reveals that the highest spiritual truth is in the heart of each individual, and serious seekers of the truth will find that once they reach the depth of the spiritual self, all other methods should be forsaken.

Nevertheless, the long relationship between Buddhism and traditional Chinese culture means that Buddhism differs from the other social religions. There is also a connection with the once largest social religion, Brahmanism, where disappointment from believing in an absolute spiritual ruler caused some worshippers to create new faiths based on their deep personal reflection. These new faiths included Jainism and Hinayana Buddhism, which are both credited for the awakening from the social-religious manipulation of their time.

Prior to the early Tang Dynasty [618-906 CE] Mahayana Buddhism supported the rulers who defended the Chinese borders, but when these battles affected national production the emperors tried to abolish the official religion. The people did not want to give up their emotional support, however, and the religious leaders preferred to bow to their peaceful, golden statues rather than be subject to the imperfect and double-handed rule of the emperors, where one hand held the force of government, and the other applied religion.

During the Song Dynasty [960-1279 CE], the government supported Taoism over Buddhism, and later the Ming Dynasty [1368-1643 CE] saw the compilation of the Taoist Cannon. But Lamaism with its meticulous rituals, which was popular during the Yuan Dynasty [1280-1367CE], had already adopted these rituals that were also supported by the much later Ching Dynasty [1644-1911 CE]. The main purpose of this form of worship was enlightenment, although most of the lamas remained heavily chained to the rituals that are still used to govern the nomadic people in the eastern highlands of China.

In contrast, the Integral Way offers a direct form of teaching where each life must achieve the purity and benignity of their original healthy life spirit. Any emotional attitudes towards life, such as being overly pessimistic or optimistic, and being aggressive or lacking equilibrium are therefore unhealthy.

The Integral Way and Christianity

Christianity is one of the later spiritual creations that exalted female morality, although in practice the teaching applies the more aggressive male approach. The original natural societies were matriarchal, but eventually the male reproductive force took control and established a network of families and clans centered on preserving the male bloodline. Chinese ancestor worship and most social religions also grew from these patriarchal societies, which imposed the strong social competition that supported their expansion. While having a common faith can strengthen a society, and offer protection, the teachings based on the male force generally do not go deep enough to reach the spiritual truth.

Christianity first developed from the early Judaism that was a social faith practicing 'an eye for an eye and blood for blood' approach to contention. Such racial revenge was denounced by Jesus, who replaced this approach with forgiveness and loving our enemy. Later, however, the Roman Catholic Church used the teachings of Jesus to promote their version of monotheism as an advance over the earlier approaches by both Babylon and Judaism, which exalted the male creative force and tightened the rule of the clan system. Early Catholics also copied the original Hindu Brahman practices where the priests shared the bounty from any victory with the Kings, or other ruling system. Furthermore, they combined the Egyptian sun worship, through the sign of the cross, with the broad humanistic love of Jesus, and used this new approach for international expansion.

Unfortunately, the Christianity long practiced by the Roman Catholic Church is a social and conceptual establishment, rather than being the direct truth. But once the Roman Empire made Catholicism the state religion to strengthen their social control, it soon became an established custom which rapidly spread throughout Europe and several European colonies. Hence, the once persecuted Christianity was reformed to revitalize a declining regime, and from there expanded to become one of the major world religions.

The Integral Way has never supported any dynasties or religions, but maintains its independent cultural position of encouraging personal spiritual pursuit and development. There are two types of enlightenment. The first approach creates religious riddles, and the followers feel bliss as they find the answers that then need verification by a religious authority to avoid any possible misunderstanding. The riddle may be resolved, although the process could harm the value of our constructive life spirit. Thus, the Integral Way supports the other approach where real life experiences offer the possibility of overcoming all the mental and emotional riddles in practical life.

The Integral Way and Islam

Mohammed was an Arab merchant with deep spiritual knowledge who saw that the scattered spiritual customs among the many Arab tribes threatened their survival. Hence, his goal was to attain the spiritual unity of these tribes.

The Chinese see several parallels between Islam and Zhan Buddhism [Zen], and Islam may even have inspired a few Zhan Masters. Nevertheless, Mohammed's main achievement was to integrate a variety of local spiritual practices to form a new approach that did not involve any outside influences. Similarly, modern people could address the root of all racism by giving equality to the major religious faiths, and if these teachings treated each other fairly there would be no spiritual problems, just different beliefs and attitudes. To achieve this, all faiths should extend their public service to guide people back to the original nature of human life. This is because the true spiritual self comes from one source, which is the sun within Universal Nature.

The Integral Way does acknowledge that there are differences among the religious faiths regarding the attitude towards life and death. But Zhan Buddhism made an important breakthrough regarding the depth of our conscious mind, and has shown us that the essence of the deep mind can be found in the conscious capability of our physical brain. At that level, any insistence on the conscious content of our mind is foolish as there is no difference between an Indian and a Chinese mind, or between a Western and Eastern mind, and whether a mind is uneducated or highly developed. Here, there is equality, and Buddha and non-Buddha become one.

People who reach the depth of life also see that the conscious content of our mind reflects the contamination from our experiences in life. Once this is washed away the purity of the life essence is restored, and achieved individuals see life and death being as easy as removing their clothes. The disintegration of the physical body and spiritual self also brings freedom from the contamination that makes the conscious breakthrough in spiritual cultivation seem like an achievement. There is no pain during this disintegration and no need for any fanfare once such liberation is attained.

This view of life can be traced back to Chuang Tzu, while Islam dates from the faith of the early warriors who chose to die on the battlefield, rather than on their sickbed.

The Integral Way and Hinduism

The spiritual mists that arise from the many cultures within Indian society require thorough research to find spiritual clarity. We have already seen how Buddhism separated from Brahmanism, but both the major faiths in modern India - Buddhism and Hinduism - continue some aspects of the original Brahman faith. Hence, there is a kaleidoscope of spiritual expression in Indian culture, although these expressions are mainly for the general public, and the few who become achieved would need to see through all these emotional and artistic creations.

Beneath the surface of any confusion in this situation there are hidden gems. For example, the law of cause and effect, or karma, is related to the patterns formed by our genetic inheritance and behavior, and their respective connection to the laws of Nature. Religionists have then turned these influences into various deities, or a personified God, both of which are believed to shape human life. The reality behind these delusions is that the true delivery from worldly problems does not come from having faith in any deity, or a creator, but from our own personal efforts and improvements in life.

Brahmanism had value in promoting the faith in one God to wider society, although the priests soon established themselves as the agents of God. But later this religious ruling system, and the special privileges given to priests, caused much antipathy in society. Those privileges included the collection of offerings or 'debts to God' from their congregation, and were based on the belief that a good life and blessings from God are subject to having faith, and have nothing to do with personal effort, or good management.

Eventually a rich but wise man called Jain reflected deeply on this matter, and formed a new faith whereby living a disciplined, ascetic and moral life within the five precepts of no killing, no stealing, no sex, no lies and no drinking alcohol, is seen to invite blessings from God. His teaching, now known as Jainism, later moderated Buddhism.

Cultural beliefs are a strong force in shaping the mental conflicts that lead to war, but it is our responsibility to find the value of the deepest truth within each regional or religious custom. Such truth should be seen as a necessity of life, and available to all people, just like water. However, we can still enjoy the numerous brands of tea or coffee at a different level of life, as every spiritual tradition has inspired some people to look into the depth of human spirituality, and find the truth which supports the management of life.

Progressing Human Spirituality

Ever since the time of Fu Shi, Shen Nung, and the Yellow Emperor, the Integral Way has viewed God as the pure and innocent spiritual essence of humanity. God lives in the depth of all healthy people, but those who abuse their health have committed blasphemy by disrespecting their true divinity. Prayers, offerings, or an overly ascetic approach, are not refused the blessings from God, although all emotions should be subordinated to the highest essence of life. Moreover, the five precepts from Jain can be broadened to form five guidelines to supplement the basic teaching from Lao Tzu that there should be no violent force, or behavior, within the Way of achieving complete health.

Pessimistic spiritual approaches merely offer an empty dream, while the warrior faith believes that giving our life in battle is the way to ascend to paradise. These fundamental mistakes come from not seeing that living with worldly difficulties strengthens the undefeatable life substance of the soul, which is above any emotional suffering and conscious reactions. Consciously strengthening our soul is the duty of life, and nobody else can do this for us.

There are also the religious teachings that gather social support for their own establishment and expansion. These are not true spiritual teachings, but social or business schemes. Cultural detoxification from such influences is an individual pursuit, and spiritual achievement comes from an honest life that does not separate the spiritual and the secular. However, the Integral Way supports all serious people who are not discouraged by spiritual confusion, and make the effort to maintain their natural life spirit and achieve the Five Healths.

Our personal health, and especially our mental well-being, affects the health of our family, society, government, and ultimately the fortune of the world. So, we should all watch our mental health! Any emotional suffering can be easily observed by others, but mental problems are not always discovered, especially in those with positions of power, until their craziness creates a disaster. Furthermore, strong social competition can negatively affect the normality of the mind, while higher education does not necessarily guarantee the healthy performance of any given duty.

The Integral Way believes that complete health is essential for all people regardless of their status. Today the old warrior societies of the past, when learned people created religions to share the ruling power with the warrior kings, have largely been replaced by the intellectual society. But now, the majority of people in the Western world give almost half their earnings to help support the ruling establishment.

Young America was the first place to adopt the power-sharing form of rule in a new parliamentary system based on British governance. The intellectuals that now make up this system are not directly involved in production, and are smart enough to make laws that enable their re-election. This process has created a new social class that purports to serve the people, but in reality consumes much of the public purse without making any noticeable difference.

Originally all people were responsible for their own lives. Today, most people carry the burden from the continuous social competition, where only a few people can become part of the ruling class, while societies accept the need for a government to protect them as they work to support their families. If that support does not come from a healthy source other problems can arise, but in the modern, educated world it is sometimes difficult to distinguish who is trustworthy, and who is not. Meanwhile, the social burdens increase, even though the human life force and its various needs remain the same.

We all share responsibility for the state of the world, and everyone has to find their own solutions in life that avoid or minimize the human cost. Nonetheless, most cultural initiatives, old or new, have made someone else in society pay the price. The Integral Way suggests living a complete but balanced life where worldly salvation will come as an increasing number of people achieve optimum health. Put simply - to avoid the problems from being a burden to the health of humanity, each person should attain the Five Healths of a complete life. This is the new approach to the spiritual light that guides all humanity.

So far the development of the human conscious power has been accompanied by the expansion of their emotional expectations that include maximizing happiness, success, prosperity, health and longevity. There are many definitions regarding the optimum amount and quality, although all people know that their physical life is temporal. Many religions also make these desires a remote possibility to be fulfilled in a higher and better land, such as Heaven. Yet, most people would prefer to see their aspirations immediately! The irony is that they could create their own rewards instead of choosing to become disillusioned after every success, and rapidly losing any sense of happiness.

The Integral Way believes that more people must improve their mental quality to progress humanity, as developing a higher mental awareness would sharpen the need to focus on attaining all of the Five Healths in life. Universal Nature is constructive, and we should all live with our constructive life nature. However, those who choose to abandon their true nature face disappointment, and may become self-destructive, while those who do not value the health of life will not care for the health of society and the world.

Attaining all five aspects needed to complete our health and well-being expresses a strong sense of duty towards life, and the health of the world depends on the number of people who can achieve this. No one should neglect their duty to engage in this campaign to save the world. But also be aware that many people currently involved in the numerous social, environmental and political campaigns to save the world are unable to take care of their own lives, and some even partake in such action to avoid their own problems.

Very few humanistic services align with their worthy goals, and the real problems in society are often more influenced by the views and emotions of the majority, rather than any rational resolutions by their political and social leaders. Even so, everyone, and particularly those with a high position in society, should engage in the duty to improve their own mind and personality as this could help to save the world. The foundation for a healthy world is not difficult – it is just the way that all parents want their children to live.

The Universal Integral Way stands for the humanistic effort in life. This teaching was developed by the achieved people from many generations, who widened their humanistic care to include the public. Some people may feel the scope of this work is too much to handle, so I have produced seven books on the Path of Constructive Life for modern spirituality that are especially for them. In simple terms, all of the Five Healths are achievable in our life, and we could all be happy when our emotions return to the purity of childhood.

Due to widespread immaturity, and the growth of malicious competition, the world of today is not safe, and recent history has shown that many serious mistakes have arisen from the immature vision and behavior of some elected political leaders who lacked the required spiritual qualities. If we understand the matters of the world we must not put immature people in charge, but find the correct help from our own healthy minds.

Life can never be separated into the secular and the spiritual when we follow the Integral Way. When all our activities meet the healthy requirements to safely accomplish both the secular and spiritual aspects of life, the deepest nature of a healthy human life is complete. But also remember that pursuing too many options can cause confusion.

I choose the sun to be the ruler of my mind,
Let its brightness shine on all corners of my mind.
The sun is the Heavenly Father of my soul, and all human souls.
Thus, no one should turn back from the source of the spiritual light in life.

There are four seasons in human life that relate to the climatic variations each year. All seasons are great to those who live a constructive life.

Grand Master, Yo San, Ni

Chapter 14

Cast No Shadows

Confucian scholars who stiffen the original teachings of Confucius
........are guilty of killing his real life spirit;
Buddhist monks who rigidify the lessons from Sakyamuni
.......are guilty of killing his true message;
The creators of Religious Taoism
.........were guilty of killing Lao Tzu's sincerity and innocence;
Christian clerics who manipulate the message from Jesus
.........are guilty of killing his heart;
When the original teachings are killed,
.........the essence of each sage's wisdom is lost.

From Diversity to Unity, 1996, revised by Hua-Ching Ni, 2013

The old social religions continue to offer the broad support of an established spiritual faith to the public, although most of these beliefs do not go deep enough to bring the true happiness found from a completely healthy spiritual life. While we do say that each generation should not be sheltered under the mental and emotional shadows cast by their ancestors, neither should they stiffen nor kill the true spirit and teachings of the great sages.

Moreover, we are all deeply related to our wider family – and our temperament, disposition, sentiment and emotions all come with some inherited problems. At times these tendencies will help us to handle a situation with ease, or they could increase the difficulties. There is also the possibility of a problematic fortune, sometimes known as karma, which is a simple word for describing our inherited spiritual responsibility, whether or not it is a burden or a gift in our life.

To paraphrase the *I Ching*: there is more to celebrate in families that accumulate good deeds, and more to suffer in families that accumulate bad behavior. Most people know this hidden reality, so the elders help the young to better understand the good behavior that accumulates spiritual merit.

We can look at our own life – if we feel bad that is a shallow emotion, as occasional clouds cannot overshadow the brightness of life. So, if our life is difficult we do not need to respond with radical actions, but let these difficulties slowly resolve to experience good 'karma' later in life. This will also prevent casting a shadow on our descendants.

All this has been observed for over 8000 years, and just as negligent moral behavior by an ancestor can still bring us misfortune, our own negligence can increase future difficulties. These patterns are more easily observed in the Chinese families that have existed for thousands of years, and there are now hundreds of families whose names can be traced back to their original family lines that date from the Zhou Dynasty [1122 -256 BCE], which formally established the patriarchal society, and by the time of the Song Dynasty [960-1279 CE] the records show around a hundred family branches.

A recent Chinese census shows that many more new family names have been added as the population rapidly grew. Some new names were given to repay a grace, but often a popular name of the time, or the name of a much admired noble, was adopted. Other families chose a simple, easily acceptable name that implied desirable qualities, such as having strong vitality. This means that the bloodlines of people in a larger family group with the same name, often amounting to millions, may be less pure than those where the name has a smaller population, such as the Ni family. The main meaning of Ni is 'smallest baby of the family', and this seems to have kept the Ni family small!

Nonetheless, the situation or 'fate' of the descendants of any family does not depend on their name, but on whether or not they carry the spiritual merits and demerits of their ancestors. Inherited genes are already known to affect our physical features, and we should also know that these genes affect our spiritual, emotional, and overall tendencies or patterns in life. Most non-Chinese cultures do not pay close attention to the spiritual and mental condition of their ancestors, but the Chinese believe that each new life represents many previous generations.

This means morally protective disciplines do not only benefit the current life, but extend that benefit to future blood connections. In this situation there is no need for outside discipline from society, or from artificial religions, as the standard for each Chinese family is to honor the life of both their ancestors and that of future generations. Thus each life can be said to stand for the moral condition of all humanity, and any social-cultural measures to regulate people have less weight than the family disciplines.

In India this continual spiritual process is called karma, but the invaders who came from the north misused the concept to create a religion that enslaved the original inhabitants of the sub-continent. That religion has now affected Indian culture for over 3000 years, although the wise people in Indian society would do well to put aside any previous wrongdoings from the caste system, and value the original meaning of karma. In life there is personal karma, family karma, and social karma, but spiritually Indian society still carries the burden from the karma of the old Brahman culture.

The sun is the ruler of our mind,
The sun is the Heavenly Father of our soul.
We worship the light that creates no shadows.
Likewise, our soul should cast no shadow on any other life.

Live constructively by facing all situations in life without frustration.
Grand Master Yo San, Ni

What then is the Best Spiritual Option?

Adults easily encounter the emotional frustrations related to maturity, while younger life tends to be over-confident, or have high expectations for the future. However, everyone should include objectivity in their basic life training and keep their emotions neutral.

Wu Wei [無為] includes having an objective mind, an undisturbed mind, and a mind free from any pressure, which is also the most effective mind. This further requires frequent self-attunement to ensure our emotions remain healthy. In addition, we need more people to know the deeper value of spiritual neutrality, and the unification between doing [有為] and non-doing [無為]:

Our minds may be active and continually rush about,
Or they could be inactive and remain quiet.
However, a mind that has attained Wu Wei *transcends all this.*
The practice is not to push away either side,
But reach for the internal unity in each life.
This signifies the unification of Yu Wei *and* Wu Wei,
Where the active and inactive mind are able to come together.

The deeper meaning of many Chinese sayings can be hidden, although they still offer useful reminders. Moreover, do not totally rely on translations as many of these cannot give an equivalent meaning:

世事之常, 多出自惹.
People often create their own aggravations in life.

欲速反遲, 欲先反後.
What is wanted in a hurry usually takes us longer,
And what is wanted first may occur later.

达先遭窘, 益反見損.
If we set a high goal for the world we may first experience frustration,
While seeking benefit can also find trouble.

欲高先下, 欲雅增俗.
Reaching high comes from below,
Although the distance increases with too much attention on appearances.

弄巧成拙, 欲霽先雪.
Clumsiness can be seen when we exhibit cleverness.
Yet, the first snow comes from a clear sky.

毀之在先, 成之在後.
Prior to accomplishment there can be destruction.

欲蓋彌彰, 欲省反費.

The more we cover things up, the clearer the trouble,
And if we seek to save a little, we may find the costs increase.

欲速不達, 欲升先墜.

Haste can cause waste,
And soaring high always starts from the lower position.

因曲求直, 欲逸反勞.

What is crooked seeks to be straight,
And if we seek leisure we may find toil.

求貴先賤, 因寬而嚴.

Yet, the distinguished come from the undistinguished,
And looseness can be appreciated by applying rigor.

欲閉先開, 求靜厭喧.

Furthermore, what is shut was once open,
While those tired of noise seek quietude.

順从自然, 心不两馳.

So, be single-minded in following the course of Nature.

但能从常, 不生阻障.

Obstacles seem easier with an objective mind.

人生阻障, 生于緣求.

Obstructions occur when the mind keeps seeking.

有格外之求, 生額外之憂.

Anxiety increases with rapid demands.

天福本現成, 人禍反難避.

However, some blessings are not so hard to attain;

The hardest aspect is in evading our self-created troubles.

多緣自造, 誰人之咎?

Whose fault is this?

為之所當, 行之理直.

When doing what has to be done, behave correctly.

不怕辛勞, 苦障自泯.

Fear increases the toil,

While the courageous find that most difficulties disappear.

A constructive person is not afraid to take on a moral duty, no matter how difficult.

Grand Master, Yo San Ni.

A peaceful mind is more blessed than sitting on top of the world, so the best option among all the spiritual beliefs should be our peace of mind:

The peace that can be enjoyed does not come from striving.
Any freedom attained is gained from the 'being' above,
And independence is for those who subdue their desires in life.
Spiritual perfection comes from being normal,
While spiritual sainthood means overcoming the crippled emotions in life.

There are no dark shadows in the mind that follows the sun,
And when the soul unites with the sun, there is light.

A constructive mind sees many options, but never possesses too many inclinations.

Grandmaster, Yo San, Ni

Part VI

Choosing an Effective Direction

The only correct choice
is to have faith in the deepest truth of life.

Chapter 15

The Deepest Truth in Life

People need to have faith in life, and this faith should come from the truth because an untruthful faith unbalances the mind, while too many faiths can scatter the mind. Thus, the only correct choice to repair our mind is to have faith in the deepest truth of life.

By now we should know that the deepest truth is that the sun is the Heavenly Father to all human life. Today, many conceptual beliefs and much conjecture have separated most people from this truth that is fundamental to both the Integral Way and the health of humanity. But if people really wish to return to the spiritual truth, the sun holds the only answer as it is the true source of the conscious power which is unique to human life.

The earliest people viewed the sun as their Heavenly King, and above all earthly kings, although that concept still explains Nature in terms of the human world. There is also a physical connection among the heavenly bodies that is similar to the human family, because the sun rules the destiny of all the planets in this part of the Universe. Hence, earthlings should be happy to be led by the sun through their deepest sense of life, and it is proper to view our lowly species as a begotten child of the sun. In this context, the sun is more like our Heavenly Father than any person, although Lao Tzu believed that human life remains in the womb of the sun.

We should also perceive this direct physical and spiritual connection between the sun and humanity through our conscious power, because we receive our physical life force from Earth, and planet Earth and all life on Earth are a part of the solar system. That is, the sun is the source of all planets, and human life was conceived, born and developed from planet Earth. However, the barren Earth has had to work with all available support - internal and external - to develop both her own 'self' and that of humanity.

The early people intuitively knew that their Heavenly Father was the sun because the males received an erection every time the sun began its daily cycle, while the eggs in the female body were nurtured by the reflection of the Heavenly Father through the Moon. But modern people also need to know that our Heavenly Father, the sun, possesses three types of potency - physical, mental and spiritual.

This physical potency is known by all earthlings, while the mental potency determines the growth of our mind by constantly stimulating the brain through the light of the sun, and other heavenly bodies. At the spiritual level, all people receive their small soul, the main part of their life, from the big soul of the Heavenly Father. Some people are able to return to the Father at the end of their physical life, but many others lose their soul on the journey of worldly life.

Human civilization is also a product of stimulation by the sunlight, although the level of civilization differs due to the various internal and external influences from earthlings. Also be aware that although the light of the sun forms life, different effects are produced when the light beams intersect with other forces in the environment. Early humanity was able to communicate directly with the forces of Nature, but as their conscious and conceptual capability grew, they began to create their own world and faith in life. Yet, the Heavenly Father still lives in each person's life as their soul and conscience.

Our soul and conscience represent the light of the Heavenly Father if we are upright, straightforward, righteous, just, fair, and considerate in life. When the soul and conscience is strong, that person's behavior reflects the qualities of their Heavenly Father. But when the soul is weak it is usurped by the mind that only works for the small self, and lacks the broad and all-embracing approach of our Father in Heaven. This means that a developed mind with little conscience can create much trouble for wider humanity.

A growing arrogance, which denies the grace of the source of life, has caused people to become ungrateful. So, they continue to develop conceptual beliefs that offer small benefits to a few, but lack the broad, all-embracing nature of Heaven. Sometimes they even deny the life given by the Heavenly Father, and choose to go against the harmony of Nature. Nevertheless, people with a strong conscience should maintain their faith in life with the openness of the Heavenly Father, in spite of all the difficulties and social pressures. We just need to seek the balance between nurturing our natural health and the pressures of modern worldly life, while remembering the true destination of our soul.

At a time when most people were ungrateful to the Heavenly Father, Jesus of Nazareth was grateful and told people: 'I come from my father. The love of my father is great, so I am able to reach you all'. He left these honest words so that we would all love each other, just like the Heavenly Father loves us all. Can anyone really separate their life from the Heavenly Father, and declare they are on their own? If we are honest, we would choose to be like Jesus, who clearly said: 'I come from my Father, my Father is in me'.

In ancient times people wondered which of the many heavenly bodies of light in the vast sky was their Heavenly Father. There are many of these heavenly bodies, but the only one that is the Heavenly Father to all the planets and their satellites in this part of the Universe is the sun. Humans are also the only life with the potency from all three spheres of their Heavenly Father, as no other heavenly body has the strength, or is close enough, to support the human life force. Jesus knew this important reality at the time when other people practiced a hypocritical cultural belief to distinguish themselves from others.

The conscious power endowed to humanity enables people to see beyond the physical sphere as they manage their lives, but their minds often complicate what is perceived. Their minds also possess the freedom of imagination, although this is constrained by their physical limitations. Thus, people might seek the Heavenly Father elsewhere, but can they really go beyond the sky? Of course many people still have a visual or conscious block which prevents them from appreciating this reality, while others loftily perceive the sun as just another moving star. However, the sun does not care what people believe, and is more like a parent who only wishes all their children to be healthy and live properly.

Many of our troubles come from deviating from the nature of our life, given by the sun, and only the wise are able to perceive the source of the spiritual life of humanity. The sun is definitely our Heavenly Father, but seeing this is a matter of growth. Few people perceive this reality, and most prefer to follow a small artificial faith, although the correct use of our internal sun is to radiate its light to all other life. Whilst this light reflects differently on each brain, the different visions are easily adjusted once our mind has attained sufficient growth, and the maturity to know its particular short-comings.

Open-minded people are able to admit that creating small faiths is part of the process of human growth, although they should also consider whether people could have survived and developed on Earth for so long without the support of their real Heavenly Father. Yet, most forms of human worship neglect the true source of life, and no one is more ungrateful than the people on Earth who do not recognize the sun as the Heavenly Father to all existence within the solar system. Instead, these people prefer fictitious stories, often established to dominate or manipulate others, that frequently lack the heavenly qualities of straightforwardness, uprightness, righteousness, justice, and fairness.

For example, some early leaders used a majestic image of the Heavenly Father to establish their kingship and control society, and later several religions took yet another cultural direction using that image. But if we look at the past 2000 years it is easy to see these grand words were not matched by actions that genuinely took care of the people, and some leaders even used their position, or conceptual faith, to shield evil deeds.

We all know that Earth could not survive without the sun, so there should be tremendous gratitude towards the Heavenly Father, the sun we can call God, who supports us all. One of the greatest emotional poisons to humanity, however, is the arrogance used to debase others. People have created numerous conceptual beliefs to support their arrogance. And once they continue to hold on to their pride, physically or conceptually, during the process of attaining spiritual growth they invite many troubles into the world.

All people on Earth are members of the big family we call humanity, but the only common source of each life is our Heavenly Father, the sun. When the bright sun forms the center of the human world, Earth could become a paradise where all people lived together harmoniously, and allowed each other an equal opportunity in life. But we also need to be aware that the main source of worldly trouble comes from being overly selfish when treating other people. So, whenever we abandon the everlasting openness of our Heavenly Father, we should remember the common source of our life force.

Although the sun is the only source of life for all earthlings, some artificial faiths use metaphors for the reality of Nature to support the small lives of their believers. Most of these metaphorical images represent the sun, but some beliefs use other powerful natural images, such as the stars, the planets, and thunder. Earthly images like mountains and the ocean are also a useful source to stimulate human creativity. Nonetheless, it is very wrong to seriously insist on a metaphor to support the superiority of some tribe or society, and ignore the reality of Nature that is open to all people and other earthly life.

Recognizing the truth that the source of all life is the sun requires spiritual growth, and attaining mental maturity, accompanied by the spiritual growth from real life experience, is the true fruit to advance humanity. This is one of our guiding spiritual principles, and includes being ready to accept those who choose to follow their own religious beliefs.

A Healthy Humanity can Achieve Divinity

A truly healthy life can attain divinity, or we could say that divinity is the healthy life of humanity. But people neglect what is near and reachable to pursue what is far and unreachable. Similarly, some old cultural beliefs that were created to discourage wrong-doing have become a serious scar on the original health of human nature. Jesus was an exception and promoted an open and honest view, which provoked his tradition, although such honesty comes from the naivety found in the original nature of life.

There is no need to retell the story of Christ, but we can explore his background as it relates to the growth of human spirituality. Jesus was born into a respected but arrogant tribe around 4 BCE, which suggests there is a price to pay from having a spiritually arrogant attitude towards others. He was born with a deep spiritual calling and a farsighted vision that believed in treating all people equally. The main theme of his teaching was that we must all learn to live together for the common purpose of survival, rather than being solely concerned with our own life, or country. He also hoped to modify the arrogance of his own people, as he saw that the growing tension and tribal superiority in his region only created more obstacles for the survival of humanity.

Jesus promoted the open, accepting and loving heart that has always been gifted to humanity by the sun in the sky. In his straightforward way he wanted wider spiritual recognition of the fact that the openness, light, and warmth of the radiating sun is our God, the creator of Earth and its inhabitants, and of all the other planets in the solar system. His deep spiritual nature also observed the hypocrisy of the artificial faiths that harm people once they became too distanced from the reality of Nature.

The sun is the biggest influence in our life, as without the sun there is no human life. The sun also conditions all aspects of our living, such as the health of our physical and emotional being, our intellectual potential, our ability to make a living and form healthy social attitudes and connections in life, and most importantly, the health of our deep soul. If correctly fulfilled, each of these fives spheres is able to draw support from the sun to provide a happy, healthy and successful life.

Overly confident people who deny the support from Nature, and believe all achievements come from their smart mind, will only trust their own actions to get the best opportunities in life. But Jesus suggested that people who turn away from the sun to favor mental concepts, like religions, are practicing hypocrisy, and committing a real sin by keeping their Heavenly Father away from other earthlings. On one occasion he even hinted that people who turn away from their real father, the sun, are like the prodigal sons who lose themselves in the jungle of worldly life to such an extent that they cannot return home.

Jehovah, the thunder God, represents a healthy function of Nature. Yet, this powerful image has been used in some regions to create a conceptual religion, similar to the early worship of the planets Jupiter and Mars. The newer faith in Jehovah, the thunder God, to replace God, the Creator, came from a struggle for survival. However, the divinity of the real creator does not need any name or awesome conceptual image. Thunder has the force to bring dramatic storms and floods, and occasionally directly kills life, although people still trust that thunder is part of the adjustment within Nature. My work, *Spring Thunder – Awaken the Hibernating Power of Life*, can help to manage this force in life, which may be annoying, but has no particular interest in threatening life on earth.

Any mental deception within this newer faith in Jehovah may have come from the intention of providing a softer approach than the usual brutality found in the frequent struggles for survival. But human survival goes much deeper, and cannot be achieved by a thunderclap, or any other form of violence. Some early sages suggested the survival of humanity requires a broad nature, like the sky, which can accept the real God in Nature. This differs from the beliefs in a conceptual God where people express their devotion to a name or symbol. Those beliefs may help to create social strength, but why not just keep our faith in the real God as the authority of human life at all levels, which is the sun.

Around six to eight thousand years ago the wisest people believed that the greatest teacher of survival is Mother Nature, who is centered by the sun in this corner of the galaxy. They then cited eight spiritual examples from Nature for people to follow:

The force of the sky shows us how to develop our life;

The force of the earth shows us how to develop great tolerance;

The force of fire shows us how to give light and warmth to others;

The force of water shows us how to flow smoothly in life;

The force of the wind shows us how to revive the gentle flow of life;

The force of the rain shows us how to lubricate or moisten the earth to produce life;

The force of the mountains shows us how to be self-contained and independent;

The force of thunder shows us how to brace the self and awaken our hibernating life.

What is most important is finding the balance among these eight forces. The force from one clap of thunder in spring cannot remind all hibernating life to return to the active world because this also needs good coordination and cooperation among the eight natural forces. That counsel on survival, and living a balanced life, is valued by the Integral Way, and also suggests developing a deeper vision to effectively manage a healthy life, regardless of the conditions that may bring us good fortune, or misfortune.

Cultural forces in society can be either beneficial or harmful to people, and sometimes are more influential than any physical force. But whether healthy or unhealthy, all cultures are capable of producing both happiness and trouble. Jesus' teaching came from a deep understanding of humanity, gained by living in a difficult situation. However, even a good teaching can be misunderstood or misused. So, Jesus' experience of life and subsequent misuse of his teachings remind us that even God may fall into the pattern of human fortune – although the responsibility for this belongs to humanity, not God.

Lao Tzu said: 'good fortune and misfortune give birth to one another', but usually they are paired. Jesus has been called the Messiah, the Savior, Christ, and other names to comfort people in need of help. Yet few people seriously follow his real intention. His own society rejected him for viewing human survival differently, and his true vision for universal harmony has never been fully realized. His teaching has also been misused by cunning people who formed large religions based on their own views of his words and actions, rather than his broad vision of universal love and harmony.

Intellectuals tend not to respect Jesus, but they should still credit him for two important influences in modern life. His teaching has helped to uplift the humanistic ethic in the world, and he indirectly inspired the development of political democracy. Hence, he continues to live through the cultural and ethical progress in some societies, although his spiritual merit to humanity is stained by the confused practices of many churches.

So, where can we look for help to improve the troubled world? First, we need to fix our own understanding and beliefs while there is still time to pull away from the quicksand of the artificial cultures and beliefs that threaten the health of humanity, and human survival. Divinity exists where people are willing to make humanistic improvements without insisting on an opinionated ideology that undermines any real benefit from the efforts made. This sense of divinity can be recognized in the people who practice self-denial to serve the broader welfare of humanity, but is often lacking in modern intellectual life, which tends to be only interested in satisfying the personal ego.

Perhaps we should all recognize Jesus as one of the greatest helpers of humanity. I have a deep appreciation for his righteous vision and real humanistic efforts, and although I am a non-Christian, I share his deep spiritual concern. The Universal Integral Way is centered on and worships the pursuit of justice, fairness, and respect for the Heavenly Father. Fulfilling that vision requires the spiritual growth of all people, and worldwide spiritual cooperation by all ethnic groups and countries. Spiritual progress is a universal venture, although everybody must be their own spiritual savior before offering help to others.

Social improvement means bringing benefit to all people. Hence, social progress cannot deny humanistic love, and all healthy ruling systems, democratic or otherwise, would offer divine respect for the lives of others. This is because God is also another name for humanistic love, and when humanity is totally healthy everyone will express godliness. But if anyone becomes sick, God is denied, and no one can enjoy godliness.

Chapter 16

Revive the Spirit of Humanity

The earliest people had the greatest faith in their sense of humanity, given by Nature. But once they discovered the strength of their mental concepts and beliefs, exemplified by the Babylonian tradition, they established numerous religions that soon spread throughout the world. These religions often became a long lasting spiritual custom, and are still used as a social or political tool to influence wider society. More recently, a few intellectuals have developed ideologies that influence society in a similar manner, although both approaches can have disastrous effects, or create social turmoil.

The cultural environment of humanity is like a public well where all people take the water, and if someone dirties or poisons that water, everyone will suffer. Cultural environments are much larger than a public well, however, and so the harm can rapidly spread from one region to another when there is no protection. But how can people expect protection from God when the concept of God differs so widely?

Cultural change is a gradual progress, particularly with spiritual customs, and it takes a long time to awaken people, who may then form a new faith by adjusting their old faith. Later, there might be further corrections and adjustments until the world becomes awash with the numerous faiths. This process may help to develop the human conscience, but it can also undermine the spiritual value of these new religions.

New religions also emerge when people on poor land look for better land in their quest for survival. This has been the source of expressions like the Pure Land, Shambala, and Shangri-La, all of which have become an element in a new faith. One example was when people from various parts of the Middle East, and later Europe, sought new land and discovered the large, fertile lands of the Indian sub-continent. Many people then rushed into this area, and modern Indian society now exhibits a range of ethnicities and cultures.

These immigrants carried their old influences, and eventually a new religion developed to serve the growing society. This religion was structured by the Brahman 'constitution' that had established four main social castes: Brahman - priests, Kshatriya - warriors, Vaisya - farmers, and Sudra - tenant farmers and servants. Brahman priests were the highest caste, seen to be favored by God, followed by the ruling class. Then there were the general workers and their families, and finally the local minority groups who formed the lowest class, or slaves. This structure enhanced the already strong racial separation and social prejudice, but people accepted their permanent role in life as their fate, or karma.

Many of the immigrants had come from religious families that did not make a real living, and followed their original cultural customs which supported the holy people in society. Some were nobles, or had royal titles, while others had various occupational skills, but they all expected the local inhabitants, or slaves, to look up to them. Although most people in this society accepted their fate, outsiders believed the racial division was unjustified. But the new teaching of Buddha from Sakyamuni, based on his awakening that all people are equal, had little influence on the Indian people, who continued to accept their 'fate' that determined both their occupation and whom they could marry.

Moreover, the people born into one of the inalterable social classes because of their bloodline accepted their spiritual karma. This meant having an unchangeable destiny, no matter the advantages or suffering encountered in life, although karma should only be accepted as an extension of our personal spiritual responsibility for the deepest sense of life that shapes our behavior. This is a universal spiritual fact, but we also accept there are natural influences that disadvantage some lives. Hence our spiritual task is to modify these natural shortcomings. When karma is seen as a personal fate decided by God, and alleviated by making offerings through a priest, it is a form of religious manipulation, as is the Christian belief that God directly punishes the soul.

Our behavior can also be spiritually affected by a direct blood connection, and although subtle, the effect can still be observed. This means that each life carries some spiritual responsibility for the new life they bring into the world, because that life may suffer some karmic responsibility, good or bad, from carrying the genes of their ancestors. Thus, spiritual responsibility lasts forever by constantly forming the spiritual essence, or root, of each new life. That is a universal spiritual truth which should be known by all people.

Chinese people believe this spiritual responsibility extends to the enjoyment or suffering by the children of the family, and the *I Ching*, or *Book of Changes* records: 'when a family accumulates good deeds, there is always something to celebrate, and the happiness extends to future generations. But when a family accumulate bad deeds, something sorrowful will be left to their descendants'. As the *I Ching* is a book of observations, these words come from the deep human experience over many generations.

Karma and other similar theories were developed by religious professionals to control people, although these professionals would be the first of the castes to be flung into the fire, based on their scale for measuring the justice of God. Often these early concepts are like a double-edged sword, but the message for modern people is to practice discernment, as even the most useful creations may have a harmful side. Yet, spiritual responsibility should be accepted as universal spiritual law, because observation shows that people are truly spiritually responsible for whatever they do, while forcing others to accept a social injustice as their unchangeable fate is both unhealthy and irresponsible.

The irresponsible use of karma pressures people to obey a religion by promising a better life next time around. But when the *I Ching* suggests that life is cyclical this describes the law of Nature, without any religious manipulation or bias. Being a good person is a natural duty, and needs no outside intervention. Good behavior yields peace, relaxation, security and prosperity in life, while immoral or improper behavior yields the opposite. Check the people around us – those seeming to build a good life based on immoral behavior eventually suffer if they do not pay their debt in life, as will their descendants.

People strive for money or power, but seeking improvement within the law of Nature is wiser. As the Chinese say - for ten years the water flows east, and for the next ten years it flows west. That is, everything changes, but good emotions offer direct support and the reward is health. Similarly, true happiness is rooted in the condition of our deepest consciousness, and reflected by our behavior in life. In contrast, society is like a bus we ride for a certain distance! Allow the natural changes to happen, and know that religious and social views often contain prejudice. Whether or not these are accepted depends on the level of our personal growth. It is correct to fulfill the natural obligations of family life and society, but fruitless to follow any demands that oppose the natural order of life.

People who follow their natural healthy life force usually attain success as God helps all those who align themselves with Nature, but mechanically following religious rules or demands does not send people to Heaven. Doing whatever is healthy for life and society is the best opportunity to guarantee a good life, both now, and for our descendants.

Natural Evolution

Natural physical evolution, which is generated by the spiritual essence of life, always progresses upwardly, while emotional inertia keeps the life force down. But how do you discuss this matter with all the people who believe they will go to Heaven?

First, we must understand that genuine spiritual service needs to be very careful with any social involvement to avoid further religious manipulation. In the West the New Age teaching wronged a whole generation. Some of their teachers may have had a genuine humanistic purpose, although many used the teaching for their own support while creating an irrational burden for their society. I hope this chaos is now over, and that the new focus and hope is for the spiritual health of humanity, and universal harmony.

All people are one family, although their spiritual attainment differs. So, the focus of the Integral Way is on mutual help, whereby the spiritual pride of the early seekers should be replaced by an open friendship towards all spiritual teachings for the sake of the suffering world. Those who can accept the plain honest way of spirituality, with no separation between the various beliefs, can enjoy a good life that accepts all people. This good will can extend to supporting their existing religious obligations, but when people remain in poverty and suffer social injustice, conscious people should also be aware of the source.

External religious beliefs are but small shadows of the true nature of life in that they teach in a framework where few people see the deep spiritual truth, and social progress is gradual. In India, Jain and Sakyamuni reformed Brahmanism, which later led to the religions called Jainism and Buddhism. Sakya was primarily against the inequality within Indian society, and used self-reflection to replace the Brahman view that burdened and constricted the life of many people. But in China, Zhan Buddhism developed to improve mainstream Buddhism, and sought to guard the benign nature of organic life.

Zhan Buddhism was derived from the teaching of Chuang Tzu, who opposed the lordly approach of the male mentality, and chose the freedom of being outside any unnatural social establishment. Essentially, Chuang Tzu held a widely different view from Sakya, as he believed: 'my humble life, and all things and lives share the root and grandness of the one life of Nature, Heaven and Earth'. This expresses the spiritual self-sufficiency of human life, where nothing extra is needed to complete each life. I trust Chuang Tzu. He was a spiritual giant who aspired to being a 'genuine human' and never considered emulating Buddha.

Then there was Hui Neng [638-713 C.E.], the sixth patriarch of Zhan, who was invited to a private audience with Hong Ren [弘忍, 601-674 C.E.], the fifth patriarch, where he was asked if he was there to seek the dharma. He replied: 'the life nature of a humble person is no lesser than that of a holy man, but I would like you to confirm - did I miss anything in the teaching that is seen as spiritual and holy?' That is a clear pronouncement, because before Chuang Tzu there was no artificial cultural establishment, only the social edicts of the king that very much went against the natural life of the people.

At that time India was influenced by several artificial religions. Buddhism had progressed from Jainism to improve the social condition of the people, while the previous Jainism had progressed from Brahmanism for similar reasons. Hence, the real practice was spiritual progress as people were stimulated by the two great teachers, Jain and Sakya. There was also some compromise to the existing customs, even though the strong social customs and nature of the people in India meant the new teachings were not as popular as the predominant religion, Hinduism, which has retained the greatest public support.

We recognize some spiritual progress in the world, although many people are still unable to find real improvement, or face the true nature of life. Moreover, some unhealthy corners in the religions continue to prevent the genuine, healthy growth of humanity. The spiritual progress that would enable true happiness in life requires the removal of all public manipulation from our social and religious teachings. Unless people are treated fairly and truthfully they will not respect these teachings, and there will be little progress.

Spiritual customs also need to make room for the progress that comes from the people themselves. Sakyamuni lived in the sixth century BCE and developed a growing antipathy to the spiritual style of Brahmanism, but today we can still observe a form of Brahman Buddhism in Bali where the people have taken the mixed influences in their culture to develop a highly colorful spiritual life. If enlightenment is less valuable than maintaining an ancient custom, Bali offers an example of how to improve such customs.

Return to the Honest Faith in the Sun

The most powerful God is the vast sky within Nature that freely supports all life. The many conceptual creations called God have only caused confusion, but people prefer to be amused by these tales, rather than place their faith in the true God. Thus, fiction has become more powerful than the reality. This is because the real God cannot be easily influenced, while a conceptual God is often used to manipulate the public. God treats everybody equally as we are all the children of Nature. That is the real practice of the true God, although we all need to develop our own spirituality to reach universal divinity.

At its depth the concept of Brahma is another name for the Creator, also called the Holy King of the Golden Wheel, the sun. There is no problem with this image of Nature, but once the image is adopted to uphold a religious faith that then persuades people to follow only one custom, the public expression of spirituality soon turns into a private business. Most spiritual teachings have given the priesthood a monopoly to manage the relationship between the natural reality and the followers of that faith. Yet, having a direct faith in Nature and the sun is much healthier than the fictitious stories promoted by religions.

In the many small galaxies within Nature, the depth of the sky is God, and we could be similar to one of these galaxies once we attain a high level of development. But as Earth is closer to the solar system created by the concentrated force of Nature, the sun that relates directly to all earthly life is seen as our God. Thus, our choice is either to interpret the creative force of Nature from its visible reality, or as the receptor of this reality.

Six to eight thousand years ago the author of the *I Ching*, Fu Shi, did not view Nature as either the Creator, or the great Receptor. He used just two words to describe the forces and manifestations of the wholeness of Nature – the strong force was *Qian*, 乾, and the soft force was *Kun*, 乾. Since then, many people have attempted to anthropomorphize the vastness of Nature for the convenience of the human mind. Yet, the human mind can move closer to the reality of Nature through spiritual cultivation, and a developed soul can find that the creator of the solar system is the sun that also created human life.

The entire solar system and its planets were formed from chips off the fireball, which remains as the core of the solar system, the sun. This system cannot be managed by our conceptual power, although spiritual development can help the human soul to know more about Nature. Fu Shi possessed an objective observational power without any intellectual training, and had already achieved his soul through spiritual cultivation before producing the *Book of Changes*. Spiritual development from self-cultivation can produce an ability to relate to the spiritual sphere of Nature, and that door should remain open to the wise people who wish to spiritually communicate with the hidden potency of Nature.

Now we have established that our real God is the sun within our small solar system, but the solar system also spins with the Big Dipper, while the large group of stars under the North Star spin with the constellation that the early Chinese called the Weaving Maiden. That is, humans ride on the solar system, the solar system is one of the riders on the North Star, while the entire North Star system rides on the Weaving Maiden, who can then take us to the subtle origin. All this can then be anthropomorphized with the single title, Mother Universe, for the people who wish to seek the depth of Nature.

We were not dumped on Earth, but our birth and life on this planet are supported by the sun, so we should all offer our gratitude, and acknowledge the sun as our God. The sun seeks nothing from its various passengers, but fulfills its godly nature, as do all other heavenly bodies that practice the constancy interpreted as the Way. I do not know who trained Fu Shi, Lao Tzu, and Jesus, but they all saw the sun as the stem [帝, from the sense of 蒂] of this group of heavenly bodies we call the planets.

The spiritual quest within humanity comes from our minds, while religions were formed to manage society. But if we seriously seek the source of our life, the sun is the serious answer, and no conceptual creation can replace the reality that our conscious capability is stimulated and supported by the light of the sun, the moon, and the stars. Hence, most cultures and spiritual faiths in the world are different interpretations or metaphoric expressions of the sunlight. As different views there is no problem, but problems arise when these concepts are used to manipulate society, or provide a living for a few select interpreters. The universal truth from Nature pays no one, although this open truth is constantly overshadowed by the fictitious beliefs that only tell and sell part of the reality.

Around 2500 years ago, Sakyamuni did not accept the conventional spiritual beliefs of his time, and sought a wiser way to live. He also wished to help others, and taught that everything in the world is sublime - the sky, earth, water, clouds, etc., but most sublime of all is our life. Making the ordinary things of Nature and life, which most people take for granted, as the basis of his spiritual education, shows that he respected his own life, and the life of all others. This can be viewed as good teaching with some progress, in spite of all the Buddhist monks who live off his faith and tend to disrespect worldly life.

The God of Nature supports everyone, but the God who lives on the lips of many religionists is meticulous in finding the faults that rule all lives. That image may stop some evildoers, but even the most upright followers of these religions must accept the demands spoken by a man of God. Whether or not the true God makes such demands depends on how those religionists interpret divinity. The Brahmans made people practice sacrificial offerings to attain blessings and the mercy of God, but also lived off those offerings. Taking this example, if any government ever asks people to pay taxes for the sunlight, it is not new as the Brahmans did this when they took the offerings to God, while Buddhists still accept the support of their sponsor without any further obligation.

So, here are three prayers to the true ruler of humanity from the Shang Dynasty [2207-1707 BCE], which operated a very religious ruling system:

Dear Heavenly Father,
Thank you for providing greater humanity, including my own life.
In my life I have witnessed your generosity towards all lives.
Using this precious guidance, I am willing to retrieve all my anger,
Antipathy and displeasure towards any offenses by others.

Dear Heavenly Father,
Please help the growth of your essence in all human life,
So that we may move under the guidance of your light
To become fair, just, and beneficial to all.

Dear Heavenly Father,
Thank you for providing the support in my life.
Each daily meal sustains my inspiration,
And my awareness that all things are transformed from your light.
Thus, I am able to take in the substance of your light in various forms
With the great hope that my life will become wiser and healthier.

Chapter 17

Respect the Lessons from the Past

Timelessness of Lao Tzu

We can trust the words of Lao Tzu, who was active around 2500 years ago according to the only verified record from the historian Shih Ma-Chien. Shih Ma-Chien also mentioned that Lao Tzu lived for 160 to 200 years, and was respected as a keeper of the government archives during the Zhou Dynasty. He has continued to be respected to this day for his short book that still provides the most mature view of humanity.

Lao Tzu's book can also be trusted to express the faith at the time of Fu Shi, Shen Nung and the Yellow Emperor when the divinity and morality of Nature was recognized as the standard for the healthy nature of humanity. The original faith was that God and people are one, and that Nature provides for all life equally with no demands. This means when people conduct their life correctly, they are naturally supported by Nature. This 4000 years old truth remains valid today, and I warmly recommend Lao Tzu to all my friends.

Lao Tzu also mentioned that that Tian, 天, sky, or Heaven, is both the provider and supporter of life, without any sentiment whatsoever from Nature. Hence, offerings are a human custom, not a demand from the sky. In early China there were no religious obligations, although it was customary for the kings to sacrifice cows as an offering to the sky, and later the people shared the meat. Divinations to assist decision making and attain public support also occurred on these occasions, and were an important political event for thousands of years. Even so, people were not subjected to any unfair religious customs.

The God of Nature is a moral example to humanity, but some people wish to seek special favors from the spiritual world for their own ends. So, eventually, the Way that had been practiced in early society became divided. One direction remained with Nature, while the other began to expand their rule over others, and used the public gatherings that made offerings to the sky as a means of increasing that power. This heralded the beginning of the first conceptual religions to replace the open and honest faith of the early people.

Conceptual Gods need rewards to be pleased, while the original Way teaches following the generosity and kindness of Nature, because Nature supports all people who conduct their life correctly. One way supports the organic condition of life, while the other way establishes a ruling system. But when the social and political interference strengthens, the Way and the natural tolerance in life tends to retreat. Based on his writings, it seems that Chuang Tzu also disrespected the way of kings and preferred to live apart from general society, rather than pay the price for receiving a high title.

Both Lao Tzu and Chuang Tzu offer the world plain and colorless teachings compared to most conceptual religions. China did not have the same spiritual experience as India, or other parts of the world that produced colorful religious teachings. So, Lao Tzu's teaching represented the earnest honesty of the early people, who recognized that Nature is truly divine. Hence, it is more truthful than the later cultures which symbolized and decorated Nature, and increasingly placed demands on people. However, the way of kings promised to protect society and maintain social order, so people accepted these conditions to improve their security and soon lost much of their natural earnestness and honesty. Unfortunately, this direction is the foundation of most mainstream societies today.

Lessons from Sakyamuni

At 29 years old Sakya did not agree with the Brahman view of divinity in his society, and retreated to the forest to explore life through meditation. A starved body can clear the mind, so fasting became one of his spiritual practices to suppress an overly active body, and improve the clarity of his mind. After much contemplation he then produced his own teaching, based on the doctrine of emptiness, which proclaimed that the world was Godless, and life had no soul.

Sakya therefore missed seeing that the conscious self is the soul of a formed life with a brain, and that the functions of this brain are provided by the light of the sun. His conclusion had come from endangering his life through severe fasting, so the real Buddha was like a skeleton with breath, unlike the fleshy statues found in Buddhist temples. Many Buddhists think that the salutations received by the statues of Buddha illustrate the rewards for becoming like Sakya, and seek a similar reward. But if they took on his real philosophy, it is likely that the number of worshippers would decrease.

After his enlightenment Sakya released the truth gained from his meditation to his close followers. This is expressed in the four Sutras: life is bitter suffering; life is the sum total of bitter suffering from the unavoidable processes of birth, aging, sickness, and death; liberation can be found by eliminating all suffering through the renunciation of worldly life; and the true Way of a life without burdens can be reached by an enlightened mind. During his 49 years of teaching, however, he never allowed any of his followers to record his words, so these Sutras came from the memories of a range of followers.

Nonetheless, Sakya's literary ability and talent for leadership was extremely high, and he was well accepted and sponsored as he constantly traveled with his disciples. The main theme of his teaching in the large volume of sutras is that there is nothing worthy of attachment in physical life, and the only real wisdom is to be free from all worldly entanglements. His own model in life was to possess nothing besides his physical body.

For the people who expected a higher kingdom, he recommended Nirvana, the peaceful mind. His worshippers make the Kingdom of Buddha their destination, but Sakya did not enjoy any type of kingdom. He preferred being a beggar king where there was no congress to point the finger at him. Later, his wife became a Buddhist nun, and his son also became one of his disciples. Hence, Sakya spiritually fulfilled his duty of being a man and a father, and in Indian terms he lived a long life spanning 80 years.

Above all, he enjoyed spiritual freedom and independence, although he was unable to deliver spiritual equality to his people, who were more interested in physical survival. He is now popularly believed to be the great awakener of life, but I worry about him being used by the people who seek an easy life instead of working to awaken the deep human conscience. Is a life that denounces all worldly interests spiritual? Or is serving others without any personal interest or ego a broader approach?

It is also interesting to note that no matter the changes to Brahmanism made by Sakya, much of his new approach merged with the old Brahman teachings after he had gone. But there are five precepts to awaken the conscience of life that are common to Jainism, Buddhism, and folk Taoism. This most valuable gift to humanity should be adopted as a universal spiritual discipline - no violence, and absolutely no killing; no stealing whatsoever; no lewdness; no telling lies; and no strong stimulants.

Contribution of Shamanism

If having faith in the sun is compared with all other conceptual faiths, it is the biggest faith. If all the social religions are compared to Shamanism, the latter is a small practice, although it served the practical needs for healing and attuning life for the earliest people.

Spiritual phenomena appear when people are weak, or seriously ill, and about to disintegrate. The early people believed these spirits caused illness, or death, and then conducted their fear to the spirits. The reality is that the illness caused the fear of death, and fearful people related death to the spirits. So, the Shamanistic approach is to remove the self-created fear, which then improves the overall feeling of life for the patient. That is, the healing power of the patient responds to the symbolic healing by the shaman.

This practice arose from the misunderstanding that there is a separate spiritual world, although all life carries spirits. Educated people do not usually accept this, because spirits and shamans signal a primitive past. But modern researchers should consider two facts: the physical body carries numerous spirits, and the power of self-healing can be evoked by certain symbolic practices that could cumulatively create an image. This image is then sometimes misunderstood as a form from a different world.

All spiritual phenomena are produced by life, and each life contains the truth. That is, spiritual matters relate to life, not conceptual theories about Heaven.

Heaven is the spiritual achievement that comes with the willingness to be and do the best in life. This should be respected, and supported as a cultural desire, because religions often reflect the common consciousness of their community. We can agree that the ancient shamans were no higher than any modern witch doctor. But if educated people with an understanding of the new physics could reach the depth where the physical can be spiritualized, and the spiritual can be materialized, humanity would possess the secrets of the Universe.

Life starts with a single cell that developed from bacteria in places where the natural atmosphere was able to produce formed life. Once formed, however, this tiny existence, or foundation of life, is neglected. Most modern people accept the existence of these tiny cells, although only a few believe that spirits are part of the foundation of life. But when these hidden spirits were activated beyond their normal range the early people saw them as the spirits of life, and blamed them for any sickness or misfortune. We would consider that if the spirits of life, or our life spirits, are seen as untruthful, or if people do not believe in the spiritual world, the foundation of most religions is lost.

When our body is ill, the 'invaders' come from the bad bacteria in our surroundings, and our bodily spirits become the protectors that can help our life to recover. In some cases the task is too great for these healthy spirits, and that physical life gets lost. Many of these spirits, which comprise the inner life of the physical form, act as agents for our bodily organs, while others gather the sense of life and pass this information on to the brain. This is how we know what is happening to our body.

The source of all healthy spirits is the sun, although the environmental spirits relate to a specific location. Each person also carries the genes from their family bloodline, which determines their internal influences in life. These genes have already had experiences in another human form, and can communicate certain old habits to the new life, although normally they are hidden within the new behavioral patterns.

Generally, what is called spiritual is the brain that has achieved balance and maturity, and what is called physical is the body that carries our spiritual reality and soul. But the brain is usually unable to feel its spirits, which are the units of life, while the reproductive force that also carries these transformable units is very strong. At one level the brain gathers its bodily spirits for support, but at another level it is pulled into strong physical interests. To become wiser and fully enjoy life, apply the principle of balance, although ancient people believed that all spirits were the source of disease and trouble. This misunderstanding came from their undeveloped brain, and lack of knowledge about their bodily functions.

In shamanistic healing the power comes from the suggestions made to the patients, which then activates their feelings, and evokes a response from their spirits. Once these spirits are attuned, the healing brings a positive result, although sometimes the healing fails because there is no effect on the spirits. However, the power is not with the shamans, but with the patients, and whether or not their bodily system gives a positive response.

Healthy human bodies are able to feel the changes in unfamiliar surroundings because the bodily spirits transmit this knowledge to the brain. This means our conscious center remains in our brain while it is fed information by our bodily senses that are activated by the relevant spirits. Usually, the messages from our bodily spirits are symbolic, such as a twitching eye, itchy ear, voluntary spasm of the leg or toe etc., but all these symptoms are merely signals from the body spirits to our brain. These spirits are also called *chi*, which is the invisible force trained in small practices such as *Tai Chi*, *Chi Kung*, or *Dao-In*. Yet the best support for human life is sunlight, good water, fresh air, good food, and nonverbal communication with the sun, the root of all life.

The *wei chi* of Chinese medicine is the *chi*, or force of life, that protects the body from invading bacteria, and is known as the immune system in modern medicine. *Wei chi* is also the power of self-healing in the body, although this power depends on whether the natural physical condition has been damaged by surgery, chemical therapy, radiation or strong medication. Once any of these methods have been applied, the opportunity for self-healing has largely gone, although realizing the Five Healths in life can alleviate some of the troubles that have already occurred.

Hence, spiritual development includes being careful of external approaches, and respecting the vital bodily chi that supports self-healing. Moreover, the *Classic of Internal Medicine* from the Yellow Emperor stated that self-healing should occur when the body feels well, rather than waiting for any sickness. This preventive approach was also adopted by the ancient tradition of seeking spirituality immortality.

Some ancient people also developed practices that attempted to gather and use the bodily spirits to perform various spiritual powers. Some are healthy, and some are not. Using such power for healing diseases can be healthy, although 'developing the eyes and ears to see or hear things beyond the general physical capability' can go either way, depending on how the practice is applied. For example, 'affecting the weather by changing the rain or stopping the wind' can offer a worthy humanistic service, but 'finding a suitable physical partner' is best left for the development of a natural and mutual attraction.

Discovery of this spiritual reality soon led to the development of various 'magic' practices, both black and white. Some of these are obviously unhealthy, or superstitious, and unworthy of our attention, but we should all agree to enhance our healthy *chi* through regular exercise, and other practices that strengthen the health of life.

Belief in Insubstantial Chi

In everyday life chi is the sensation of warmth, or cold, and pain, or pleasant bodily feelings. Insubstantial chi is also the bridge between our formed life and the unformed life energy of Nature, which can be seen as the 'substance' at the deeper level of the physical world. But when this chi is on the verge of being transformed into the bodily light that is the deepest substance of life, it may appear as a formed being when various changes to our bodily sensations send that message to our brain through a dream.

There are many different practices to conduct this transformable *chi*, and for everyday life the best are those that enhance our physical health. But people who wish proof on whether or not external *chi* actually exists can experience the opportunities given by Nature. In some locations the different bacteria or *chi* form a special atmosphere that is felt by most people, and these places are usually the most suitable for family life. In Chinese culture the practices that locate and channel this *chi*, are called *feng shui*, or good wind and water. This art, also known as geomancy, can identify locations with a subtle atmosphere, which our bodily spirits then sense as pleasant or uncomfortable.

Bodily spirits are a more sensitive 'organ' than our five common sensory organs – the eyes, ears, nose, tongue, and skin. Their existence can be known through certain spiritual practices, which I describe in my books, *The Quest of Soul* and *Nurture Your Spirits*. These numerous tiny spirits adhere to every inch of our skin, and generally hide within the form of life. But a starving body, or a life on the verge of danger and death, can easily experience this spiritual phenomenon.

Are these visions real? Images are structured by the bodily spirits that relate to our brain, but in normal life these hidden partners use incomplete dreams to communicate their message. When our *yang chi* or reproductive force is strong, the messages can be very clear, and when our vitality is weak, we may be punished for some spiritual error. This response persuaded some early teachers to create a religion based on their experience with bodily spirits, and later other people interpreted this as a conceptual image.

There are now numerous religions because the condition of each brain differs, although all religious teachers are affected by the reflective light of the sun on their brain. Our *chi* energy also reacts to our emotions and thoughts, and then responds through our deeper conscious self, the living soul, or center of our life. The initial reaction can include a response from our nervous system, which is related, although *chi* cannot locate in a fixed position. However, it does respond to various healing techniques like acupuncture.

Sometimes our *chi* even responds to our conscious system with a lifelike 'form' that is invisible to others, because it is just a manifestation of *chi*, rather than a physical being. For example, a young man may drown in a foreign country, and at the same time his mother or wife may see his wet body return, although unrelated people are unable to receive this information. As this experiential knowledge cannot be verified by modern researchers, it remains outside the general understanding of life.

Value of Deeper Spirituality in Nature

The spirituality of deeper Nature is independent, although it lies behind all of the conscious activity projected by our mind. Human spirituality, however, operates at the deeper level of the substance of life, and is neither holy, nor unholy – it is just the potency of Nature that is able to transcend all emotional and conscious experiences. That is, our mind responds to various internal and external conditions with suitable actions and reactions, but when our conscious functions depart at the time of death the spirituality achieved through spiritual cultivation and attainment can transcend these responses.

Moreover, the pursuit to be a holy being, such as an angel, or Buddha, cannot really be fulfilled in the conscious sphere of life, although the purification of our life spirits is a realistic pursuit to develop and strengthen the self. And while the spiritual potency of Nature never really leaves us, this purification can be achieved through conscious effort.

A healthy life may witness numerous bodily spirits during this search, but that experience is interpreted differently by those who have a spiritual purpose. Our spiritual potency, or subtle substance behind the describable level in life, is associated with a change in our consciousness, so these experiences will always have many interpretations. We respect all healthy interpretations, as they all come from the same foundation of life, the sun.

Internal harmony is a spiritual achievement that is possible for all people, while universal harmony should be the common goal of all healthy teachings. The Universal Integral Way also recommends being above all sentiments and emotions to cohere with the reality of Nature, and the natural healthy functions in life. Hence, our public service suggests that our members support the teaching by becoming examples of a healthy life, and help to eliminate any spiritual prejudice by adopting a trans-religious approach.

Achievement at the subtle level is also possible. While we cannot describe spiritual health, it is illustrated by healthy, self-reliant people without greed, hatred, or attachment. All conscientious people and seekers of the Way would do well to adopt no aggression as the basis for universal spirituality. This does not suggest retreating from the world, but choosing to attain all five aspects of a completely healthy life - a healthy body, mind, emotions, and spirit, plus healthy financial support, and healthy social connections.

These five healthy qualities express the wholeness of our precious life from Nature, which is sometimes lost in the religious standards of saints or martyrs. Periodic retreats can help us to reflect and focus on our real needs, and this has now become an important spiritual practice. Yet, most spiritual seekers focus on their emotions, and neglect their own bodily and spiritual experiences to admire those of others. A weakened life can be supported and improved by more self-discipline and organization, rather than adopting an external program from a social or religious faith, but there can be no real spiritual gain through imitating the superficial style of any conceptual teaching.

Some forms of Shamanism still exist in rural areas, such as Mongolia. But generally, the early misunderstanding about a separate spiritual world was extended into the conceptual beliefs that created a Heavenly paradise beyond our worldly life. In the deepest truth there is no other spiritual paradise outside the real spiritual world of the human body, where the hidden spirits operate as entities within our specific organs. When we are partly asleep, however, our brain may perceive these spirits as different people.

The Shamanism used for healing and exorcism still contains the highest healing power - the sun that is the source of all lives in the solar system. In contrast, the many conceptual beliefs were developed to support the mind, although the real achievement comes when the mind is open, and is able to identify the conscious self with the light of the sun.

Their long evolution has given people several qualities that place them above the other animals. At the physical level, all life is constructed from cells, but humans also possess an inherent moral sense of life, and have developed the conceptual mind that then created numerous cultures in the world. Sometimes their higher moral qualities, such as justice, fairness, uprightness, righteousness, sincerity, and the love for all life, will conflict with their conceptual mind, although they are able to express those qualities in some situations. But this duality also means they are too ready to trust a belief if it acknowledges the value of spiritual discipline, and avoids unsuitable religious expansion.

While the passive evolution of humanity is possible, a subjective effort to improve ourselves is more meaningful, and should be the focus of all generations, in order to prevent our inherent spiritual faith from dying. No teaching should refuse to make progress, but few people challenge the convention of using one image to rule their spiritual life. Meanwhile, no real help is given to reaching the spiritual truth or seeking to progress the spiritual growth of humanity. Instead, most people today inherit a spiritual teaching that has so far brought both benefit and harm to humanity.

We should all become more spiritually responsible in the world. This is because people with spiritual dignity, who respect self-discipline, differ from the majority, who beg favors from a conceptual God. This situation can only be changed when there is a wider spiritual understanding that Nature is the foundation of all life, and there are three levels of attainment for humanity - physical health, mental health and spiritual health.

Spiritual fantasies may harm the clarity of our spiritual vision, or set the goal too high by imposing unrealistic disciplinary regimes that go beyond the normal spiritual purpose, or a healthy life. But any spiritual approach should also acknowledge that some people will still seek higher attainment, so the ancient teachings need to be modified to progress the true spiritual growth that results in the wisdom of spiritual maturity and a childlike body.

We cannot return to living a totally natural life, although we can learn to absorb the principles from Nature into our daily life. The general principle is to fulfill universal harmony, and because the substance of life is *chi*, this principle is fulfilled by cultivating our *chi*, or vitality. We also need to naturally combine the spiritual and secular aspects of life, and acknowledge that spiritual development is both practical and useful and relates to how we manage and enjoy life. This includes being more self-reliant, and having less dependence on money to find outside happiness or excitement.

I will now give another example of how the deep spirituality of humanity relates to Nature. During the late Han Dynasty an achieved master, Zhang Tao-Ling, gathered the higher achievements of early Shamanism, and shielded these with the teachings of the *Tao Te Ching* to establish Folk Taoism. Since that time, all of the many forms of Taoism have used Lao Tzu's name. Zhang's teaching was known as the sect of the Heavenly Teacher, and conducted healing and exorcism through the written talismans and ancient dances from the time of the Great Yu. Yet, both practices, which continue to support the Zhang family today, are really symbols of the sun and the Big Dipper.

We can still find help from Nature during troubled times. Shamanistic practices just used the various natural phenomena to convince patients they had become too scattered, or taken the wrong direction, and needed to be pulled back into their bodily life. The real secret is that the healing power is within each of us, and although these practices are very colorful, they only offer a small service to humanity.

The highest spiritual practice of all is to respect our own life, and all other life, and to achieve both internal and external harmony through having a supportive living environment. Lu Dong-Bin established the principle for nurturing life by combining spiritual and mental practices with bodily exercises, and later Chang San-Feng applied this principle to create *Tai Chi Chuan*. He is a good example of absorbing this wider spiritual principle into bodily movement and was reputed to have lived for 400 years. The slow *tai chi* movement can be applied as a martial art and, if done with the correct understanding, can also become a preliminary step to improving our self-control in life.

Chapter 18

The Spiritual Strength within Change

Essentially people are 30 per cent desire, 50 per cent emotion, 19 per cent knowledge and one per cent rationality. Our spiritual strength is not a myth, but it only comes from sublimating our many desires and emotions, and avoiding the lower spheres of knowledge. Yet, most people are unable to live with the plain nature of life due to their general disposition, and the various temptations and challenges generated by their many needs, desires, and emotions.

Even so, it is the strength of our spiritual power that enables us to live with the plain and natural truth without looking for external stimulus or support, although the people who only live with the plain truth may feel dull or bored, and constantly seek external help or excitement. Real spiritual achievement means never feeling dull or bored with the natural truth of life. Our extensive emotional search for the truth, and the popularity of the colorful religions, however, shows the practical and emotional need for such teachings. So now we will explore the ongoing search for the truth, and the need for colorful rituals, through the contribution from four wise men and one wise woman during the development of several versions of Buddhism after Sakyamuni.

The Example of Buddhism

In the first century C.E., when many people searched for a savior in life, the sense of Buddha from Sakyamuni was broadened through a new form of Buddhism known as Mahayana, or the big vehicle, established by leaders such as Nagarjuna [龍樹], and Maitreya [彌勒]. Sakya came from a family who used spiritual teaching to help people in exchange for their respect and support, and the new Hinayana Buddhism, or small vehicle for the quest of self-preservation, also became popular through one of his uncles.

Mahayana Buddhism sought a better world by establishing a new social-spiritual order within the religion. But once the priesthood needed material support the original concept of Buddha as the awakened one, who became achieved through meditation, soon became mixed with the sense of God, the heavenly ruler. However, the Buddhist monks lived by begging, rather than the arrogant Brahman style of being an agent of God and using that privilege to take obligatory offerings. Buddhism has become very popular in Asia, but both the large and small vehicles for teaching have benefited from changing the image of Buddha from the awakened one to the ruler in Heaven, or another outside spiritual world.

As the Asian population increased many of the early nomadic people sought more fertile land for their survival. They called their dream for the perfect land, Shambala, or Shangri-La, and as this dream grew in their hearts it became spiritualized as Pure Land Buddhism, the most important and popular sect in China. This form of Buddhism helped many people find hope, or a home in the spiritual world, because believers are promised a better life when they return to the earthly world. There is also immediate fulfillment from the many religious festivals throughout the year that give the farmers and other workers much joy, as well as relief, from the unceasing physical and mental toil.

Most people need something that gives them emotional hope, and an example to live up to. Thus, Buddhism prospers under the name of Mahayana in China, Japan and Korea, and as Hinayana or Theravada in Thailand, Cambodia, Burma, Laos, and Sri Lanka, while the Vietnamese take an eclectic view. The ability to give godly support is the real attraction behind the survival of the many religions and sects, yet few believers open their eyes to the fact that the true grace comes from the light of the sun.

There is another truth to be grateful for in the above countries, which is the fertile earth and bright sunny weather that allows several harvests each year. Hence, the real God is the help given by the land and the sky, so the worship of Buddha could also be taken as a spiritual symbol for the good earth. Help from Nature takes many forms, which is why there are numerous teachings and much spiritual confusion.

Generally, we make no distinction between the forms of support from Nature that offer us free help every day. Yet, people happily accept and support the many beliefs that promise help from a conceptual spiritual world. While we do not equate the worship of religious statues with the primitive worship of idols, some religions did develop from the early customs that made sacrificial offerings to the sky. Both approaches provided the religious tolerance that hides many primitive desires, but we now need to cleanse all forms of primitive or brutal behavior, including symbolic images, to reveal the spiritual truth.

In Tibet the worship of Buddha is directed towards the sun. People could not survive in this high terrain without the sunlight, and the Sun Buddha or Sun God is worthy of people's devotion. This Buddha is used to express the trust and gratitude of the people, and also given the highest authority. An open Tibet, where the entire culture praises the sun, would be a great religious capital for all sun worshippers in the world. Tibetans live in very lean conditions, but still have the faith to donate a third of their income to their religion, although the lamas rather than the Sun God are the recipients of this generosity.

Visitors to Tibet may be confused by the numerous names and statues of Buddha, but they all relate to the light of the sun, and the walls and small flags everywhere show the essential mantra: *Om Muni Padme Hong*. In this context *Om* is the sound that requests a gathering of the divine, *Muni* means the light, and *Padme*, or the purity of the lotus, is used to express the radiating light. Finally, *Hong* is the sound of starting a fire or a light, and used to enhance the effectiveness of the mantra.

This mantra is easy to use but if English is preferred say: *the light of the Heavenly Father shines upon me, and I embrace the light of the Heavenly Father within.* The sound Hong can also be used alone to mean lighting up spiritually, or rejecting all evil things and thoughts. Hong also expresses the explosive sound of a thunderclap, and those with faith in the Thunder God can chase away any evil with this sound. Yet the sun makes no sound at all as it rises from the east and passes through the high sky.

Four Wise Men and One Wise Woman

Spiritual development does not come easily, and is often like a relay where each runner passes the baton to continue the race until the goal is reached.

Philosophically, people accept this, but religiously they do not. So, here is a story about the wise teacher Sakya who refused to write books or let anyone record his teachings. He gathered many followers, and each time they met to eat the food given by the farmers, the teacher also had to feed them with wise and eloquent words. Sakya was a good philosopher and the group enjoyed travelling with him, because he was an excellent lecturer, and also offered the experience of visiting many places.

After many years some followers felt that the party must end, and this made them unhappy, so they asked who would be the next teacher. Sakya said not to worry as each generation brings good teachers and followers, just like water flowing in a stream, where each time a foot is dipped in the water it encounters new water. He may or may have said this to escape the question on the future of Buddhism, or could have answered that after another 500 years another great teacher would come to serve the world. But whether the above event truly happened, or was said to comfort others, is debatable. The spiritual work of humanity is like the runners in a relay, where the ultimate goal is spiritual progress.

The foundation of Buddhism was first advanced by two great individuals, Nagarjuna, [龍樹], and Maitreya, [彌勒], who appeared around 500 years after Sakya. We shall call them Wise Man 1, and Wise Man 2. Chinese Buddhism was later influenced by two other important scholars, Xuan Zang, [玄奘], and Silabhadra, whose Chinese name is Che-Shiang, [戒賢]. We shall call them Wise Man 3 and Wise Man 4. In addition, there was the Wise Woman known as Princess Wen Cheng, who integrated the five teachings of Bon, Buddha, Muni, Confucius and Tao to shape Tibetan Buddhism.

<u>Wise Man 1</u>: One of the dragons or elephants of the new Buddhism was Nagarjuna [龍樹], who started the sect known as the Truth of the Conscious Mind. His book [Chinese title: 瑜伽師地論] on the higher doctrine of Buddhism adopted an analytical approach to our senses and thoughts that led him to believe that all achievement and suffering is centered on our conscious life. That is, there is no real truth or substance that lasts forever, and any pain or joy comes from the insistence of the consciousness. Furthermore, because no stage of knowledge is real or lasting, he denied the soul of life.

This view can make people withdraw from society. Neither Sakya, nor Lao Tzu, nor Chuang Tzu took this helpless direction. Rather, they showed people the way to a positive and constructive life. What is truthful, however, is that our internal emotions and fanciful mental creations are reflected externally. Most conceptual religions are not on the same scale as the approach from the deep Nagarjuna, although some Zhan masters in China came to a similar view by extending the deep truth of Nature and their healthy conscious strength to arrive at a very limited involvement in worldly life.

Nagarjuna had reached the peak regarding research on the conscious mind. The value of his contribution is to slow down the people who strive too hard for worldly achievement, and provide a corrective tool for their emotional insistence, or an unreasonable or idealistic stubbornness in life. Moreover, most people can understand and make use of this approach for matters related to the mind.

The Integral Way takes the view that all life from Nature is complete, and cannot be valued by a single cell, or any one aspect of life. An analytical approach can achieve a partial result, but never sees the value of the whole. Similarly, people should not get lost during the journey, and take courage and find fulfillment from the wholeness of a completely healthy life. But we can also take the approach of Nagarjuna, 'the dragon tree', to dissolve any emotion and its effect on the practical level of life by giving it due importance, and then allowing it to go. At the same time, value each small entity in life, as it is like a healthy tree that ultimately supports the growth of a luxurious forest.

Wise Man 2: The other dragon or elephant who made an early contribution to the new Buddhism was Maitreya, **[彌勒]**. He responded to the call for a savior in the Indian subcontinent by transforming the declining spiritual teaching into a public service known as big vehicle Buddhism, or Mahayana. This is also the source of the teaching called Pure Land Buddhism, which takes a religious approach to placing faith in the sun through a new title, Amitabah, or the boundless light, with the hope that cleansing the secular world will help people to reach the spiritual light of the Pure Land.

Of the ten Buddhist sects established in China, the most popular one is the teaching of the Pure Land, while the second most popular, especially among learned people, is Zhan. There are numerous Buddhist temples throughout China, where people visit with the expectation of receiving extra blessings or other help from Buddha. Unfortunately, however, the real practice of Pure Land Buddhism is now just a small psychological tool for aged people, who hope to live in the most blissful realm of Amitabah.

The Integral Way embraces all good dreams for humanity whether spiritual, social or political, and teaches the Five Healths to realize these dreams within our practical life. We are also open to the world becoming a Heaven on Earth. Conventional dreams have a variety of descriptions, such as the Heavenly Paradise, the Heavenly Kingdom, the Pure Land, Shambala or Shangri-La, and so on, but the Integral Way expects the realism of a complete and healthy life for all people in order to build a trouble free human society.

Wise Man 3: It is possible for a natural and healthy human mind to see what will occur or what is actually happening in an unknown place. One night Emperor Ming [8-76 CE] of the Han Dynasty saw some golden people in a dream. A few days later, some strangers on white horses from a faraway land entered the capital carrying the Buddhist sutras. They gave these to the Emperor, who then ordered a new temple to keep this cultural novelty. This was how the religious culture of India was introduced to the Chinese, but at that stage there was no intention of influencing the local culture. But during the Jing Dynasty [265-419 CE], when the five border tribes invaded China, the majority of the Chinese people came into contact with Buddhism. And ever since that time, their faith in Buddha has grown and very much influenced the Chinese culture.

The original Chinese faith in the sky, or Heaven, was based on many generations of experience with Nature, and there was no intermediary between the spiritual world of Nature and the spiritual world of ordinary people. Later the kings used the sky to build their social authority as the sons of Heaven, with the power to rule the world. The new approach from Buddhism then offered another perspective, whereby believers could become like the Holy Being, Buddha, and enjoy happiness and an everlasting life.

This appealed to the Chinese, who saw an opportunity to get much more than just serving the emperor in a life fraught with difficulties, where entire clans would be held responsible and beheaded in troubled times. Thus, the new faith offered ordinary people hope by promoting the West Heaven as the trouble free home of Buddha, where everyone could enjoy a great life. With no other thought the Chinese then absorbed the faith in Buddha, and firmly believed they would receive help and protection from the Holy One.

During the Tang Dynasty [618-916 CE], when Buddhism had become a major cultural influence, there was a family with two sons who became monks. At that time there were often disputes about conflicting sutras, and the younger son asked two serious questions: were these sutras translated correctly, or was there something missing that prevented receiving the complete answer? These questions haunted the young monk, and he became determined to make a long trip to seek the answers. This young monk was the third Wise Man, Xuan Zang, [玄奘, 596-664 CE] who started his quest in 629 CE.

A popular Chinese novel, *Journey to the West*, tells the story of his journey. This novel was written by a scholar to entertain the public during the Ming Dynasty [1368-1643 CE], but the genuine record came from Xuan Zang's own observations as he participated in all aspects of the Indian culture for over seventeen years. During that time he became fluent in Sanskrit, and learned from the great teacher, Silabhadra, or Che-Shiang [戒賢], while staying in the important ashram, Nalandu, [那爛陀寺]. When this large and highly regarded ashram was challenged by the leader of a different faith, Xuan Zang represented the ashram, and won both the debate and the respect of the Indian king.

He also translated the *Tao Te Ching* into Sanskrit when he was in India. And later, when he returned to China and became a teacher to the royal family, he translated the Buddhist sutras into Chinese. His two most important works were the Heart Sutra, and the Diamond Sutra. His 260 Chinese character translation of the Heart Sutra absorbed 600 volumes of the Maha [big]-orajna [wisdom]-paramita [delivery]-sutra, while his Diamond Sutra forms one of the larger volumes translated by a group of experts on Buddhism.

These two sutras helped to clarify the Buddhist doctrines, and have been studied by generations of Chinese families to help their emotional life during difficult times.

The Integral Way respects all spiritual teachings as part of the wider human culture, but also seeks a continuous review of the standards for holiness to ensure spiritual progress. My vision on the correct standard came from witnessing war during my early life, and observing that spiritual cultures cannot really help people to live with a healthy moral sense, because they all fail to pacify and discipline people for the sake of the wholeness of humanity. I believe when everything is correctly done, it is holy, and correctness means humane consideration and respect towards all others, regardless of their beliefs.

<u>Wise Man 4</u>: Unequivocal faith in the Brahman style sun God can block the spiritual development of humanity, similar to other stiff beliefs. But an active form of meditation that respects all personal thoughts, as a reflection on our situation and understanding in life, can allow our minds to grow and experience further spiritual development. To quote Confucius: people do not become enlightened by learning without thinking, nor become resourceful by thinking without learning - 學而不思則罔, 思而不学則殆.

Our emotions can support our spiritual faith if we allow room for the development of a healthy mind. But any overly rigid faith, whether spiritual, religious, political, or social, suppresses the healthy activity of the mind. This is illustrated by numerous worldly experiences where a specific group or society with a set religious faith has created a model, such as saints or martyrs, for its believers. That approach then blocks the long term cultivation and development of the true or master mind required to progress society.

Buddhism was an improvement to the Brahman approach, as it respects the ability of the mind to roam freely on all matters that effect individual life, and the growth of humanity. Also be aware that a scattered mentality does not reach any destination, and a rigidly formed meditation or religion is not the healthiest route. This was verified by the three wise Buddhist men, discussed above, although we must not neglect Silabhadra, or Che-Shiang [戒賢], the

Wise Discipliner, who was head teacher at the Nalandu ashram during Xuan Zang's long journey to the West. He was a true sage and well versed in several important Buddhism sutras, including those from Nagarjuna.

There is another detail from this journey by Xuan Zang that cannot be neglected. His main interest in making the trip was the possibility of learning directly from Che-Shiang. It is indeed marvelous that the supposed 110 years old head teacher delivered the book by Nagarjuna, line-by-line from his memory, to the foreign student and the entire population of the ashram. I have reviewed the Chinese translation, and feel that the teaching, by itself, is too delicate and fragile to serve the rough emotions of modern life. But I am still grateful to both Xuan Zang and his great teacher, Che-Shiang, for giving me the opportunity to witness this great work by the remarkable Nagarjuna.

The Integral Way recognizes that possessing a clear mind at that age is an obvious achievement of attaining spiritual benefit, and proves that having good thoughts and allowing these to keep flowing is a blessing. For practical reasons, however, my suggestion is to consider an important matter that may have been confused or neglected in earlier teachings - the difference between the heart and the mind. Each function serves a different purpose in life. In normal situations the heart is humanistic, while the mind offers the intellectual capability to serve the practical needs in life. Both are important, but when our mind becomes overly extended, the burden can ruin our health, and when the heart is overly extended, this may lead to a state of helplessness.

Conventional spiritual teachings exalt the function of the heart and give it a holy name, like Buddha, to teach people to restrain and discipline the mind, which they see as unholy. This is because our mind is associated with our desires and emotions, while our heart relates to the organic health of life. Know that the impulsive mind can be like a wild horse, but do not forget that it can also assist the heart to accomplish great deeds in life.

The Wise Woman, Princess Wen Cheng: During the seventh century CE, the Tibetan King requested a marriage partner from the newly established Tang Dynasty in China [618-906 CE], and Princess Wen Cheng was the royal daughter chosen. Wen Cheng, meaning 'The Accomplishment of

Civilization', was not her real name, but she did achieve long lasting political and cultural peace through her leadership in integrating the five spiritual teachings in this border area to form Tibetan Buddhism. Those teachings were Bon, Buddhism, Manichaeism, Confucianism, and Folk Taoism.

Manichaeism is the backbone of Tibetan Buddhism, and Sakya's Buddhism represents the conscious exploration of the mind. Confucianism supports religious rituals and family order, while the Folk Taoism that practices the worship of deities and heroes provides the natural medicine to support a healthy life. Bon, or the worship of the black, implies hiding from harm, and the other local folk religions practiced from the time of the Great Yu preserve the worship of the mountains, lakes, and other natural features.

Tibetan Buddhism also preserves the chemical refinement of the immortal medicine from the Jing Dynasty [265-419 CE] that can be used to help certain physical illnesses. The biggest contribution, however, was to conceptualize the sun as the central Buddha, rather than an artificial statue. In the snowy highlands, where the average elevation is around 4000 meters, it is always clear that the sun in the sky is the most precious gift to life.

Most external religions use popular cultural expressions from the time they were established, rather than emphasizing the highest truths of life. Princess Wen Cheng knew that the culture of any society is deeply related to human nature, and the real needs in human life, although most people prefer to pursue various cultural diversions. So, she gathered and integrated all the local cultures and beliefs to form the practice of sun worship using the most elegant decorations. The result could be seen as the most expensive cosmetics ever, but this religion saved that ancient culture from much of the male expansionism, and associated struggle and loss of life, for over a thousand years.

The Integral Way salutes Princess Wen Cheng as one of our great leaders, although the accomplishment of her spiritual vision also illustrates that 90 per cent of human culture and 50 to 70 per cent of politics is cosmetic. However, 99 per cent of human conflict is purely for appearances, or having something to boast about in the world. But we do have to admit that male expansionism should be restrained, and that the direction taken by Princess Wen Cheng was meaningful, if overdone. Nonetheless, the real development of humanity comes from every person who continues to seek the balanced way of life.

PART VII

Focus of the Integral Way

True spirituality
is the dissolution of all conceptual frameworks.

Chapter 19

Personal Transformation

In the Integral Way our heart is physical, but it is also host to the hidden spirits that form part of our benign life force. During the day these spirits live near our eyes, and around our head and face, and at night they withdraw to our heart. In most religions, this aspect of our heart is represented by God, or Buddha, while our cooperative life spirits are called guards, or Bodhisattvas. Spiritual cultivation means finding the balance and harmony between these two aspects to accomplish a good and healthy life that benefits the world.

When we practice active meditation, we channel the mind without stiffness, or restraint. Our heart should be like the sun, because physically our heart is the sun, while our brain is the moon, and our other internal organs are the planets. The deepest benefit comes when the internal transformation uplifts our lower desires, and we seek moral interests, such as the Five Healths, to help us achieve a useful and balanced life.

Hence, all healthy personal cultivation should consider the deeper nature of spirituality, as discussed below, while sharing our concern for the cultural health of the world.

Is the Spiritual Truth Formless?

In the deepest truth, our spiritual life is both formed and unformed. The unformed is mother of the formed, and the formed is an expression of the unformed. However, the spiritual truth is not necessarily formless as it has the spiritual strength to create form from the unformed. But also know that all form is an expression of the deepest truth of Nature. So, in spiritual teaching, which is more truthful - the formless, or the symbols that represent form?

Making statues is both an art and a craft, although Zhan Buddhism, which is based on reflection, worships the formless truth of the nature of life. Other expressions of the new Buddhism adopted the worship of statues from

Alexander the Great, who brought the art of statue making with him when he conquered India, where it became a new cultural fashion. In many cultural circumstances East is West, and West is East, but that is not enough, as all people need to come together regarding their spiritual beliefs. The Integral Way is always willing to offer the foundation to help accomplish this goal.

Modern people live in the shadow of their cultural heritage, and the stone statues they worship were made by people. In contrast, the flesh and blood that shapes human beings is made by the sun. These beings then recreate their own image using precious materials and call them Buddha, or God, or the Holy One, to express their love for those forms.

It is natural to express love towards all creations from the beloved Sun. Look at the mountain caves throughout China that were carved into numerous stone statues of Buddha by the ancient warriors, who wanted these forms to represent their immortality. Yet every good deed and practice is precious, no matter its form, although there are also many statues and portraits that represent the cultures that destroyed all forms of life.

In the areas where various religions, such as Judaism, Christianity and Islam, originated from the Babylonian culture, many people believe that the spiritual truth is formless. That is also correct. Both positions – having pride in a formless God, or worshipping a statue that represents God – are forms of communication among the believers, who need some symbol or concept to express their formless spiritual faith.

That is, both form and no form are names that represent universal spirituality, but if either position is insisted upon, or the innate flexibility of the human mind is blocked, this expresses spiritual immaturity. Symbolism is unavoidable when attempting to uplift people's spirit, and although language is only another symbol, conceptual insistence does not express our higher levels of spirituality.

All cultures are an interpretation of the sunlight, and variety is the essence of our cultural creations. Conversely, uniformity expresses the ambition of young rulers who reject or suppress difference to more easily manage their society. Hence, universal spirituality is ultimately inexpressible, although no one should destroy any form of cultural expression for more convenient social communication, or to gain recognition or power.

Unifying people through insistence on one religion limits our spiritual growth, so we respect all differences as we adhere to the unity in the deep spiritual realm. Healthy spiritual education can include understanding the many differences, although each person should ultimately pursue their own maturity and achievement. No matter the spiritual teaching and expression, however, all cultures are expected to pursue their own health and be supported by the divine help from the sky. The real help comes from the light of the sun, the mother to all human civilization, which is the force that supports the growth of our constructive creativity, and its ability to benefit the lives of all people.

Spiritual worship also supports people's emotions, regardless of their living conditions. In pre-Christian Europe the people worshiped Jupiter and Mars, and during the fifth century, when Mohammed created Islam, his ascension, as described in the Koran, has been interpreted by some scholars as his return to one of the planets. My belief is that he wished to achieve himself by reaching the spiritual realm. But the result is the same for all spiritual seekers - what is projected can be discovered at the end of the journey. That power belongs to all people who concentrate on their personal achievement, and should be valued and respected without any need for comment.

Moreover, a religion can uplift the moral condition of humanity, although cunning people may use those teachings to manipulate others, and sometimes even good deeds can become mischievous. The outcome relies on the achievement of the believers, but a good, clean faith that connects to the broad spiritual reality is invaluable to progress the humanistic direction in the world. This is the goal of the Universal Integral Way, and we support all responsible teachers. But also note that their achievement will differ depending on the approach used, and that each practitioner has their personal limitations.

Hence, the nature of each religion relates to the development of the human mind, which means its influence depends on the public emotion. The true requirement should be whether or not it is healthy. Any country or race that allows their national or ethnic faith to become arrogant towards another faith or country can create a crisis. When this occurs the strong faith of the believers may transform into the confidence that makes them think they are better than others. They are not, although their arrogance makes them yield to all manner of meaningless, unworthy, and unhealthy forms of contention.

In recent times, several countries have betrayed themselves by being over confident about their superiority and physical force. There are also examples of groups that have insisted on their religious superiority for over 3000 years. A strong spiritual faith can become part of the strength to survive, but this position often invites trouble and creates unavoidable disharmony, while any spiritual growth attained is tainted with the smell of blood.

All cultural creations come from the sunlight, and the sunlight does express difference, although being arrogant is too high, and excessive humbleness is too low. But some people do achieve the ever-spring that expresses the Chinese expectation. This should be our spiritual goal so learn from the good examples, and avoid fixed beliefs, while being open to progress. That is the path to mutual cooperation and the survival of humanity.

Also be aware that each generation and life will face obstacles. Hence, practicing the broad faith of the Universal Integral Way, and promoting spiritual cooperation among humanity, does not necessarily reduce or prevent the competition for survival. We cannot neglect our biological background, although we are the only species with the ability to cooperate with others and progress our spiritual qualities in life.

Around 2000 years ago the early Roman leaders adopted part of Jesus' teaching to form a new religion. That development continues to cause confusion as Judaism is the mother of the original Christianity, although Judaism and the teaching from Jesus are totally different beliefs with the same spiritual root. This confusion is regrettable as the newer Christian religions now teach from both the Old Testament and the New Testament.

Often the serious differences were not noticed by the newer Protestant Christian leaders, who trusted that that the social formality adopted by the Roman Catholic Church was still suitable to gain public support. Nevertheless, an objective value of the Old Testament would be to remind people that holding on to a stiff spiritual faith frequently intensifies the struggle with other people, because many of the believers may think they are different, either consciously or unconsciously, and distance themselves from others.

The Old Testament also carries some of the Babylonian heritage where the natural forces on Earth were exalted to be the Creator. This great Creator still refers to Nature, although Jehovah is usually exalted to be higher than the Creator. Worshipping the Creator can be a broader faith than having faith in Jehovah, but it is still a psychological belief. Even so, the belief in Jehovah, thunder god of the desert, established monotheism, and has a clear social purpose.

We do know one thing for sure - when the black spots on the surface of the sun increase, there will be more thunderstorms on Earth. This could also symbolize further physical and emotional stress in the areas where the conceptual differences from over 3000 years continue to create tension. Needless to say, the sky remains the source of all existence, and the natural faith in the sky offers an honest mental practice, as well as the broadest support to human life. True spirituality is the dissolution of all conceptual frameworks.

Personal Spirituality Influences Cultural Health

Widespread confusion on the nature of human spirituality, and its influence on cultural development, has long obstructed international cooperation. Thus, the Universal Integral Way has taken on the duty of clarifying the spiritual situation in the world, with the hope of increasing our understanding of the numerous cultures that now exist. There is no reason to discontinue these cultural differences, but there is an urgent need for a new approach to spirituality that is above such differences.

Our review of the larger spiritual cultures has indicated that most are either a sentimental expression of the human spirit, or a means of gathering a social force to compete or conquer in the world. Moreover, the diversity of this expression has long created much hostility among people. To counteract this, the Integral Way proposes a new spiritual benchmark to apply to all people. This standard is the attainment of a balanced life with a sound body, a sound mind, and a sound spirit, which is also supported by a sound financial situation and healthy social connections.

Everyone is capable of seeing the importance of all of these five qualities, where each influences the soundness of the other aspects. Finding this common ground in life is also influenced by the psychological situation and cultural background in different societies, and some are more constructive than others. But when the Five Healths are a common goal to improve life, the only difference is the choice of living constructively, or destructively. People with a constructive attitude are creative, and always make both ends meet. Hence, this is the standard proposed to achieve a healthy human spirituality.

Once people stay away from the confusion of worldly life, they can clearly see the value of living constructively. So, first obtain the spiritual clarity to live above this confusion with its colorful cultures and social fashions. Yet, worldly pressures and demands leave little time to reflect, and most people are unaware or confused about the correct goal and true rewards in life. They may also be the victim of a religious system, or a destructive political system, or an unfortunate social condition. This problem has existed for many generations, which only shows that most people have not gained sufficient maturity, or clarity, to manage the wastage in their lives.

These matters do affect our health, and may come without invitation, or even being noticed. Influential people frequently misapply their power in a manner that unconsciously victimizes others, although eventually they end up being the victim of their own improper desires when their ventures fail to bring them the real gains in life. Many people will say we are all equal, but in the rough ocean of life there are bigger and smaller fish, just like in the real ocean. In spite of this, the Integral Way chooses to believe that Universal Nature is constructive, and the world evolves both forwardly and upwardly. Thus, the Way of the Universe is simultaneously horizontal and vertical as described in the *Book of Changes*.

A partial vision can encourage people to surrender to an incurable condition, or accept their suffering from physical ill health, or social toxicity and poverty, or an unclear mind, or spiritual immaturity. Meanwhile, governments and social trends continue to shape society towards a problematic destiny, while religions offer a false escape in the hope of another world beyond the current life. Politically, however, they all help to increase the social struggle - internally and externally- through their lack of spiritual depth.

The Integral Way wants people to develop a clearer vision so they are better equipped to manage life. When our body initially makes contact with the world it experiences both good and bad situations, but later on our mind learns to master our body. If our mind does not grow from these experiences in life, however, that mastery can cause trouble. This means we must first master our mind to understand the deeper reality of life, which includes attaining knowledge on the inner partners that work within our consciousness.

In a general sense this deep conscious group forms our non-verbal spiritual life force. Although it is not as apparent as our physical brain and mind, it still manages that mind, whether developed or otherwise. Thus, our personal happiness or pain in life relates to the condition of this group, which includes representatives from up to seven generations of our blood lineage. The truth is that no life ever learns or develops enough, but the will of life continues to strive, and God represents the greater flow of the life spirit in all of us.

At the current stage of human development, the physical mind largely ignores its partnership with the spiritual mind, and often remains at the animal level. Yet everyone has a group of internal spirits that participate in the management of the health of their mind. Unhealthy minds are messy, and a confused mind can ruin a life, while an unachieved mind has limited functions and lacks circumspection. These are all common conditions in the modern world.

There is no physical trace of the life spirits that act as backseat drivers in our minds, although they can be traced spiritually. These spiritual phenomena are often personified as existent but separate beings, while the unified spiritual and mental functions of our mind are seen as angels or devils. If they are personified as our own life, this is part of our spiritual function. And when the image is seen as a spiritual vision, this still comes from our internal group of spirits, although our mind may believe the phenomenon is external. That effect is produced by our spiritual function, which has accepted a conscious suggestion to our deeper consciousness to appear as a separate being. But also know that such phenomena indicate that our life has not yet achieved spiritual unification.

True spiritual power comes from the clarity attained from overcoming such confusion, and when our spiritual strength grows, the increased clarity of our inner spiritual group will then improve both our conscious mind and overall bodily life. Hence, spiritual attainment is a matter of developing the spiritual functions in life, as our mind cannot grow without this internal help.

Furthermore, true spiritual growth comes from real life experience. Trying to escape life blocks our internal growth, while spiritual cultivation means approaching life as a source of inspiration, and an opportunity to serve. Buddhism complains about the emptiness of life, but devaluing our life experience also denies the spiritual function, because self-awareness is the substance of our spirituality. Once our life is denied this function, it is no more than our basic instincts. Social religions and other external beliefs do reflect the subtle substance hidden in the mind, although they are unable to distinguish that being and non-being operate at different levels in life. Some teachings also suggest good disciplines, such as living a pure life, even if the nature of this pure life remains unclear.

There is also the choice of becoming a truthful being in the Universe by fully attaining the Five Healths in life. The first three - physical health, mental health and spiritual health - are inescapable, whether or not we choose to retreat from our worldly duties. The other two - social health and financial health - can be expanded or reduced in life, depending on our personal growth and circumstances.

The Universe is constructive, but if any one of the Five Healths is lacking, that life cannot be constructive. We support all people who have attained the Five Healths, whatever their contribution, as in the integral truth there is no difference between those who achieve much and those who achieve little in society, and whether or not they are distinguished. What is important is the value of the well-being achieved from completing all five aspects of a healthy life. Moreover, any social leader who does fulfill these five basic requirements is disqualified from serving the health of the world.

Some religions have devalued secular life to promote a Heaven that leads to spiritual failure for many of their believers. Spiritual failure means having the spiritual weakness of being unable to function in secular life with all its pressures, although overcoming those pressures leads to spiritual awakening. There are also the religions that encourage racial struggle, and societies that support living off other people. Both approaches rely on an empty pretext to establish practices that lack the truthful foundation of life, and deny the basis of a healthy society.

Finding the Deepest Unity

The deepest truth is that the sun is the true source of human life, which possesses the highest conscious power of all life on Earth. Some early people also viewed the sun as the Heavenly King above all earthly kings, but most people today have become separated from this truth by their numerous mental concepts and social creations. Although these early views of the sun still explained Nature in terms of the human world, there really is a physical connection among the heavenly bodies that is similar to the human family. This is because the sun rules the destiny of all planets and stars in this part of the Universe.

This means we should be happy to be led by the sun through our deep sense of life, rather than perceiving the sun as a ruler. It is also proper to view our lowly species as the begotten children of the sun, because the sun is more like our Heavenly Father than any human being. Lao Tzu, however, thought that we still remain in the womb of the sun. Nonetheless, our true spirituality includes dissolving all conceptual frameworks to embrace the reality of Nature. Originally, *Tian*, 天, the sky or Heaven of the natural faith, was interpreted as the Heavenly Law, 天理, in daily life, and provided the spiritual unity that guided Chinese behavior and society for 8000 years.

This broad faith in Nature, whereby all people accepted they were equal and equally supported by the sky, is the highest legacy from the earliest people, although there are no written records. There were several interruptions from a few powerful people, who challenged the spiritual orderliness of society, but the many spiritual differences that later became religions largely grew from the development of our conceptual mind. Even so, spiritual unity remains absolutely essential for the health of humanity.

Jehovah is one of the many names for God, and also the name of a Jewish ancestor. Allah is another name for God, and could even be the name of an Arabic ancestor. We should all respect the names of our many ancestors, regardless of their origin, because at the deepest level our common ancestor is the sky. Most people would find the true nature of the sky too vast to comprehend, but they should trust the closest divinity to human life, which is the sun that initiated this part of the Universe.

People commonly give names to all lives and things, although each being is just an interpretation of the energy from the sun. Our earliest ancestors did not have names, however, and we still respect their contribution to human life. But should any name, such as Jehovah or Allah, be above all others? This depends on whether people are able to perceive the reality that we are all equal under the sun, and need to embrace each other. If we continue to insist on all the names given by our ancestors to the various divisions made in the world, we will miss the real concern. That concern is finding the way to come together to help each other overcome the many dangers facing the modern world.

We should also understand that although our life comes from the sun, our differences have been influenced by the many environments on Earth. Primarily however, more people need to consider that the depth of their life contains the sky, and that Nature created all people to be the smaller 'suns' on Earth. Thus far, no earthly mechanism has the ability to destroy the source of our life force, which also means that no name or concept can be more important than the reality of our life, and all other life on Earth.

In a harmonious world no one would insist on the differences related to our birth, or education, or even natural superiority, although all these variations do exist. Generally however, our natural disposition relates to the reflection of the sunlight at our birth, and this differs depending on the time of day and the yearly cycle. But being humble is a virtue related to developing the higher self-awareness and consideration for other people that would eventually strengthen the harmony in the world.

To quote Lao Tzu: 'a little is easily grasped; too much is confusing'. Look at the sky, where the many light bodies influence both Earth and all earthlings. Yet, the Romans with all their knowledge did not know that the sun is the root of the entire solar system, and the basis of our cultural expression, or that the many different human dispositions merely exhibit the influence of the sunlight on each life.

'Catholic' means universal, liberal and broad-minded with a connotation of justice, fairness, and balance, but the Roman Empire used their new catholic religion to increase their control over European society. What they really wanted was absolute authority on Earth, although they lacked the vision to guide a healthy humanity. Unfortunately, the people at that time were taken in by their various schemes because they lacked the knowledge to see that the vast reality of Nature needs no artful human promotion.

If Christianity was really upright and truthful much human suffering would be avoided, as many mistakes and troubles arise from their socialized form of spiritual leadership. Jesus was very clear - the Heavenly Father, or sun, in the sky is fair to all lives. But the Roman Catholic Church did not want to make this truth any clearer because the image of Heavenly leadership could be used to proclaim their authority while they developed fictitious beliefs, like original sin, which kept people coming back to the church for help.

The sun is always in the sky, although it was Jesus who saw that the relationship between people and the sun is similar to that between a father and his children. His teaching is clear, but the story of his crucifixion is used by the church to manipulate the public. If that event truly happened it was clearly Jesus' choice to return to his Father, as all small life on Earth must eventually return to the big life in the sky. Thus, the accomplishment of his life, and his return journey to the source of life, is really a glorious story. If the priests had had any moral sense they would have made it clear to the public at the beginning that faith in the Heavenly Father, the sun, is also faith in Nature. Justice and fairness is natural, and any injustice or unfairness comes from the people who mishandle various matters. That would have been the most truthful faith on Earth, and worthy of the meaning of the word 'Catholic'. Who on Earth could refuse such spiritual truth?

Around 6000 to 8000 years ago all Chinese people had faith in the sun, which was seen as an example of openness and brightness. Their emperors were also seen as a symbol to express this faith, and were expected to behave like the sun in the sky. The broad blue sky, *Tian*, also produced the Heavenly Law that shaped the common spiritual faith, and at the head of the emperor's throne was a wooden tablet saying: 正大光明 - righteousness and honor. Yet, the sun has always been the God to all people, and not just the Chinese.

Lao Tzu respected the principle of *Wu Wei*, meaning not going against the nature of life, and his teaching of the Way follows the way of the sun. There are no special benefits from following a conceptual faith that only denotes a group of people who separate themselves from others. However, Lao Tzu called the people who followed the sun, and exhibited no cleverness or guile to get more from life, the wise simpletons. Chuang Tzu may have overly extended this view from Lao Tzu, although he also influenced the creation of several religions, including Zhan [Zen] Buddhism.

Many people today still want to be special, and use religion as a broker to make a deal with the spiritual world. Religionists are frequently the active partners in this deal. For example, in the Pacific Islands the people were once happy to live with their faith in the natural reality that the sun would continue to shine on them. Then some preachers built them a Christian church, even though these people with their faith in the sun God were in no way lesser than the believers in the God of this new church.

Religionists often wish to sell a religion with unnatural beliefs to people who already possess a sound belief in the natural reality. Christian churches have been very active in areas like the Pacific Islands, and remote mountain areas, where they attempt to replace the existent worship of a real God, the sun in the sky, with a written form of an artificial belief. These concepts may be sweetened with free milk powder, or used clothes, and the real attraction is not so much the words of the preacher, but their charisma, or hard work, combined with a small material gift.

If a wealthy society wants to help rural people by supporting a teacher, or a new building, or giving people goods, they do not need any other justification for their charitable work. But converting people to a foreign concept, instead of confirming their already honest living as they tackle various hardships, only seeks to replace their real holiness with an idea of how to enjoy a new form of holiness. Modern city folk could learn much from the people who live in remote societies where there has been no crime for many generations. They have produced their own ethical rules from the original nature of their life, and held on to their faith in the sun much longer than the inhabitants of industrialized urban areas.

Does teaching faith in a conceptual God really turn people away from following the spiritual example of the sun? Our ability to conceive ideas can explain Nature, but we are unable to create anything that competes with Nature. This gap in our mentality is very clear, although it is still the source of much confusion. One example is the above mistake, made by most spiritual teachings, when they wrongly apply a conceptual approach to establish a new belief system with the intention of replacing the reality of Nature.

Much human dishonesty has been based on this error and approach to public teaching, which has little real value if it makes people disrespect life. Moreover, people with a bright life based on an honest means of making a living are already in paradise, and should be encouraged, rather than being told to seek a paradise elsewhere. Instead, many people like to be entertained by new ideas, or fashions, and other distractions that replace their real needs in life, and are frequently side-tracked into unrealistic ventures.

Religionists, politicians, and business people are all guilty of taking advantage of the innocent and others who lack the vision to see their real needs. Hence, most people have lost the ability of managing their life in a healthy way. This is the real spiritual problem today, because the lack of growth in our overall mental health means the whole world remains unhealthy. Meanwhile, only a few people realize the problems in life need a solution from life, rather than seeking an emotional fantasy, although watching a good movie can help to relax our mind!

Furthermore, some social groups turn the religious or political approach to solving problems into a psychological weapon for social expansion, or aggression. In these cases the first thing to go is the underlying concept or belief. Look at how some societies have used their spiritual beliefs in the past. We tend to remember the devious minds, and the conflicts that left unresolvable troubles, while the healthy minded remain unknown. This legacy is far away from the interests of the sky, or the real concerns from God.

Unfortunately, it seems that the low moral condition that has made modern people crazy started with the shamans, priests and other religionists. This is because conceptual beliefs can spiritually take people away from the natural wisdom of life, and some people even completely abandon the correct path to follow the other helpless animals on Earth.

The real teaching from the sun comes from example, not words, and can be easily perceived as:

Having an open heart towards all other life;

Having a bright mind that never hesitates to ask, or to learn from others;

Always expressing our brightness in everyday life;

Being straightforward when seeking an explanation on a complicated matter;

Behaving in a manner that can be revealed to others.

The Fountain of Everlasting Life

In the deepest truth the sun is the source of the human soul, and represents the healthy nature of all life. Hence, we should all clearly recognize that the sun is highly qualified to be our Heavenly Father, even if we apply a conceptual measure.

The sun is also the source of human civilization. People are able to absorb and transform the sunlight, but our constant misuse of that life force has created all manner of trouble for wider humanity, and the unhealthy development of civilization is only one illustration of how far we have deviated from the nature of the sun. Yet, the sun is the source of our civilization and should be healthy, so what has really created the on-going troubles?

All people receive the light of the sun equally, although different conditions related to our genetic background and lifestyle mean that once the reflection of the sunlight finally reaches the core of our brain, it manifests in a range of expressions and attitudes. This also means any unhealthy concepts, which block our inner view of reality, come from our own self-deception. That process has made the world a confusing place, where the truth from the sun that supports an honest life has been distorted by many conceptual schemes - spiritual, social, and political - some of which are even alleged to have God's blessing.

Anyone who still denies the importance of the sun to all life, or who does not believe that their life force comes from the sun, can find shallow proof by attempting to stay in a dark cave for a long time. They will then see that their blood has become white instead of red when they are wounded.

Nonetheless, the conceptual function of our mind is still a useful tool to supplement our basic life force, although its development is linked to our perception of the meaning of the words we use. Take the word 'catholic'. In terms of the true meaning of this word - liberal, broadminded and universal - a faith with that name would be upright and open, and being catholic would include serving the public without prejudice. Does any religious faith, or service, fulfill this description?

Truly being catholic would also mean practicing universal tolerance. However, the declining Roman Empire adopted that word to describe a new religious tool to secure social control over much of Europe. The Roman Empire fell long ago, while the unhealthy ambition of their religion to maintain social control has continued, and the Roman Catholic Church remains strong over much of Europe, South America, and the Philippines. This church, and many other religions, have taken advantage of people's spiritual confusion, but only created more confusion. Thus, instead of encouraging a natural, honest life, they expect their congregations to support these unhealthy institutions.

The cross has a strong conscious effect on people because it represents the reflection of the sunlight in our brain. Hence, the Roman Catholic practice of communion, whereby the congregation takes in the flesh and blood of the conceptual Heavenly Father, replicates taking in the sunlight provided by our real Heavenly Father in Nature. Roman Catholics originally based their religious form on the Jewish faith before initiating a new round of hatred against the Jews. Moreover, they adapted the Pharaoh ceremony of raising a cup to the sun during their celebration of Mass, while actively debasing the Pharaoh culture. In truth, both of these cultures wanted to rule the world.

We all share the strongest supporter of our life, the sun, with the other inhabitants on Earth. Therefore, the sun has high spiritual significance to all people with a clear vision, who see its real value as the hub of earthly life. Yet, people have built numerous churches and temples to worship false images of this great spiritual ruler and potential unifier of humanity, although our Heavenly Father never requests or demands anything from us.

Rather, our Heavenly Father has given us our life and our soul. Some people have wounded their soul, but their natural savior is still our Heavenly Father, the sun, because no one can separate their physical life from their soul. Only death is able to achieve this, although the people who use their clever minds and an incomplete life to replace the true heart of humanity can accelerate this separation process.

Harmony and internal unity in life comes from our everyday behavior, not attending the churches with their false religious images. But busy minded people have allowed the churches with their fancy names and fictitious stories to usurp the position of the sun as the real authority in our life, even though the social ambition behind the religious cloaks of many of their leaders is the most heartless sin.

According to the Dead Sea Scrolls, the life and teaching of Jesus had no conspicuous color, but the Romans distorted his teaching by dramatizing his life and death with colorful stories, including his death by crucifixion. Since then, the word 'crucify' has been used to describe people who suffer, or who are unjustly treated or persecuted for insisting on a certain belief. Yet using an artificial faith to socially manipulate people is like administering a drug, and a similar approach was later used to start many of the extreme political and social movements that eventually caused humanitarian disasters.

Often these 'reformists' want justice to replace the injustice of a religion, or political regime, but they all use the same approach to manipulate people. They then deny people their conventional, if deceptive, religious faiths as they seek to replace those beliefs with a new ideology. In reality, both forces have engaged in an unhealthy social practice, and many of the current religious, political and social reformists still make this fundamental mistake as they play people to fulfill another artificial ideology.

The Integral Way believes that all social improvements need to undergo a gradual and moderate approach to bring about a better result, which means avoiding further destruction to humanity through widespread social wastage, or bloodshed. Regimes that hold on to their radical behavior to fulfill a social concept will continue this destructive pattern, but true leaders with an open and genuine heart do not engage in such behavior.

In terms of our own life and healthy personal cultivation, we should all consider the deeper nature of spirituality, and share our concern for the cultural health of the world.

Constructive people are able to face any challenges in life.

Grand Master Yo San, Ni.

Chapter 20

Saving Humanity

Who Really Runs Human Society?

The sky, the sun, and God can all be used to suggest the organization of society. Lao Tzu defined the merits of the unchangeable *Tian* – Heaven, or Sky, or God, as follows:

> God [Heaven] gives birth to all lives, but does not own or place demands on them;
>
> God [Heaven] provides for all life, but does not insist on living in any particular way;
>
> God [Heaven] prepares for the needs of all life, but takes no credit;
>
> God [Heaven] gives and supports all lives, but never lords over them;
>
> God [Heaven] benefits all lives, but never harms them;
>
> God [Heaven] treats all lives as equally important, but favors none;
>
> God [Heaven] accomplishes all this, but takes no reward;
>
> God [Heaven] practices balance towards all life, and is never partial.

What is spiritual and what is divine in life should be measured by these eight standards, and in Chinese such merit is known as *Te*, or being morally virtuous. These are also the requirements for being a good leader, and the nature of the sky, as defined by Lao Tzu, should be the job description for all world leaders. If any leader behaves differently, it shows that their spiritual nature is either non-existent, or damaged. They may want to be respected like God, but their actions are a denial of any such divinity.

In earlier times, Chinese rulers were referred to as God, and were gladly respected and supported if they met those godly qualities. But if these leaders did not maintain those qualities, they no longer enjoyed genuine respect and support. People in power often use propaganda to boost themselves, and some cunning leaders practice all manner of manipulation to attract the public. Unfortunately, that behavior only illustrates the further deterioration of the health of humanity.

The above eight standards express the normal condition or morality within greater Nature, as well as being a clear description of the moral nature of the sun. These qualities can also be used to help people understand God. What is most important, however, is the understanding that the sun in the sky cannot be deceived. People with a healthy nature live with the sun, while people with an unhealthy nature take the opposite direction.

Respect the Healthy Reproductive Force from Nature

Our reproductive force is part of the life force that drives our daily life. Hence, anyone who disrespects the health of their reproductive force also disrespects their life, unless they correct this matter. That is, both aspects of our life force from the sun are really one, although the form and application of each can differ.

God is a term for the life force of greater Nature, and many people view the creative aspect of this force as our Creator. How then did this benign force, endowed to all life, become known as the original sin of humanity? If correct, maybe God's endowment contains a mistake. But if we deny the reproductive force in life, can a God without a healthy creative force still be God? Obviously, there can be no Creator without the force of creation, and once Nature loses her reproductive force she is no longer Nature.

Moreover, as Earth and all life on Earth come from the same source, why do people need to pay a ransom to the church for their original sin? And if God was angry each time we applied our reproductive force this would mean God had become unbalanced, because anger expresses an imbalance in the life force. In reality, any imbalance is related to our own internal condition in life, rather than coming from an external God.

We also need to understand that any ransom exacted as a punishment to allay human destruction, or modify people's behavior, still comes from our creative force. There is also the question of what is a sufficient punishment. Is the life of one lamb enough, or should it be the entire flock? Some Buddhist lamas even eat sacrificial lambs as 'vegetables' to avoid the killing forbidden by Buddha, but Jesus was kind and thought the life of each lamb too precious. So, as the begotten son of God, he decided to sacrifice his own life for the sake of the life of one lamb. By this example, he hoped to save the life all people.

Jesus could have been a good business man, but the business conducted by some Christian Churches since his time have become the source of an evil root that constantly ransoms their believers. Using the principle that blood can subdue the anger of God when God does not actually touch the blood, there has been almost two thousand years where the priests from these churches share the symbolic blood and flesh of Jesus with their congregation. This is a good show, but it is difficult to find the true heart of the church.

Know the Beloved Truth

If there was no sun, there would be no reproductive force in life. Our reproductive force comes from the sun, and the mating season of most other life is linked to seasonal changes caused by the relative position of the sun and Earth. What then, can be more sinful than the attitude that misuses our reproductive force to create mischief in society?

The so-called original sin is really the healthy life force that exists within our body and mind, which join together to produce all of the constructive projects that assist our life. And since our life force is also able to produce good deeds with a divine quality, it is untruthful to describe that precious endowment as the origin sin of humanity.

Thus, no one on Earth should be confused about the reality of having a natural faith in the sun, or deny that the sun is the Heavenly Father to Jesus, and indeed, all humanity.

The Savior of Healthy Humanity

The idea of a human savior came from people who felt helpless during troubled times, and expected some divine intervention as a reward for their strong faith. But the true savior, the sun in the sky, came and never left, and remains just towards all life on Earth. Do we really think people living in conceptual darkness with confused beliefs can save the world, or should we acknowledge the true value of the sun in our life?

Contrary to popular belief, Jesus has been the only teacher with a deep conviction in the sun. He was also the only person of his time and region who saw that all the troubles in the world came from denying this great teacher in the sky. Yet, all earthlings should have this understanding, and hold a deep faith in our Heavenly Father, or one God, the sun.

Ti [帝], the God of Lao Tzu, is also the sun. Yet, the deepest and most perceptive observations of Nature indicate that her valley is much deeper than our solar system, and even the entire galaxy is only a part of the Way. This profundity of Nature existed prior to the birth of the sun, although the sun is still qualified to be our real God as it influences all human life, including those who attempt to measure the Universe and the Cosmos.

Faith in the sun is universal, but the Egyptian Pharaohs used this faith for political advantage by driving their own people into slavery with the excuse that the pyramids would identify the important seasonal changes due to the relative position of the sun and Earth. This venture also heralded the concept of finding immortality underground, which was believed to be linked to the position of the sun at night and mid-winter.

Jesus had spent his youth in Egypt, and seen the pyramids, but could not ignore the fact that slavery produced these magnificent buildings in the desert. Therefore, this wonder in the world is also a permanent memory of the spiritual shame of both that society, and all humanity. However, Jesus also saw the truth that the soul can be immortal when it radiates to become a healthy light to all other souls within humanity.

Around 6000 to 8000 years ago, the Chinese developed a line system to measure the light of the sun, and in the *Book of Changes*, *Ti* [帝出震], or God, rises from the East. This affirms that the sun was once the universal God to other early people, and not just those who lived in the desert, or high mountains, or on remote Pacific Islands. Furthermore, there is no shame in modern developed people having a strong belief in the sun, which has five enduring divine qualifications to back any claim of being the real God of humanity:

The sun is kind to both the kind and the unkind;

The sun is upright to both the upright and the unreasonable;

The sun is civil to both the civil and the uncivil;

The sun is wise to both the wise and the unwise;

The sun is faithful to both the faithful and the unfaithful.

In all situations the sun also allows people to discover which matters might become the real shame in human life, as well as giving them the opportunity to both discover and truly see the real shame or other shortcomings in their own lives.

These five divine qualities in the nature of the Sun God were then developed into the five upright forces that are able to bring us success, prosperity, happiness, health and sufficiency in life. My book, *Enrich Your Life with Virtue*, also discusses the twenty-five healthy constructive forces that can enhance our lives. But my inspiration to continue promoting the constructive life to all people comes from the life force given by the great father of humanity in Heaven.

My recent series of seven books on the integral approach to living a constructive life is intended to help the people who would like to emit the essence of the sun as they enjoy a complete life. While I have carefully produced this work, the one certainty to enrich all of our lives is the Heaven we call the sun. Hence, early to rest and early to rise is still the best advice to attain complete health.

Many of the people who disrespect Nature have encountered numerous obstacles in life, and because some of these troubles came from natural phenomena they developed a mindset that likes to compete with Nature. Even so, no one can really separate themselves from the nature of life, although people keep trying to invent substitutes, such as spiritual faiths, or social ideologies, or scientific theories.

Those concepts and beliefs only sharpen the confrontation between the two natural energies in life, which then intensifies their duality. As each side reaches an extreme, they express this duality as holy vs. unholy, divine vs. evil, Satan vs. God, angels vs. the devil, paradise vs. hell, grace vs. punishment, and so forth. This exaggeration is an emotional response, and can make people frustrated with the plain reality of life. They may then seek help from God using the religious style, although there are now other interpretations to make the ordinary achievements in life seem absolutely miraculous.

At these times, and with other ordinary matters in life, comedy is often the best remedy to alleviate the tensions – praise to the Lord for such a wonderful performance!

Jesus is the Light that Dispels Darkness

Jesus was born at a time when people's conceptual minds had started to grow to the point of undermining the genuine nature of humanity. He called the many new false creations that went against the plain and honest reality of life - hypocrisy. But his deepest heart prompted him to tell the truth, so he became a spiritual teacher and leader.

Jesus' own life demonstrated the truth he had learned from his Heavenly Father, the sun - always be open, straight, candid, honest, and warm-hearted. The sun constantly lightens the world by giving us its life force, which is a divine quality. Thus, identifying with the divinity of Nature is to identify with the light, while Jesus is the light of humanity.

He frequently used parables and metaphors in his teaching, and his parable of the prodigal son hinted that most people had long lost their humanity, and needed to return to the bright truth exemplified by their real father, the sun. His teaching is also very deep, and when he said - 'I come from the Father, and shall return to the Father'- he was referring to the sun, the source of all life on Earth.

The seven most important messages from Jesus' teaching can be simplified as:

All people are the children of their Heavenly Father, the sun;

Everyone is able to live through drinking the blood of their Father, which means absorbing the light of the sun;

People should also eat the flesh of their Father, which means all the natural products on Earth that have grown from the light of the sun;

No human being can deny that Nature is the source of their life;

All human blood is colored by the light from our Heavenly Father, the sun;

Only the Heavenly Father has the power to produce the color of each life;

People who shed blood on the unrighteous battlefields of war disrespect the blood of the Heavenly Father.

Spiritually our soul comes from the essence of life within the Heavenly Father. Evidence from people on the verge of death is that if they are able see the light at the end of the vortex, or tunnel of life, they can return to this life. But once people developed their conceptual mind they began to neglect the fact that their life comes from Nature. If they cannot accept that truth, they should at least be kind, avoid bloodshed, and accept all other people in the world, just like the light of the sun.

Jesus, who identified his life with the light of the Heavenly Father, also left us five important spiritual guidelines:

Love all people equally as we are all spiritual creatures. Our primary duty in life is self-care without overly extending our self-interest, or becoming reliant on others;

Forgive the mistakes of those unable to see the bigger picture when they overly extend their self-interest and cause trouble to others;

Never hold hatred towards another person. They may really be expressing our own self-created or inherited darkness;

Treat all people as a friend, rather than as an enemy;

Never seek revenge when someone has offended us.

Jesus has been promoted as the symbol of morality for around 2000 years, together with a suggestion that faith in Jesus will heal all our troubles in life. In reality, most people's problems are created by themselves. However, Jesus' divine nature is best illustrated by the fact that he did not seek to avoid trouble when upholding the cause of loving all people in the world. For this reason, he is indeed a great example of universal morality.

The Universal Integral Way also recognizes that the sun is the source of all human cultures and spiritual teachings. For example:

Judaism represents the strong afternoon sun;

Islam represents the sun at high noon;

Roman Catholicism represents the sun on a hazy day;

Jesus' own teaching represents a fine day from early morning to late afternoon;

Sakyamuni represents the bright moon.

The Heavenly Father is Forever

In the *Book of Changes* the image of the creative force comes from the sun, and the image of the receptive force comes from the earth and the moon. Achieving balance and harmony between these two forces is the basic principle within greater Nature.

Of all the spiritual teachings in the world, none appear to have a broader intention than the original teaching of Jesus. He echoed the Way from 3000 years before his time when the benignity of the original human nature still shone in people's lives. Lao Tzu's call for universal morality occurred 500 years prior to the life of Jesus, and his work marks the maturity that should be attained by all people, and especially their leaders. Unfortunately, Lao Tzu's profound teaching has never been fully realized in any country, including China, although he is still appreciated by the deeper people in the world. Therefore, I believe that culturally Jesus has done more for humanity.

The early spiritual teachers worked at a time when people were far less educated than today. Modern people are better educated, and should have more ability to recognize Jesus as the conscience of humanity, rather than believing he is an extension of a conceptual God who can free people from all the troubles in their mundane life.

But most people who experience and understand a religious teaching know that having a clear conscience in life is higher than any belief. Furthermore, it is very difficult to cheat our conscience. Jesus gave up his life to become the light of human life, although he was not understood by his own people, who believed that their superiority came from subduing any opponent. That approach, however, has now become the source of an endless cycle of revenge among the different beliefs and ethnic groups in the world.

Around 300 years ago several groups from Europe sought religious freedom in the new frontier of North America. These people were inspired by the teaching of Jesus, and had seen that the formality of the churches was not part of his message. They had also noticed that the higher achievements from humanity came from the spiritual freedom and independence practiced in societies that valued equality among their people.

Their dream helped to shape the young United States of America, but soon this new nation became involved with the on-going tensions in the world, and today the original vision for America is stained with the blood produced by political arrogance. Moreover, the social progress experienced by this great country has not been correctly expressed to the world. The lesson from all this is that when any individual, or ethnic group, or nation, expresses arrogance, this heralds their eventual decline.

Should America or any other country in the world find a new savior? I believe there would be more benefit from reviving the essential message in the original teaching from Jesus. We could also apply our modern intellectual skills if these were guided by universal morality, as this is the basis of the humanistic principle the Integral Way insists upon for the survival of humanity. Hence, Jesus' teaching offers a way out, although ultimately we must all receive the forgiveness from God, the life force of the Universe, and seek for harmony and balance between the *yin* and *yang* forces in our life.

Puritan Christianity combines spiritual faith with faith in Nature, and modern Americanism could also be based on faith in Nature. People who follow Jesus would focus on the humanistic principle as their highest God, and any social achievements would cohere with that principle. This new humanistic faith also refines the American approach to serving humanity without threatening or competing with other societies.

Seeking short term profit is for immature people, although the entire world competes for such profit. Long term prosperity, whether personal or national, requires the discipline to develop the strength that could benefit all humanity in the longer term. But anyone with an ambition to save the world without valuing their own spiritual discipline could create a new disaster in their society, or nation, and may even endanger the world.

Instead, we should all adopt the true faith in the sun, and realize its bright, open, and joyful nature that is never obstructed by the clouds in the sky, or our own life situation. Once we develop good discernment, we could then use an interpretation of our previous faith, or other appropriate spiritual teaching, to avoid living in the constant whirlpool of a lower life. In any event, we should all realize the humanistic love taught by Jesus.

Most conventional churches were established as part of the ruling system within their wider society. Any organization within a new spiritual teaching, however, should focus on helping their members attain the Five Healths in life – good physical health, no mental shadows, a clear spiritual goal on how to fulfill universal morality without having a particular spiritual bias, the ability to practice balanced love towards all people, and the financial dignity earned through a self-sufficient and responsible life.

No social position in life is any higher than the moral condition of our society. This means we need to be centered and spiritually detached to see the true value in others, while a completely healthy person has no need to blow their own horn. Yet, spiritual immaturity has become an increasing burden with every new generation.

In a healthy world we would all come together to form a clear, collective vision for our life - both spiritual and secular. We would also know that our secular life is no lesser than our spiritual life and that spiritual maturity and true achievement is attained by the experience and lessons from our own life, rather than regularly attending a church.

Part VIII

The Ultimate Spiritual Truth

The sun is our dutiful ruler
and offers openness and acceptance to all!
Grand Master Yo San, Ni

Chapter 21

Ally Your Spiritual Life with the Great Sages

Lao Tzu is our friend whose efforts renewed the constructive Way of our early ancestors;

Sakya is our friend who is happy we all now live a regular self-reliant life;

Jesus is our friend who is happy we find his relationship to the higher spiritual truth worthy of respect;

Mohammed is our friend who supports our disciplined life as we continue to pursue our spiritual interest;

Lu Dong-Bin is our friend who supports our spiritual interest when we do not neglect our healthy life.

The sun provided the strength of the humanistic heart in these great sages, although we can all live a truthful life as we fulfill our basic needs in the world. We should also extend our friendship towards other people as we pursue the Five Healths to accomplish the true duty of life. Real spiritual progress and achievement would be more respected if there was no spiritual partiality. Our own achievement, however, begins with the dissolution of believing in a single image to project the spirituality of humanity.

By now we ought to have a clearer picture of the three basic aspects in life - the physical self, the mental self, and the spiritual self. We should also be more aware of the nature of our social and financial life that connects us with other people. But what is the true self behind these five selves? People who wish to find their true self as they pursue the Five Healths would consider the following factors regarding their spiritual faith as they engage in their practical lives:

Life is spiritual, and each life carries the genes from previous generations. *Our temperament, disposition, sentiments, and inclinations*, which form our internal life, are therefore all related to the past.

Our personality and character are also influenced by the land and other geographical features from our place of birth.

Human beings developed from the overall life flow within Mother Nature. Each geographical location belongs to a smaller part of this flow, and the life flow related to our particular family or clan is but a fraction of that smaller flow. Hence, we are merely tiny beings at the end of the overall life flow. Nonetheless, all responsible people value their own life, and respect all other life from Mother Nature.

Following a traditional religion can raise the dilemma of either losing ourselves in that belief, or forgetting the heartfelt devotion of our ancestors as we cast aside their beliefs. So, here is a three point approach to finding the balance within this dilemma:

- First, we respect our ancestors;
- Then, we respect the history of our society. We do not need to change the history of our family or nation. Rather, we value any glory, and take any humiliation;
- Finally, and of utmost importance, we develop an upright character.

A healthy life is a complete life. Physical health alone is not enough. Our physical health affects our mental health, and our mental health depends on fulfilling our physical health. Moreover, a team with only two partners accomplishes little, and we all need some outside support, as sometimes our healthy physical strength may suggest using force, while our healthy mind refuses to cooperate with anything that threatens our life.

Financially it is not how much we own, but how well we manage what we have. And once we attain financial health we are further supported by a trouble free mind that expresses our spiritual health. But if we mingle with the wrong company to earn a living, this expresses our lower mind, and in the bigger picture we may cause disharmony within other important social connections. Any shortfall can damage our spiritual health, and relying on a strong social influence could also lead to greater disharmony in wider society, while there are many historical examples of heroic lives that ended in misery.

All this relates to how much we need in life, although the real needs of life are few. An unhealthy mind does not see that the true compass is balance, and allows the whole life to become extreme. Social pressure is not a reason to lose our healthy balance in life. Over the past 150 years China has suffered tremendous social pressure, and many young lives sought the opportunity for adventure. Eventually, the ensuing irresponsible behavior caused much trouble and damaged society, and the whole nation paid a heavy price.

Many difficulties in the world come from trying to resolve another difficulty, and this applies to personal troubles as well as society. These problems arise through a loss of balance, or as Lao Tzu said, calmness. But how can we achieve and maintain balance in life when so many people are intent on getting something from someone else, and various aggressors continue to keep the world busy as they pursue unreasonable ends?

Perhaps the spiritual principle of balance ought to become a common religious belief, because individually or collectively, balance is the key to safety. If this is denied, any solution to a problem can increase the trouble. Respecting this principle requires a mature mind, but an examination of the above may help us to see something new. And, as most people see things differently with maturity, the world would then change for the better.

One man clearly recognized his physical connection to the sun, and called this relationship 'father and son'. That is true for all people, but many have a conscious block that prevents them from appreciating the reality, while others loftily perceive the sun as merely a moving star. These people would prefer to ignore their real connection to our closest source of life, and our ability to perceive - the sun. The sun does not care about our attitude, and whether or not it is treated religiously, although being religious still relates to living in a healthy manner. Rather, it is more like a parent who wants their children to be healthy and behave correctly. Nonetheless, the conscious power endowed to all human life offers everyone the chance to suitably manage their own life within Nature, and beyond.

In fact the light from the open sky is the real source of our spirituality, while the light from the sun has the strongest influence. This means our mind still adheres to the nature of the wider physical sphere in the world, even though most people are constrained by their mental blockages. Hence, in our everyday life, our mind possesses the freedom of a wild imagination, while our body must operate within its physical limitations.

Nature offers the spiritual depth of life to us all. Trouble comes when we deviate from our original nature. Yet many people remain unsure about the source of their spirituality, and only the wisest are able to perceive the true source. There is also the matter of growth, and people unable to perceive the reality may choose a conceptual belief which is far from the truth that the Heavenly Father of our soul is the sun in the sky.

The spiritual truth on Earth is very clear - the sun is the Heavenly Father of human life, and the most heartfelt offering in the vast galaxy is to place our greatest faith in the sun, and make an alliance to voyage through the rough sky. When we carry this belief of living with the inner light of the sun, we should also radiate that light to all those able to perceive the same reality. But also know that the universal light differs as it reflects on each brain, although the multiplicity of our visions can be adjusted to the truth once we attain sufficient growth and maturity to understand our own shortcomings.

Achieve the Humane Heart

The humanistic spirit within the humane heart is the true authority in our life, and the verse below on achieving the humane heart is based on the humanistic teaching from Grand Master Yo San Ni [1879 -1968 CE].

人类心: The Humane Heart

人类至贵人类心, 獸道横行此心旡.

人类復得人类心, 人世从此悦和熙.

The most valuable gift in our life is the benevolent
And compassionate nature within our heart, called the humane heart,
But the animal impulse in people often pushes this aside.
If people could only see their inner light and reclaim their humane heart,
The world would be a joyful and peaceful place.

自來人类种族繁, 地廣人稀爭不多.
各自立教固族群, 出乎向心之需要.

Many ethnic groups carry features from their geographical origin.
To start with there were only a few people on the vast land,
And no problems, but later each group developed their own culture.

人类发展从自然, 生命进展道路長.
無人能知歲与月, 一路发展求进步.

All human development is supported by Nature,
But our step-by-step journey is slow.
Nobody knows how long it will take,
Although it must constantly move forward.

生命进化有可稽, 空穴來風逞跡轍.
感乎环境神形变, 精神感通真事实.

That evolution is trusted, but each vision is incomplete,
And requires internal development before an external change.
Good cooperation between the internal and external
Means the spirit has transformed and completed that life.

現今地球未变小, 人类增多势难遏.
相和协作是前途, 互相殘害道途絕.

The problem is not that planet Earth has become smaller,
But that the human population keeps growing.
Future survival requires cooperation among all beliefs and nations,
While mutual destruction hinders further development.

人类可贵三种心, 第一可贵自立心.
第二乃是民族志, 第三乃是人类心.
There are three aspects to the healthy human will:
The first is the will to be self-reliant,
The second is the will for group survival,
But the highest of all is the will for coexistence
That comes from the humane heart.

最贵三者须平衡, 若是犯偏德不全.
个人生存贵自立, 民族生存求自强.
All three levels should be balanced, as any partiality
Creates tension and limits the function of the life spirit.
Self-reliance nurtures the healthy will power needed
To strengthen the efforts for the survival of humanity.

种族競爭仍盛极, 你死我活爭相拼.
应知同作地球人, 该当协力求出路.
When the racial or nationalistic struggle is strong,
People believe that if one side lives, the other side must die,
And ignore the fact we are all the children of Earth.
Rather, they should offer mutual help as they seek a common future.

独生排他理不正, 种族仇恨最持久.
冤冤相报何日已, 各自省悟重和氣.

Obviously, rejecting the right to survival is a misconception,
But the longstanding hatred and acts of revenge continue.
Instead, both sides should practice self-restraint, and reflect
On the importance of total harmony amongst humanity.

新的人类应自觉, 和协合作求前途.
旧日宗教怀偏窄, 放开心量求归一.
The new humanity must value the awakened self,
And a future of harmonious cooperation among all people.
Hence, any narrow religious teachings should be replaced
By the unity and openness required for coexistence and survival.

上帝本是人类心, 造作别名其实一.
各从习俗加詮解, 共同尊天天是一.
God is the Humane Heart,
Although there are numerous names for the same reality.
There are also many customs and forms of worship
Based on their common spiritual faith in the open sky.

不恃族别出生处, 但体同属一人类.
人已同尚人类心, 因何相爭不相让?
So, do not insist on your race or birthplace,
But value the common understanding that we are all human.
If everyone was able to respect the humane heart,
There would be no hostility, or on-going struggles in the world.

不因异教相迫害, 人类倒退此为羞.
无私大公作上帝, 憑此大公救天下.
There would also be no persecution over different beliefs,

But regression to the nature of the lowly beasts would be shameful.
However, being selfless and open to all would be seen as truly godly,
And this could save the world.

舊日阻礙当抛除, 从此缔造新人类.
新的人类不附群, 面对宇宙抱大同.

So, remove all the old obstacles and create a new humanity
That follows no fixed convention, or mob mentality,
As we embrace all existence, and face the future of the Universe.

Chapter 22

Honor Mother Ocean of Eternal Wisdom

For Multiple Blessings we should also honor the great Mother Ocean of Eternal Wisdom, whom Om Ni introduced in his New Year's message, 2013:

The Ocean is where all life on Earth comes from:
There is the ocean of desire where people become confused,
And there is the ocean that produces the wisdom which can take us to dry land.

There are also two kinds of blessings:
The general kind maddens the people that inexhaustibly pursue them,
While the other type embraces the essence of life.

Life itself contains this essence, and should be enhanced and strengthened, although adding too much to our life can make us unhealthy. And while the chase for suitable needs to support our life is part of our life nature, we should also be aware that wildly chasing after unsuitable needs goes against this nature. True wisdom means seeing the appropriateness of our various 'needs'.

Hence, wisdom is a highly respected quality in life, because people can become confused by their internal pressures and external needs. To overcome this, each life must learn how to grow eyes on the top of their head and be open to the sky. That means we should not use blind impulse to conduct our life, and the people that choose wisdom above all other needs, and who know when, what, and how much is enough, grow closer to placing their lives amongst the divine.

We do not invent our true spiritual life – we are born with it. Religions are a human invention and present themselves according to the situation at that time, although only those with the eyes of wisdom are able to see the limitations of these creations. Thus, there is both the everlasting essence of life, and the dust from worldly competition within the numerous religious teachings.

Our focus is on the necessities of life that will enhance the essence of life, and giving up all interests that conflict with this approach. All life is able to function on the necessities and essence of life if they choose to keep away from the over swollen aspects of worldly life that can negatively affect our nerves, and even our bone marrow.

To do this the Integral Way has combined the practices of a secular life with the sacredness of a spiritual life to remove the spiritual convention that tends to disrespect secular life. We believe in the spiritual maturity found in a simple life, which is physically healthy, fully developed mentally, and spiritually blossoming. Our intention is to conduct our life through spiritual reflection and self-correction at all times, with the hope that this approach can lead to a deeper understanding of life.

A secular life combined with spiritual growth avoids nothing, but has given up the common spiritual interest of running away from life, and replaced this with moral courage, as truthful achievement does not chase any illusions or spiritual fantasies. Instead, we make the sun, which represents our naturally healthy life force, the spiritual center of our life. That is, the Way positions itself within the ageless truth of human life.

Although the spiritual side of life is ultimately unnamable, the greatest need in human life is to reach the spiritual truth. The world has created many spiritual cultures throughout the long history of humanity to help people to reach that truth, but be aware that many of these attempts were initiated by teachers who had not yet reached spiritual maturity.

Today, people are still trying to describe the indescribable to shape and formalize their understanding, although none of these attempts can be insisted upon as the spiritual truth. The custom in most spiritual cultures is to choose a name to represent the common unnamable reality in all life, and then introduce it as a direct 'being' that influences human life. This practice has created confusion. But if we correctly understood the logic, we should be able respect any suitable name to represent our common spiritual reality.

So far, the name of our teaching has been the Way. Yet, the Way also includes the people whose spiritual side of life is still developing, and full of contradictions, such as wanting to help people or save the world as a means to lead society. However, the latter approach may come from mixed intentions and could even be seen as a form of spiritual abuse.

While we can agree that the spiritual side of life has no name, we still require a suitable name to correctly conduct the spiritual force in our life. This is similar to using a compass on a long sea voyage. So, to teach the openness of our spirituality, we have chosen a new name to take people ashore from their endless struggle in the dark sea, which is full of bitter prejudice. Thus the name we currently choose as a reminder and a goal for our spiritual direction is: ***Mother Ocean of Eternal Wisdom***.

An open secret behind this name is that it comes from the real experiences that have helped the spiritual growth of several people associated with the Integral Way. Some of the names they have used to conduct their spiritual force in life include:

Mother of the Awakening Power in Life: this is a name for the deeper self that was used by my mother to help her own spiritual life and that of her friends;

Mother of the Awakening Power in Deeper Life: I [Om Ni] have used this name to help some stages of my life;

Mother of Enlightening Our Deeper Life: here the word Mother should be Goddess;

Mother of Great Ease: this is a name recommended by the Thai Buddha, and came through a dream. Can it also be read as a plea to revive or restore our spirituality?

Mother of Enlightening All People: this is a suitable name to use at any time;

Mother of Inner Life: this is another suitable name for the deeper self;

Mother of an Ageless Inner Life: this adds encouragement to the practice;

Mother of an Everlasting Inner Life: this adds the sense that the inner life is immortal, while the physical shell is mortal;

Mother of a Blessed Life: this name refers to the source of a life with a blessed body, a blessed mind, a blessed soul, blessed human connections, and a blessed financial life. People with all five blessings should do more for those who are not so blessed.

Mother of the Five Blessings of Our Choice: this name comes from our new spiritual promotion of a constructive life with all of the Five Healths in order to improve the future generations of humanity.

Recently, I was taken to a mountain retreat in South East Asia, which bordered several countries where the spiritual contact was both valuable and fruitful. Here I also found:

The ***Mother of all Buddha of Spiritual Self-accomplishment*** - from Laos;

The ***Mother of all Buddha of Spiritual Self-realization*** - from Burma;

The ***Mother of all Buddha of Spiritual Self-fulfillment*** - from Vietnam;

The ***Mother of all Buddha of Spiritual Self-enfoldment*** - from Cambodia.

In these countries the people do not need my spiritual support, as they have already conquered the desire to engage in worldly conflicts and competition. Here, the conventional view is that the world is unspiritual, but they wish to build a spiritual one. Yet, all people seek self-improvement, and this includes not repeating any patterns from an unhealthy sense of life, one of which is giving up the natural health and duty of life.

The Universal Integral Way seeks to clean up the concept of disrespecting worldly people, as well as clarifying the confusion from the numerous and often competing spiritual cultures in the world. Many people have been troubled by their life in the world, or have even become spiritually poisoned by others. A healthy life spirit is not bothered by the plethora of spiritual stories and fashions, and the multiple styles of worship and rituals which block people from seeing the real spiritual value of life. The truth is that all people should live with the simple essence of their life.

Much of the current confusion only expresses the spiritually helplessness of the modern world, and our new effort is to encourage more personal development within a spiritually dutiful life. This means there should be more spiritual learning as we seek the balance in life, as well as an open style of meditation and regular practices, such as Chi Kung and Tai Chi. When we are able to see that there are no real spiritual differences between people and cultures, and that difference only demonstrates the many spiritual qualities in humanity, there would be no real obstacles to the unity of human spirituality.

Our pursuit is the balanced life, and we value all spiritual growth as people reach for the Mother Ocean of Eternal Wisdom. This name conducts the spiritual force in our life as we seek the unnamable spiritual truth, and can be used as a prayer, or imprint, on our conscious mind to decide the spiritual direction for our soul, and its eventual realization during this lifetime. That name could also be used to stand for the convergence of a new effort to improve the spiritual health of humanity. We would accept any name for this great purpose, and do not fight for a spiritual brand. We only seek mutual cooperation to find the one deep spiritual connection with the light of Mother Universe.

Moreover, we insist on refusing the continual spiritual confusion. All spiritual creations from the past are part of the historical background of humanity that we wish to put behind us as we move away from the incessant divisions in our problematic world. Hence, our new spiritual life is based on the deepest reality of life, rather than shallow emotions.

This means we also agree with the spiritual depth from all human achievements, past and present. We respect spiritual maturity, and would like to be inspired by anyone in the world with this quality, because the spiritual function of the world is to enlighten both ourselves and other people. Once we discover this, we are able to achieve everything.

We do not need to be born talented, although all people with spiritual sincerity and honesty are equal to the sages. But we do need to know that we were all spiritually open at birth, and may now need to rediscover how to embrace the essence of the sky and the earth. When we follow the Heavenly Heart, we respect the sky as Heaven, and the health of Mother Earth and her people as part of Heaven. This Way is not new, but thousands of years old, and has always offered people this opportunity.

This approach means we should appreciate every opportunity to renew our life. And once we have chosen a name to direct our spiritual force at this stage of life, we can directly use that name as a prayer by rotating a string of beads in our left hand. That is only one way, and is not required, although it is necessary to fulfill or live up to the standard set in our prayers. We can also use the chosen name to smooth our emotions, or privately quieten any confusion in our mind. The chosen name represents our spiritual service in this life, and is related to our individual spiritual status and desire for improvement.

Who is Mother Ocean of Eternal Wisdom? The mother is Nature, and people are her offspring. But when her children overly trust their smartness, they create trouble. Thus, their mother must inspire them to save them from themselves. How should they repay her? They should not create trouble for each other, and love Mother Nature and Mother Earth the best they can - this is the way to the salvation of humanity.

Chapter 23

The Correct Spiritual Expression in Life

This message from Hua-Ching Ni [Om Ni] in early 2013 clarifies the substance and direction of the One Universal Faith in life as expressed through the Integral Way.

When we are spiritually healthy we are not opinionated, and remain quiet while we provide for our practical needs. We also keep an open mind to observe and learn as we slowly become more centered and neutral, which is the correct way to conduct life.

We also need to correctly recognize the times in life when some spiritual phenomena may appear, such as when a relative dies. But if we live unwisely, and are not concerned with our spiritual health that manifests as calmness, firmness and balance in life, even our everyday life experiences may express spiritual confusion. How should we react to any spiritual phenomena encountered? Just treat these worldly spiritual experiences with no more, or no less, emotion than any other balanced reaction to a life situation.

My work on reviving the original Universal Faith in life and humanity has the purpose of strengthening our healthy spiritual force, rather than continuing the conventional confusion about spiritual matters. Discussions on our soul, or past lives, or the future of the world and society, often raise questions and make us wonder. The correct response is to just receive the information as given, without any imaginative embroidery, as our emotions can easily develop these images into stories that add further confusion. Similarly, the original spiritual confusion came from people who could not handle their spiritual experiences accurately and instead offered stories.

The recent name to help us guide our spiritual energy and direction in life, Mother Ocean of Eternal Wisdom, was chosen by Dr. Mao with an active group of spiritual friends, headed by Dr. Dao, who were also inspired by a wider circle of students and friends. Similarly, I do not accomplish these books alone and give credit to my many helpers all over the world, who share the universal heart that wishes widespread spiritual improvement so that all people can live in peace. Who guided us to this new direction? There is only one source – it is Mother Nature, who also offers me help at 3am in the cold winter mornings as I write these words.

Recently I have been inspired by the local people who use the image of Buddha for their personal support, but also endeavor to earn a living to support their practical life. In that sense, the statue of Buddha has been positive in that their belief has helped these people to build a good life, rather than running away from life. In a deeper sense, the image of Buddha can also be used to exemplify someone who has gone through many worldly troubles, and their efforts to accomplish this correctly have brought spiritual liberation.

But healthy spirited people have no need to live like a monk or a nun, as spiritual experience is very subtle and takes many forms. For example, the very different spiritual significance of the Mother of Great Ease is her encouragement to not struggle with the world, although both approaches may help a ruler to maintain peace without using force.

Yet, the people who are able to live with the world without becoming attached to worldly desires have had to fight their own wars in life before they were able to lessen their personal desires, and be qualified to work with others in the effort to cool down the fiery mood that leads the world towards war. Ultimately it is the cold mind that wins the battle for living a decent life, and in this regard the teaching of the Way requires no special name. Hence, farmers, laborers, and other honest workers are free to shape their own healthy spiritual service, and there is no reason to fight over the different styles.

During the rough years I followed an open and natural way of spiritual cultivation, but never defined how it should be done. Now I have found proof from the spiritual world that all spiritual achievement must come from our own efforts. Thus, the Way of personal spiritual cultivation is spiritual self-reliance, combined with a good faith in life. Nature is the God that is really the open sky. And as the sky is ruled by the sun, the sun is our real creator. This also means that the conventional promotion of God as the ruler of human life ought not to be applied to influence or take advantage of the general public.

Spiritual development is part of the duty of all life, and although anyone can be tempted to give up on this effort that approach cannot bring the true blessings in life. Those with spiritual sufficiency, however, know the importance of spiritual improvement, as nobody can reach the spiritual heights without the continual effort that leads to self-awakening.

Popular Buddhism has denied the soul its purpose of unifying and cleansing the conscious self, although both functions are important in our spiritual life, and offer people the opportunity to live selflessly and spiritually merge with the light of the sun. Moreover, the sun has already merged the best souls of humanity. In contrast, those who rely on community support throughout their life can weaken their mortal soul.

There are many situations in this world. Lao Tzu was an archivist for the Zhou Dynasty, and developed his philosophy from a historical viewpoint. This perspective led him to believe that spiritually humans are still in the womb of the Universal Mother. Sakyamuni lived in another time and place, and developed his philosophy on the non-existence of the soul, and its ego, to evade the many struggles in the world. Thus, Buddha defined the holy life as a clean life where the substance of life no longer exists, while his many believers must continue to follow the natural law of being reborn to live on Earth.

We acknowledge that anyone can develop a conscious view of life, although the substance of all human life will remain subject to the laws of Nature. The lifestyle established by Jain and Sakyamuni sought to eliminate all worldly entanglements to avoid or escape pain. On the other hand, the teaching of Lao Tzu offers the option of embracing the simple essence of life, which has the power to strengthen our life as we face its various challenges and difficulties. When our spiritual purity and wholeness have not been damaged by the world, this is a real victory, but we must also be aware that a painless soul is achieved by overcoming all the pain in worldly life.

Hence, genuine spiritual achievement has to include spiritual self-fulfillment, self-realization, self-enfoldment, and self-accomplishment. Being like Buddha may mean having a painless spiritual life at all times, but choosing to be a monk or a nun is no guarantee of freedom from spiritual pain. Rather, the real Buddha is just like anyone else who must pay the price to live in the world. The wise are able to pay a reasonable price for the right things, and the achievement from a life of spiritual self-cultivation and discipline brings our own choice of happy moments in life.

Lao Tzu's vision was that all life is equal in its original, benign condition, and is in harmony with the healthy nature of universal life. Conversely, being sentimental is to be the slave of a yet to be liberated soul, which pulls down that life. Furthermore, both Lao Tzu and Chuang Tzu, two great masters of the Way with a deep psyche, disagreed with the kings and other people in power who used rank or class to attract people to fight in order to obtain more land, or receive special privileges.

From their experience this leads to the corruption of society and eventually humanity, while Chuang Tzu frequently mocked those rulers in his writing. But we should also know that any social establishment with official ranks, or a religious faith of any denomination, can be structured to attract this aspect of human nature, which is counter to representing the true nature of humanity that comes from the universal nature of life.

Some people may now ask how much of my own work on this truth is credible. I welcome the examination of all my work before anyone uses my services. I attained my spiritual nature and ability from many years of living a quiet life, and engaging in broad spiritual research. I have also worked through the bulky volumes of the Taoist Cannon, which is a large collection of many generations of spiritual pursuit in China. My explorative study took the modern intellectual approach to verify which aspects are the truth, and which are pure fantasy. This process verified three important matters:

> *Human life does indeed have a soul*, which is able to survive the end of our physical life.

> *Each human life contains numerous tiny bodily spirits*, and even our ears and nose hide a large army of these spirits. I have no intention of taking people back to the stage of Shamanism, however, and only suggest that these spirits should be respected for helping the healthy functioning of our bodily life.

> *The acupuncture points and meridians discovered by the early Chinese really exist.* This system protects our physical life when it is exposed to natural harm, and we could expect a self-recovery that would be enhanced with acupuncture or herbs. In contrast, heavy modern medicine sometimes harms our natural capability to heal.

I also recommend new research on these matters regarding several problems connected with people's spiritual faith, as well as their physical life and approach to healing. It took many long years to undertake my spiritual research, and several more years for my physical body to produce the light that proves the possibility that a soul can become immortal. But it only took seven days to verify the tiny bodily spirits that are our partners in life. However, it has taken me many more years to report these discoveries to the public, and there are now over fifty titles in Chinese, and over eighty in English, of which several are unpublished.

Why did I work so hard in this direction? Humanity is now at a crossroads where we can either continue on the path of materialism, or choose to recognize our three partners in life – the life spirits, the soul, and the physical body with its mind. Bodily spirits are just physical particles that form the hidden beings in our life. They can be verified by the experiences of sound minded people, but they can also cause insomnia and sexual desire.

But the best spiritual guidance is still an open and balanced life as any narrow or radical belief, or extreme behavior, can endanger our life. The bulky Taoist Cannon remains available, and those who lead a dutiful life are welcome to pursue a direct spiritual experience with other spheres of existence. Although the management of this bulky tome requires a high mental capability to make the information clear, being able to attain the essence from many generations of effort could be likened to receiving a large fortune.

Regarding the wider cultural contribution, the value of the family principle within Confucianism is also important in our life. Similarly, the social discipline found at a certain stage of Christianity seems to do better than other religious societies, although it can be tight and constrictive like many older societies. But it does show that when people respect the spiritual side of life they are less violent than many societies today. We only need to look at all the modern cultures that emphasize personal free will with little social discipline, and where much of the personal discipline promoted is unhealthy.

In the East, where Hinduism and folk Taoism support the farmers and laborers, the many colorful festivals and customs have helped to stabilize society, although this long standing and harmonious situation is now being disturbed by the social rivalry between various groups. One example is the events that occurred in China between 1966 and 1976 where the approach was subnormal, and added nothing to the much needed growth of humanity. We agree that the existent practices from the old folk religions should not be taken over seriously, but their approach can offer useful information to our spiritual research. However, Buddhism with its loose cultural shape could go in either direction, and any spiritual help will depend on the individual's personal achievement.

Why do I not give people the practice for verifying their spiritual reality right away? I have only one more matter to test - whether or not my life can do any better than those who choose to be ignorant about human spirituality, and I await an answer from the internal support given by the nature of life. Of course I continue to live as normal a life as possible. Yet, I cannot confirm the practice necessary for maintaining this normality - my great faith in human life. The nature of life produces what is needed in life, and so far, so good. Thus, I take the normality of life as the prime faith for both myself and most people, and agree there is no need to engage in all the great spiritual disciplines.

Nan Haijin, 南怀瑾, an enlightened cultural leader in China, lived for around 94 years on only one meal per day for much of his life while he made his contribution to saving the old culture after its politically misguided destruction. Yang Sen, 楊森, a Chinese scholar and general, practiced conventional sexual Taoism and produced more than 40 children during his 96 years of life. There have also been some conventional scholars who lived a good, clean life and reached over 100 years, such as Chen Li-Fu, who lived 101 years, and Madame Chiang Kai-sheik, who reached 106 years. Moreover, many farmers in the remote mountains still live for 110 years, and beyond.

Hence, I also believe that the real value of the old traditions should be more widely known and further tested. The people mentioned above illustrate the value of a long life free from heavy medicine, but we are all involved in the experiment of testing the modern influences on our own life. For example, in recent times the 10,000 years old China has been forced to modernize for her survival, and who knows for sure whether the blessings will be greater than the problems created. Even so, a good and healthy faith remains important in all of our lives. This is how we shape and conduct our life force, and it could also save us from widespread personal misbehavior and social disaster.

As ordinary people the best we can do is to match our life with the reality of our given nature. Similarly, each nation cannot rely on an artificial face lift. Rather, they should concentrate on recovering their cultural confidence, as most of the old cultures still represent the essence of human life. We could also apply modern research methods to confirm the old beliefs, which would soften or reduce any excessive pride regarding the advancement gained from modern technology. Of course we would expect this research to truly serve the health of humanity, as well as advancing our new endeavor of promoting the humane heart and humanistic principle in all aspects of our life.

Life is the Flow

Next to me flows the river of the Far Away Mother,
[Mae Yao[13] in Thai means Mother of the Remote].
Above me, a group of stars move across the dark sky.

---

13 Editor's note: Mae Yao is a sub-district of the Chiang Rai area in North Thailand and influenced by the Mae Kok River, which joins the Mekong River near the Chiang Zhong border crossing to Laos. Spiritual influences in this general area were mentioned in the previous chapter.

Inside me, each organ functions according to its mood,
While further inside, my blood continues to circulate normally.

It is still, but the invisible flow of the air
And the gentle breeze envelops my bodily life.
Looking into the deeper level,
Time is invisible, and space cannot be traced.
But once they join the existence of all things and lives,
They are beyond caring how they are noticed.

The Universe is not so far away,
It can be within me, though it is also outside of me.
This is because the time and space that frame the Universe
Also stretch their 'being' both inside and outside of me.
Is my being separate from this time and space?
Or is it part of the time and space that lives outside of me?

These 'beings' [time and space] can be rough, and uncaring.
But we can choose to have nothing to do with them,
And whether or not they choose to stay or go,
Although each 'being' keeps trying to have a good time,
And find a good place to stay.

They can also be very ungrateful,
And keep rushing along, with no farewell when they depart.
Should we choose to make a contract with them?
That is how worldly people like to tie down other lives,
But who really succeeds?

The early Chinese named this team [time and space] the Inconstant.
They called daytime the White Inconstant,
While nighttime was called the Black Inconstant.
Those people did not want to be the prey of the Inconstant,
So, they started the pursuit of an Immortal life.

All earthly life is shaped by the day and its light

That produces the sense of the White and Black Inconstant.
Defeating this pair means learning to ride the light of the sun.

Human life came from the integration of the sun and the ocean.
Thus, our soul of life is endowed by the sunlight,
And our mind is influenced by the 'watery' moon.
This means our brain is receptive to the sun, the moon and the stars.
But Immortal life means returning to the birth of the Universe
That is beyond the framework of time and space.

People have created numerous small religions over time,
While the Universe maintains the freedom to continually
Cross the threshold of being and nonbeing.
To the nonbeing of the Cosmos -
Being is nonbeing, and nonbeing is being.

In the world of beings [existence] we call things and lives,
Nonbeing is the Mother of all those things and lives,
Meaning we are the children of that Mother.
Yet, what we insist on usually cannot be insisted upon.
Setting our life vision on what cannot be insisted upon
Has far more value, as non-insistence is the religion of the Cosmos.

The Cosmos can also be seen as an enormous oblong egg
That contains a multiplicity of small worlds.
But what people generally insist upon as the truth
About that big egg is mainly untruthful,
Because all truths and untruths must return to infinity.

This means it is evil to call our Mother 'Zero Truth',
But we could say the integral truth, or the total truth.
I would prefer Mother Truth not be given a name at all,
Although Mother Universe carries the constructive truth
That fulfills the life nature of the Universe.

This cannot be denied.

Those who deny the spirit of the truth of life, deny life.
And if the health of the nature of life is denied,
The living truth is also denied.
Hence, behaving negatively is a denial of life.

All life is ultimately immortal,
While immortal life enjoys the Universe
Where being and nonbeing are equal.
This means they are part of life, and life is part of them.
But both the truth and many untruths are part of my life and yours,
As they come together to form our life on Earth.

What then should be our real worries in life?
Our unfaithfulness to fulfill each moment,
Or even those two villains - the white ghost and the black ghost,
Who have teamed together and tried to steal my good time and space.
Or it is me who has tried to steal their possessions for my own use?

No matter……..
Once the wise Lieh Tzu enjoyed his immortal ride on the breeze of life,
And I now quote from a work that carries his name.
My work, *The Universal Subtle Law*, also wished to preserve his words.
But I can still hear his laugh as he murmured:
'How can you make me work with mortals again?'

Should the pursuers of the immortal truth of life still partner
The earthlings who are preparing for the next world war?
The real difference between the two is:
Choosing a life of immortal pain,
Or a life of immortal joy.

Epilogue

Twelve Supposed Creeds of the Great Way

A message with much love from the Omni-traveler, Hua-Ching Ni, April 2012

First Understand the Spiritual Values from the Past

All seekers of the spiritual essence in life should objectively review the spiritual experiences from the past, as no one should continue to carry a banner that has been used to fight another human being, whether physically or spiritually.

Around 5000 years ago, Chinese society developed a style of leadership that placed no demands on others as they offered help to all people in need. Many of their leaders are unknown, but those who are include Fu Shi, Shen Nung and the Yellow Emperor. Later, various forms of spiritual worship became part of the social schemes that managed the increasing population in the world. Some of these new services were socially manipulative, such as Brahmanism, while others were more thoughtful and benign.

About 2000 years later, Zoroaster took the agent of fire, Agni, to establish his worship of the everlasting flame of life. This hidden or spiritual agent represents the soul in each human life, and when their flame goes out that life is no more. My understanding of this belief is that the sun remains the vast soul of all human life, and the four maidservants to the bright king are the four seasons that influence all life on Earth. While this spiritual metaphor was the basis of the early Persian belief it is less popular today, although Zoroaster's intention is a healthy example of human creativity.

Later, the young Jesus forged his faith in the Heavenly Father from the beliefs of ancient Egypt and Zoroaster, and was persecuted by the resulting social conflict. But during the second century C.E., a young Syrian, Muni, continued to carry the essence from Jesus' teaching. However, Jesus' good name was soon taken over by the Roman Catholic Church, which continued the style of the Egyptian Pharaohs, but used Jesus to hint at the worship of purity, or the spirit of young life. Yet, the image of Jesus should represent the light of the humanistic spirit within all people.

Lao Tzu lived 500 years before Jesus, although both men presented similar Heavenly qualities, including humanistic love, forgiveness regardless of racial or any other differences, not holding enemies, and never engaging in physical contention. Their spiritual attainment is also similar, and correctly expresses the spiritual development of humanity during the 500 years between these great teachers.

Lao Tzu represents maturity, and Jesus represents bravery, but both men sought an end to the practice of revenge during racial or tribal struggles by suggesting we meet any hatred with morality. This illustrates their divine quality, although the story of Jesus' life is more dramatic. Unfortunately, Jesus was repeatedly rejected by his own people, so the great Way has fostered this orphan, and now waits for his own people to reclaim him.

Around 600 BCE, Jain represented the spirit of detachment and nonviolence. In a confused world most people deny the privileges gained by others, but the wealthy Jain practiced self-denial from all worldly comforts and emotions, and is indeed a model for serious seekers of spirituality. Also be aware that while the deep denial of physical desire to strengthen our spiritual power is harmless to others, this approach could be harmful to the practitioner.

Spiritual purity is still a worthy goal to pursue if the ecstatic or extreme disciplines that made Sakyamuni popular are modified. Yet, Buddhists often discount the spiritual purity of life - if you do not agree, ask Sakya for the answer. Sakyamuni himself, however, represents the spirit of a peaceful mind and pure consciousness. His merit was gained from spending six years in the forest fasting and meditating to discover his personal spirituality, and eventually he attained what he sought. His literary achievement was also great, although most of his followers miss seeing the purity of the truth in his teaching.

Sakya also eased the way for all seekers of spirituality, even though Buddhists monks still find numerous excuses as they apply his 'discounted' approach to achievement. For instance, there is no last judgment on whether a believer has attained spiritual purity because their faith in Buddha liberates them all. But most people already know that extreme physical practices weaken or harm the physical body and its spiritual strength. Who then are the true Buddhists?

However, I have a strong understanding and appreciation of both Jain and Sakyamuni, and agree with their original disciplines, although our family does not create any artificial conditions to induce suffering. Rather, we take the discipline when and where there is a situation in life that delivers the need.

Nonetheless, Lao Tzu most represents the harmony that exists within the original spiritual nature of humanity, and the completeness of a wholesome life which should always be respected. His merit is in restoring the social style of the early leaders, like Fu Shi, Shen Nung and the Yellow Emperor, who freely served the public need for development, and never imposed their own interests. Moreover, many women also followed and served these great sages, and this contribution has strongly influenced Chinese society.

Confucius represents the spirit of delivering the true virtue and orderliness in life. I once said that Lao Tzu could be seen as the father to Jesus, while Confucius could be seen as his elder brother. But Jesus also represents the spirit of the broadest love and forgiveness, and he would be open to any spiritual adjustment by his own people to embrace the entirety of humanity.

Judaism has long represented the spirit and faith of survival in the face of adversity. In difficult situations we all have a healthy interest in our own survival, although we should still be open to finding a solution beyond any contention or strife with others. Thus, Jehovah the Thunder God should also represent the well-being and survival of all people.

Then there is Islam, which represents the spirit of devotion and surrendering to God. And the Hindu beliefs that represent the spirit of uniting with God through the sincerity of their religious practices, combined with their everyday duties in life.

I hope this summary of the major spiritual influences from the past brings a new understanding and some adjustment to your personal beliefs. Once we are enlightened we will see the God in both ourselves and Jesus, as well as in all the other great teachers.

The Twelve Supposed Creeds

1. The Sun is the Creator and provider to all life in the solar system. Hence, the Sun is the God to all earthlings, and those who object can choose to move away. If the fire or light that symbolizes the soul inside a physical life is quenched, that life is also extinguished. This means no human belief can be higher than the reality that all life is part of the Sun.

2. Thus, Jehovah, or the Thunder God, is no higher than the Sun God, but represents the release of the male life force. Without that force, no new life is possible.

3. Although all people are the children of the Sun, they should also be open to joining the source of the wider Universe, and the orderliness of the Way, or Milky Way. Can anyone live beyond the galactic orderliness we recognize as Mother Universe?

4. When we recognize that what is material is also spiritual, we cannot separate our spirituality from our physical life, although a deeper understanding can be applied in situations that lack the convenience or cooperation of the physical sphere of life.

5. If a religious establishment extends its good will towards all humanity, they still have spiritual value, but if not, they deny the value of their own existence, regardless of size.

6. The pursuit of Heaven through a harmonious world should be the only reason for all spiritual establishments. Heaven never interferes with human expression or survival, but religions and societies do.

7. Heaven on Earth can only exist when everyone values the right of survival for all humanity, with no exception. Hence, governments and

other social organizations ought not to adopt a ruling system, or enforce an unhealthy lifestyle, which denies the natural sense of life.

8. Higher spiritual reality has two vital qualities - the strong but insubstantial substance of the soul, and a strong awareness of the needs of others. This can also be interpreted as respecting the universal right to survival, or the belief that God favors all lives.

9. The main goal for humanity is continual self-improvement, and finding Heaven on Earth means practicing harmony and never engaging in contention as we apply Heavenly or impartial love in all situations of life.

10. The health of our spirituality, both individually and collectively, is the real strength of attaining a healthy life. Sometimes it may seem that scheming and being negative, or even evil, brings success, but that is just a momentary bubble compared with finding the depth of universal life.

11. True seekers of the spiritual essence in life do not deny the interests of others, as we all grow at different rates. Nevertheless, our true spiritual strength is expressed by our efforts to fulfill our responsibility of completing the Five Healths in life - physical health; mental health, including emotional health, conceptual health, and the health of the deeper consciousness; a healthy life spirit that is beyond all the emotional and conceptual shadows in life; healthy social connections; and financial health.

12. The health of life is the strength of life, and higher than any of the many physical, or material, or mental and emotional needs in each life. Thus, personal spiritual gain comes from how much we have transcended our vulgar desires, rather than any social recognition we are given.

INDEX

A

Amitabah 188, 189

B

Black Inconstant 247, 248
Buddha 36, 78, 103, 115, 116, 117, 118, 119, 120, 121, 137, 140, 164, 167, 174, 180, 184, 185, 186, 187, 189, 190, 192, 193, 196, 197, 215, 236, 237, 241, 242, 243, 252
Buddhism 21, 25, 76, 88, 115, 121, 137, 138, 140, 141, 142, 167, 168, 175, 184, 185, 187, 188, 189, 190, 191, 192, 193, 196, 203, 207, 242, 245

C

Cheng, Princess Wen 187, 192, 193, 194
Che-Shiang 187, 190, 191, 192
Chi 7, 40, 43, 177, 178, 179, 182, 183, 263
Chi kung 7
Chinese New Year Spiritual Renewal Ceremony 25
Christianity 88, 139, 197, 199, 206, 222, 245
Classic of Internal Medicine 178
Classic of the Yellow Court 40
Confucius 29, 35, 75, 94, 95, 96, 97, 98, 99, 147, 187, 191, 252
Cultural leadership 60

D

Dao, Dr. 240
Dead Sea Scrolls 212
Demons 44
Diamond Sutra 190
Dong-Bin, Lu 183, 226

E

Eight Further Disciplines 26
Eight Treasures 7
Emperor Ming 189
Emperor Shun 96
Enrich Your Life with Virtue 83, 109, 217
Esoteric Tao Te Ching 27, 133

F

Five divine qualities 217
Five Harmonies in Life 57
  Material harmony 57, 58
  Mental harmony 57
  physical harmony 57, 58
  Social harmony 57, 93
  Spiritual harmony 51, 57
Five Healths ii, 19, 21, 22, 24, 25, 29, 36, 42, 70, 80, 83, 85, 87, 89, 102, 103, 106, 107, 117, 123, 125, 127, 133, 143, 144, 145, 177, 189, 196, 201, 203, 204, 223, 226, 237, 254
  Financial ii, 19, 21, 58, 60, 65, 67, 70, 81, 82, 83, 86, 94, 105, 106, 107, 117, 118, 125, 181, 201, 203, 223, 226, 227, 237, 254
  Mental ii, 7, 10, 12, 14, 19, 21, 32, 35, 38, 40, 57, 65, 67, 70, 71, 77, 81, 82, 84, 90, 107, 117, 124, 125, 129, 136, 137, 140, 142, 143, 144, 147, 148, 155, 158, 159, 160, 163, 182, 183, 185,

188, 200, 203, 204, 209, 223, 226, 227, 229, 244, 254, 263
- Physical 7, 19, 32, 107, 155, 196, 254, 263
- Social 19
- Spiritual 19, 21

Five Universal Disciplines 25
- No strong stifmulants 26, 175
- No violent behavior 26
- Respect our own health 26
- Take nothing from others 26
- Tell no lies 26

Folk Taoists 39
Foundation of a Happy Life 83
Fu Shi 101, 110, 142, 169, 170, 172, 250, 252

G

Ge Hong 39
God in our own lives 15
Great One of Heavenly Truth 41
Great Unity and Harmony 35
Guide to Universal Spiritual Harmony 85, 133

H

Haijin, Nan 245
Han Dynasty 99, 183, 189
Harmony of Humanity 105
Health of Our Environment 105
Healthy Family Values 105
Healthy Human Faith 9, 70
Healthy Public Funding 105
Heart Sutra 190
Heavenly Father-King 5, 22, 24, 25, 27, 28, 30, 32, 33, 34, 111, 116, 121, 123, 127, 129, 130, 133, 134, 146, 149, 154, 155, 156, 157, 158, 159, 162, 171, 186, 204, 206, 207, 210, 211, 215, 216, 218, 219, 220, 221, 229, 250
Heavenly Grandpa 111
Heavenly Harmony 37, 41, 43, 47, 50, 51, 52, 53, 54, 55, 56, 57
Heavenly Heart 6
Heavenly Justice 104
Heavenly Law 53, 204
Heavenly light bodies 24
Holy Being 117, 118, 119, 120, 189
Hua Mountain 120
Humane Heart 229, 232
Humanistic love 16, 17, 24, 95, 130, 139, 162, 223, 251
Humanity
- Spiritual detoxification ii, 10

Human Spirituality
- Organic Health 7

I

I Ching 7, 20, 27, 92, 123, 147, 165, 169, 201, 217, 221, 263
Insubstantial Chi 178
Integral Way 6
Internal harmony 180
Islam 88, 140, 141, 197, 198, 220, 252

J

Jain 142, 167, 168, 242, 251, 252
Jehovah the Thunder God 252
Jesus 27, 28, 29, 30, 32, 33, 34, 35, 84, 98, 102, 118, 119, 121, 123, 124, 133, 139, 147, 156, 158, 159, 161, 162, 170, 199, 206, 212, 215, 216, 218, 219, 220, 221, 222, 223, 226, 250, 251, 252, 253
Jing Dynasty 189, 193
Judaism 88, 139, 197, 199, 220, 252

K

King Jie 93, 94

King Jou 93, 94
King Tong 93, 94
King Wu 93, 94

L

Lady of Wisdom 29, 116, 127, 128
Lao Tzu 30, 35, 39, 42, 88, 92, 94, 95, 96, 97, 98, 99, 100, 121, 133, 142, 147, 154, 161, 170, 172, 173, 183, 188, 204, 206, 207, 213, 216, 221, 226, 228, 242, 243, 251, 252, 263
Light of the Sun 9, 114
Lord of Great Harmony 48
Lord of Heavenly Harmony 43, 55
Lotus Sutra 138

M

Mae Yao 246
Mahayana Buddhism 137, 138, 184
Maitreya 184, 187, 188
Mantra 186
Marx, Karl 36, 80, 89
Mastering Chi 83
Mencius 95, 98
Moral Merit 129
Mother Nature ii, 13, 17, 29, 39, 64, 69, 77, 79, 89, 93, 116, 129, 130, 160, 227, 239, 241
Mother Ocean 10, 234, 236, 238, 239, 240
Mother of a Blessed Life 237
Mother of all Buddha 237
Mother of an Ageless Inner Life 237
Mother of an Everlasting Inner Life 237
Mother of Enlightening All People 236
Mother of Enlightening Our Deeper Life 236
Mother of Great Ease 236, 241
Mother of Inner Life 236
Mother of the Awakening Power in Life 236
Mother of the Five Blessings of Our Choice 237
Mother Universe ii, 27, 50, 79, 93, 116, 127, 128, 129, 170, 238, 248, 253
Mother 'Zero Truth' 248
Motzi 26, 74, 98

N

Nagarjuna 184, 187, 188, 192
Neng, Hui 121, 124, 167
New Path 24, 26, 50, 128
  Eight Further Disciplines 26
Ni, Hua-Ching 3, 4, 7, 6
Ni, Mao Shing 3, 4, 7
Nung, Shen 110, 142, 172, 250, 252
Nurture your Spirits 133
Nurturing a Healthy Conscience 104

O

Om Ni 134, 234, 236, 240

P

Path for Mastering the Grand Life 37, 61
Path of Constructive Life ii, 25, 27, 28, 77, 80, 145
  Evolve Heaven on Earth ii, 29
  Five Healths for a New Humanity ii, 29
  Love of Universal Mother 28
  New Universal Morality ii, 28
  One Spiritual Reality ii, 29
  Power of the Feminine ii, 28
Path of Pure Light 9, 37, 61, 64, 65, 67
  Moral fulfillment 65, 66
Political Culture 105
Pure Land Buddhism 185, 188, 189
Puritan Christianity 222

Q

Quest of Soul 27, 133, 179

R

Realization 35
Renaissance 80
Roman Catholic 139, 200, 206, 211, 250

S

Sakya 123, 124, 167, 168, 173, 174, 175, 184, 187, 188, 193, 226, 251
Sakyamuni 123, 147, 164, 167, 168, 170, 173, 184, 220, 242, 251, 252
San-Feng, Chang 183
San, Yo 3, 5, 17, 19, 22, 37, 61, 67, 146, 149, 152, 212, 225, 229, 263
Savior of Healthy Humanity 216
Self-awareness 21, 44, 90, 118, 203, 206
Self-reliant life 24, 226
Shamanism 76, 78, 175, 181, 183, 244
Shambala 163, 185, 189
Shang Dynasty 94, 171
Shangri-La 163, 185, 189
Shrine of the Eternal Breath of Tao 84
Silabhadra 187, 190, 191
Social Correctness 106
Song Dynasty 138, 148
Source of Humanity 9, 61
Spiritual health of humanity 23, 80, 102, 116, 166, 238
Stepping Stones for Spiritual Success 83
Surface of life 14

T

Tai Chi 6, 7
Tai Chi Chuan 183
Tang Dynasty 138, 190, 192
Tan Tien 41, 64
Tao Te Ching 27, 30, 133, 183, 190
The Centermost Way 83
Three immortal fields 41
Tibet 186
Traditional Chinese Medicine 76, 263, 264
True spiritual health 102
True spirituality 21, 44, 195, 200
Truth of the Conscious Mind 187
Tuan, Chen 120
Tzu, Chuang 97, 121, 133, 141, 167, 173, 188, 207, 243

U

Universal Integral Way 5, 6, ii, iii, 10, 25, 26, 30, 73, 76, 83, 114, 116, 123, 127, 134, 137, 145, 162, 180, 198, 199, 200, 220, 237
Universal vitality 12

V

Vision of the Messenger 36

W

Wayfarers 136
Way of Sakya 123
White Inconstant 247

X

Xia Dynasty 25, 93
Xuan Zang 187, 190, 192

Y

yang 16, 179, 222
Yat-Sen, Dr. Sun 36
Yellow Emperor 7, 35, 41, 42, 66, 97, 98, 110, 142, 172, 178, 250, 252
Yin and Yang 16, 179, 222

Z

Zang, Xuan 187, 190, 192
Zhan Buddhism 121, 140, 167, 196
Zhou, Duke 94, 98, 99
Zhou Dynasty 74, 75, 94, 98, 148, 172, 242

RESOURCES

Tao of Wellness Health Center

Santa Monica, CA
310-917-2200
www.taoofwellness.com

Pasadena, CA
626-397-1000
www.taoofwellness.com

Newport Beach, CA
949-706-7770
www.taoofwellness.com

The Tao of Wellness Health Center is the integral way to total wellbeing and a long life. Each patient is seen as an individual whose health is immediately affected by his or her lifestyle including diet, habits, emotions, attitude, and environment. The center, co-founded by Drs. Daoshing and Mao Shing Ni, focuses on acupuncture and Chinese herbs for complete health, longevity, and fertility.

The Wellness Living Store
800-772-0222; 310-260-0013
www.taostar.com
taostar@taostar.com

Nourishing Chinese herbal products from the 38th-generation Ni Family Healing tradition. Books on Taoist teachings to nurture the spirit and to provide tools for positive living. Tai Chi and qi gong on DVD, and guided meditation on CD. The Wellness Living Store also carries products and everything to make your life healthier.

Yo San University
Traditional Chinese Medicine & Clinic
Los Angeles, CA
877-967-2648; 310-577-3000
www.yosan.edu
admissions@yosan.edu

One of the finest and most academically rigorous Traditional Chinese Medicine schools in the United States, Yo San University offers a fully accredited Master's and Doctoral degree programs in acupuncture, herbology, tuina body work, and qi movement arts. In this program, students explore their spiritual growth as an integral part of learning the healing arts.

Chi Health Institute
Los Angeles, CA
www.collegeoftao.com
contact@collegeoftao.com

The Chi Health Institute (CHI) offers professional education and certification in the Ni family qi movement arts including tai chi, qi gong, and Taoist meditation.

College of Tao
Los Angeles, CA
www.collegeoftao.com
contact@collegeoftao.com

Learn about classical Taoist teachings transmitted by the Ni family through books, mentoring, and retreats organized by the College of Tao. The COT assists people in achieving physical, mental, and spiritual health by nurturing self-respect and by offering methods of self-improvement based on the principles in the classic works of the I Ching and Lao Tzu's Tao Teh Ching.

Chinese Nutrition: Distance Learning Course

www.taostar.com

Apply the classic concepts and power of Traditional Chinese Medicine to the selection of daily foods. Basic understanding and practical application of nutrition theories including food energetics, survey of Zang-Fu syndromes, and patient consultation. Up to 45 hours of CEU credit available for licensed acupuncturists.

Infinichi Institute International

PO Box 26712
San Jose, CA 95159-6712
408-295-5911
www.longevity-center.com

Professional training in qi healing leading to certification as an InfiniChi Practitioner. The program is designed to develop your energetic healing abilities utilizing the Ni family books and texts that relate to Traditional Chinese Medicine, qi gong, Chinese bodywork, and natural spirituality. It features a progressive, systematic program that nurtures understanding, facilitates skill development, and promotes self-growth.

Acupuncture.com

www.acupuncture.com

Acupuncture.com is the gateway to Chinese medicine, health, and wellness. From this site you can purchase The Wellness Living Store herbal products.